Simnikiwe Buhlungu

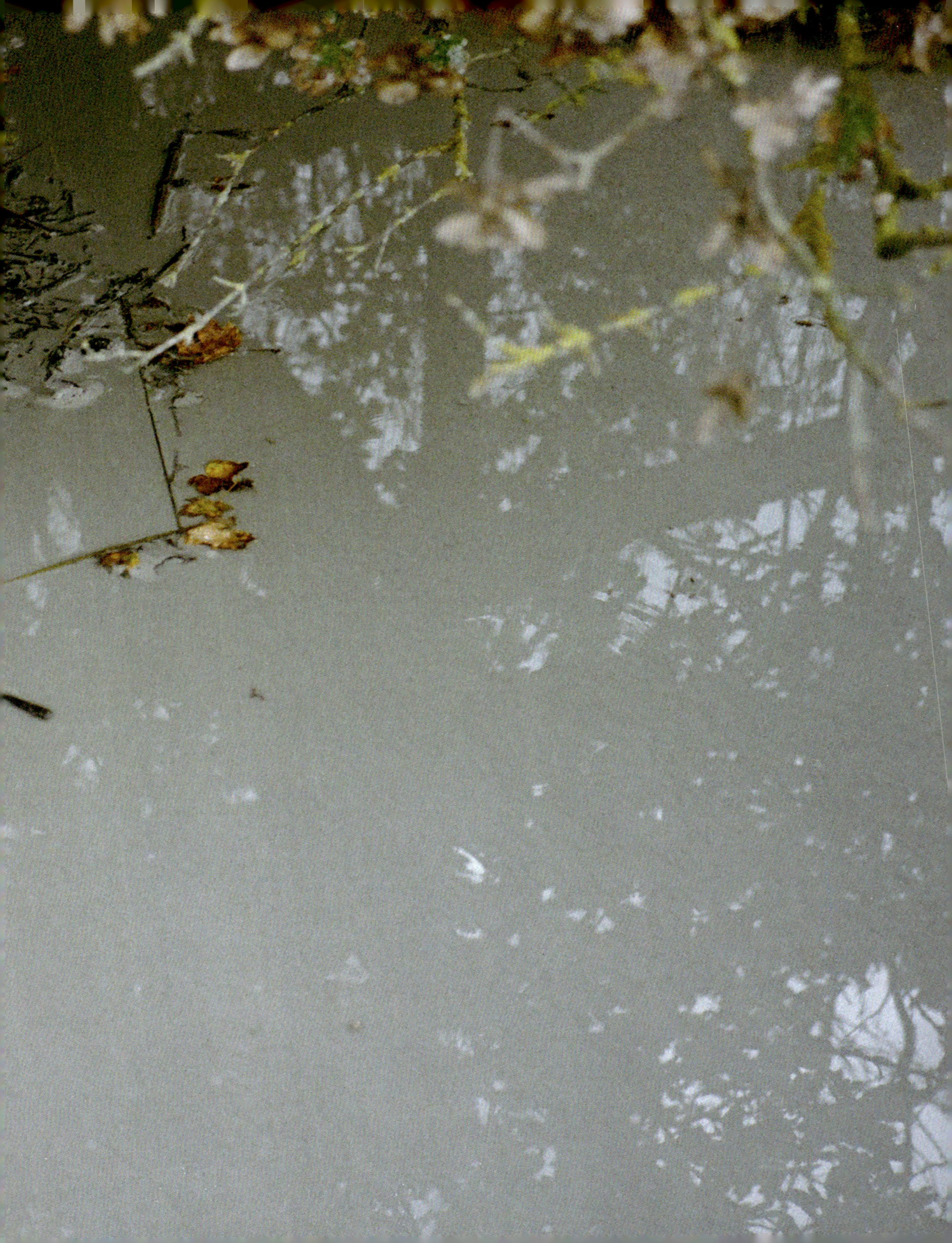

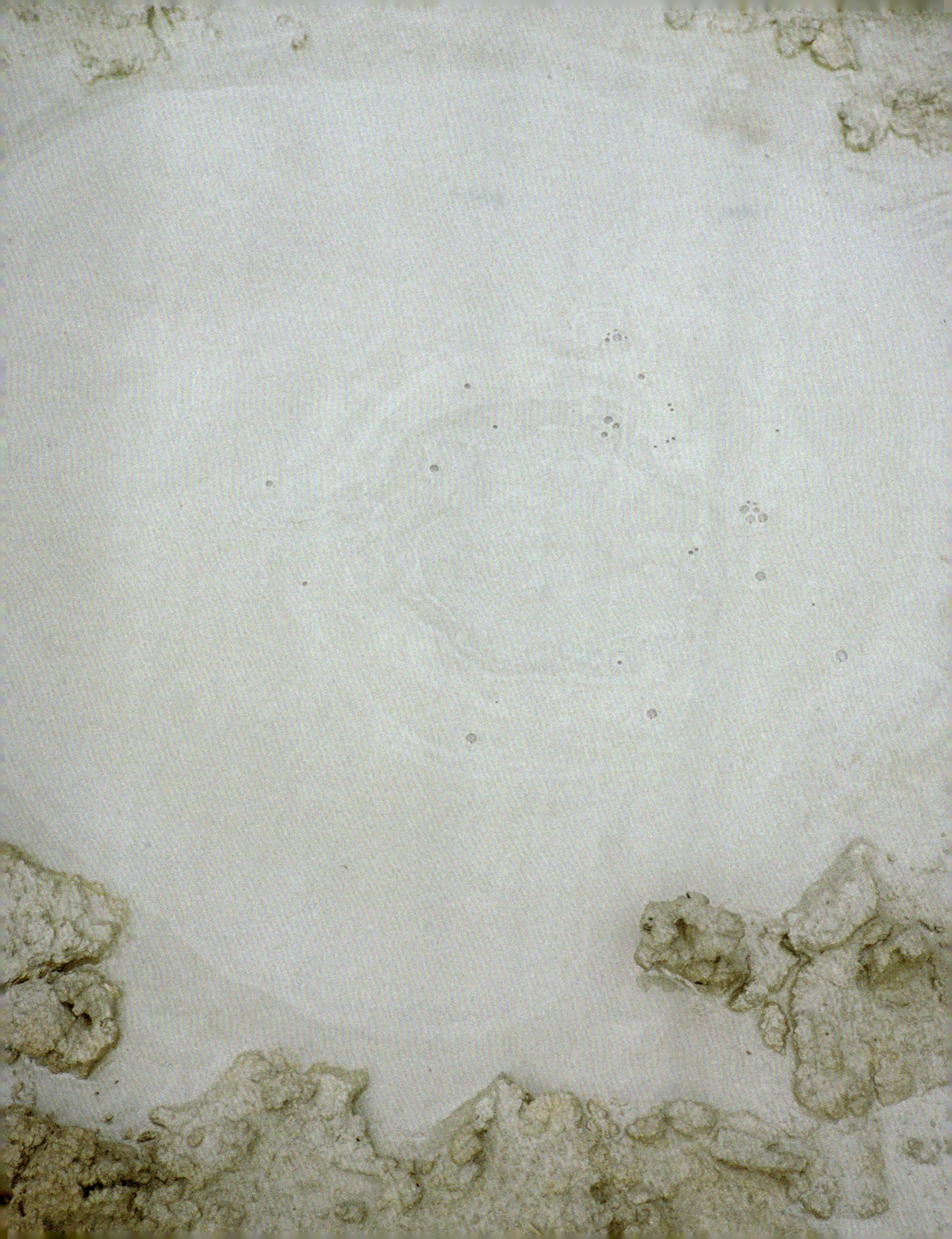

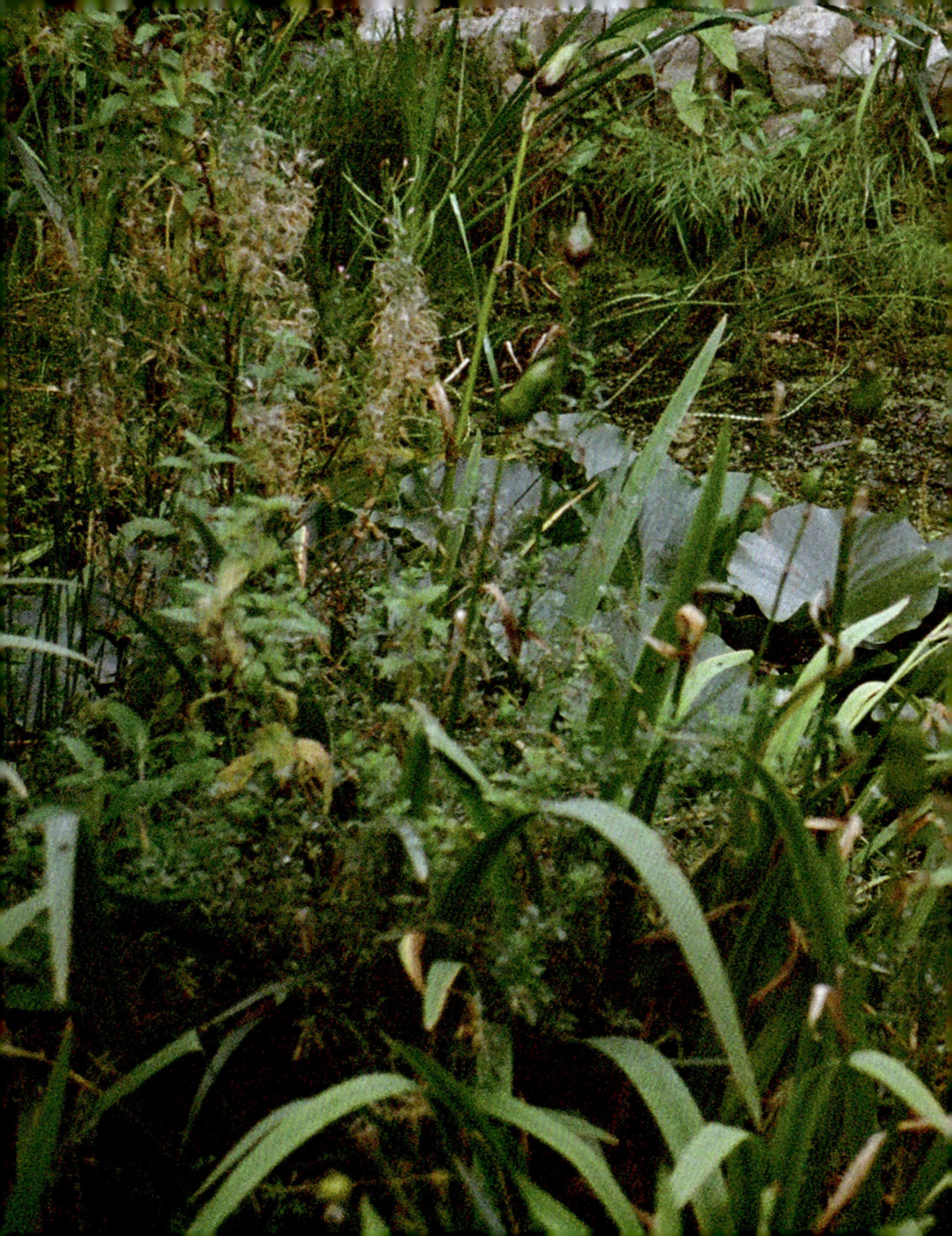

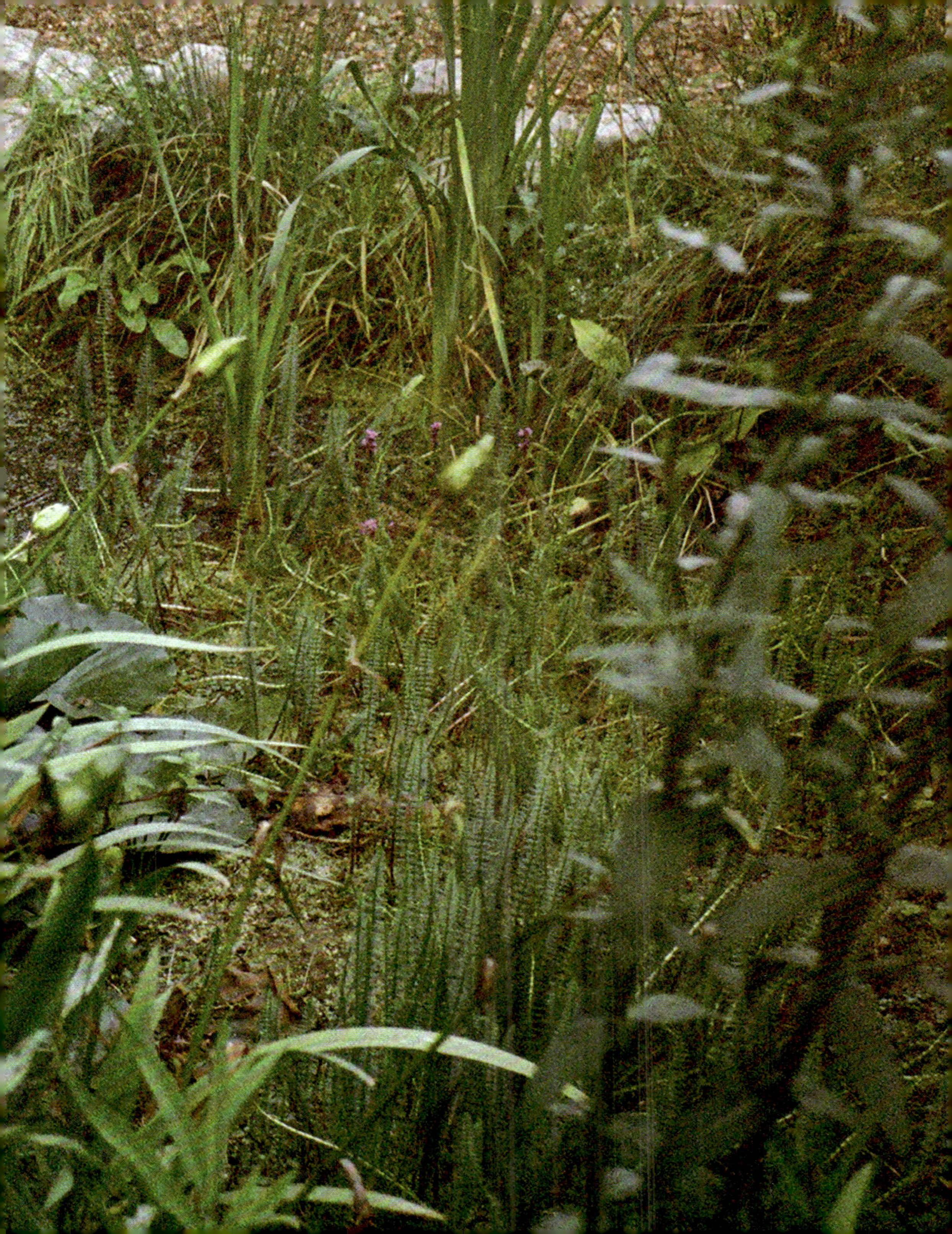

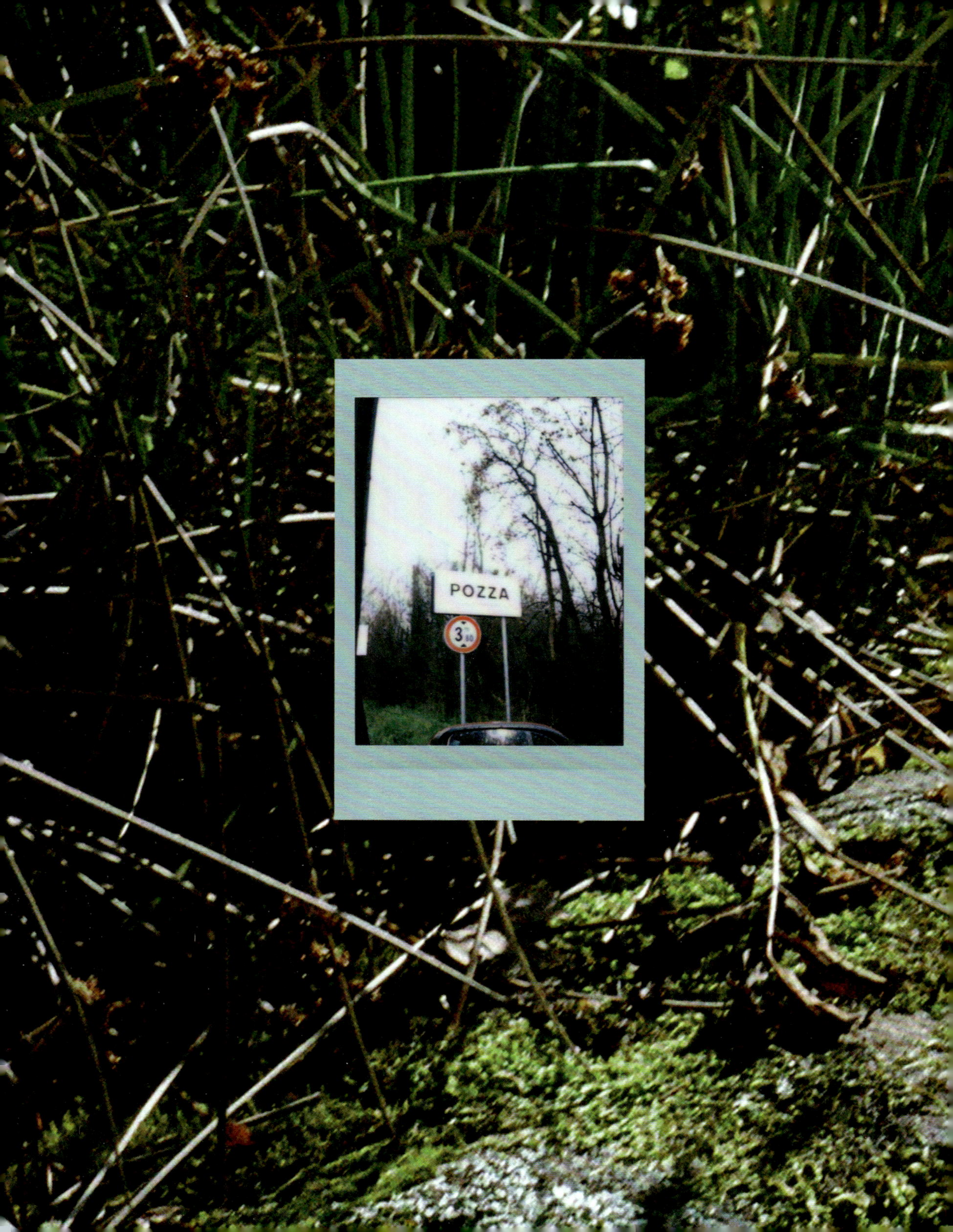
POZZA

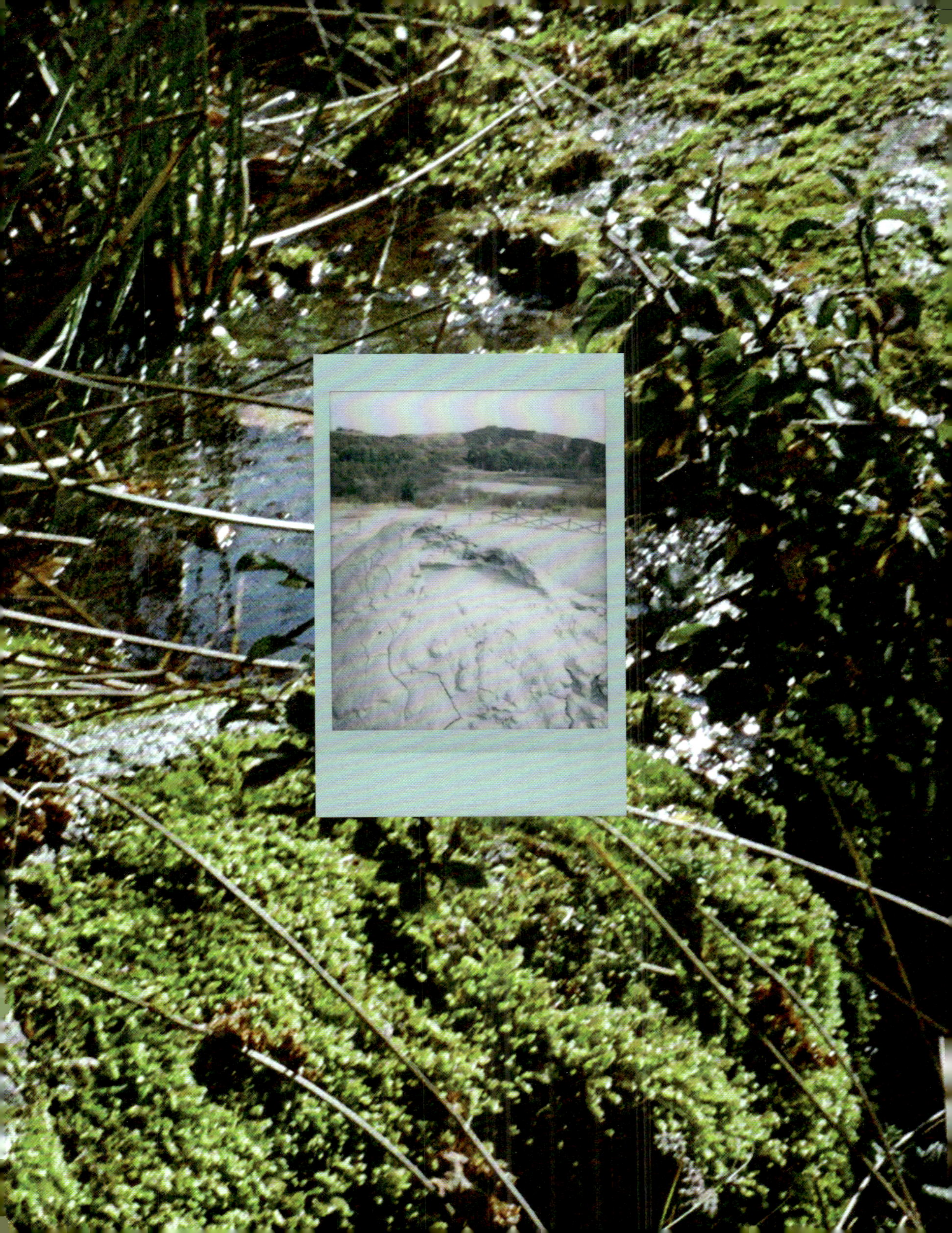

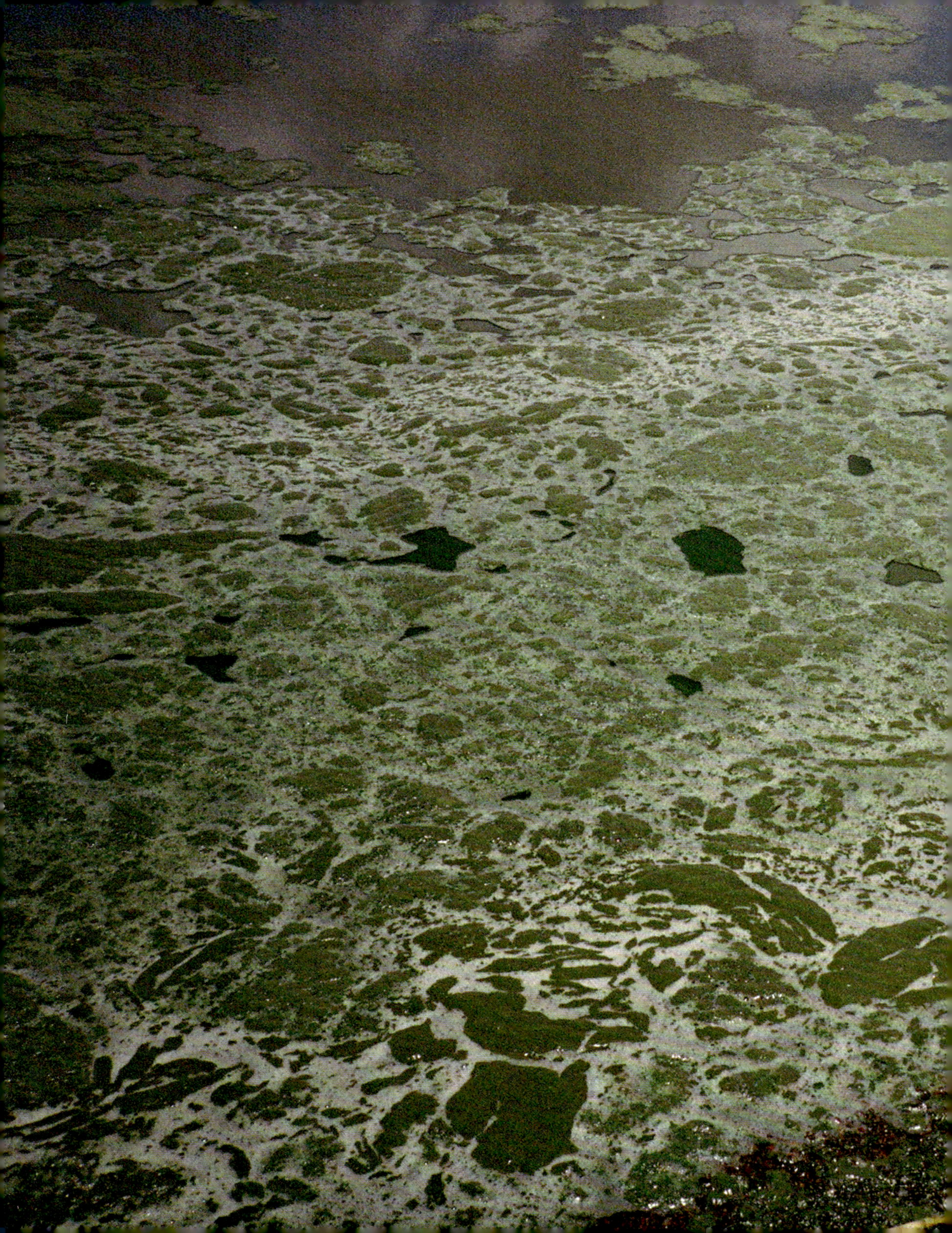

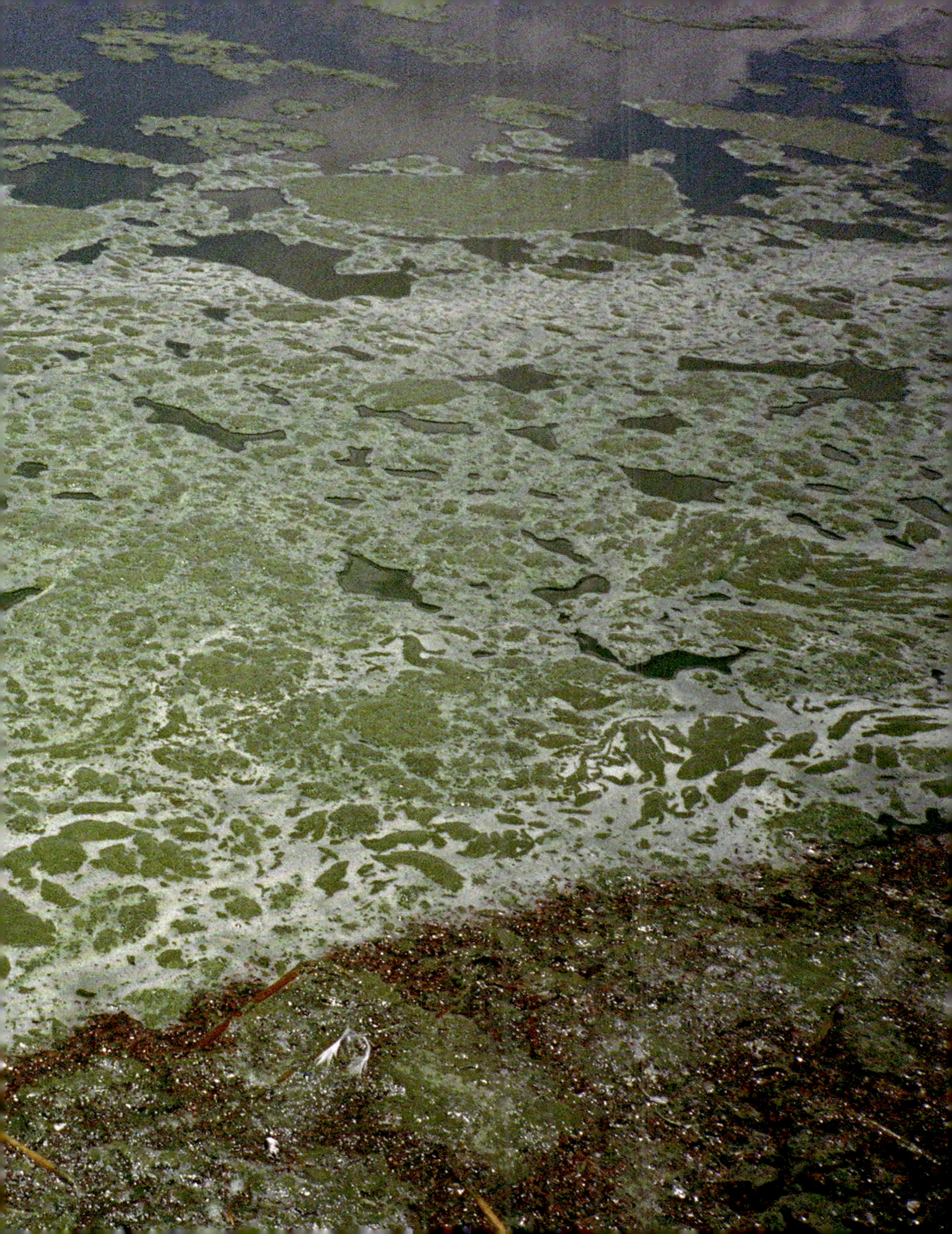

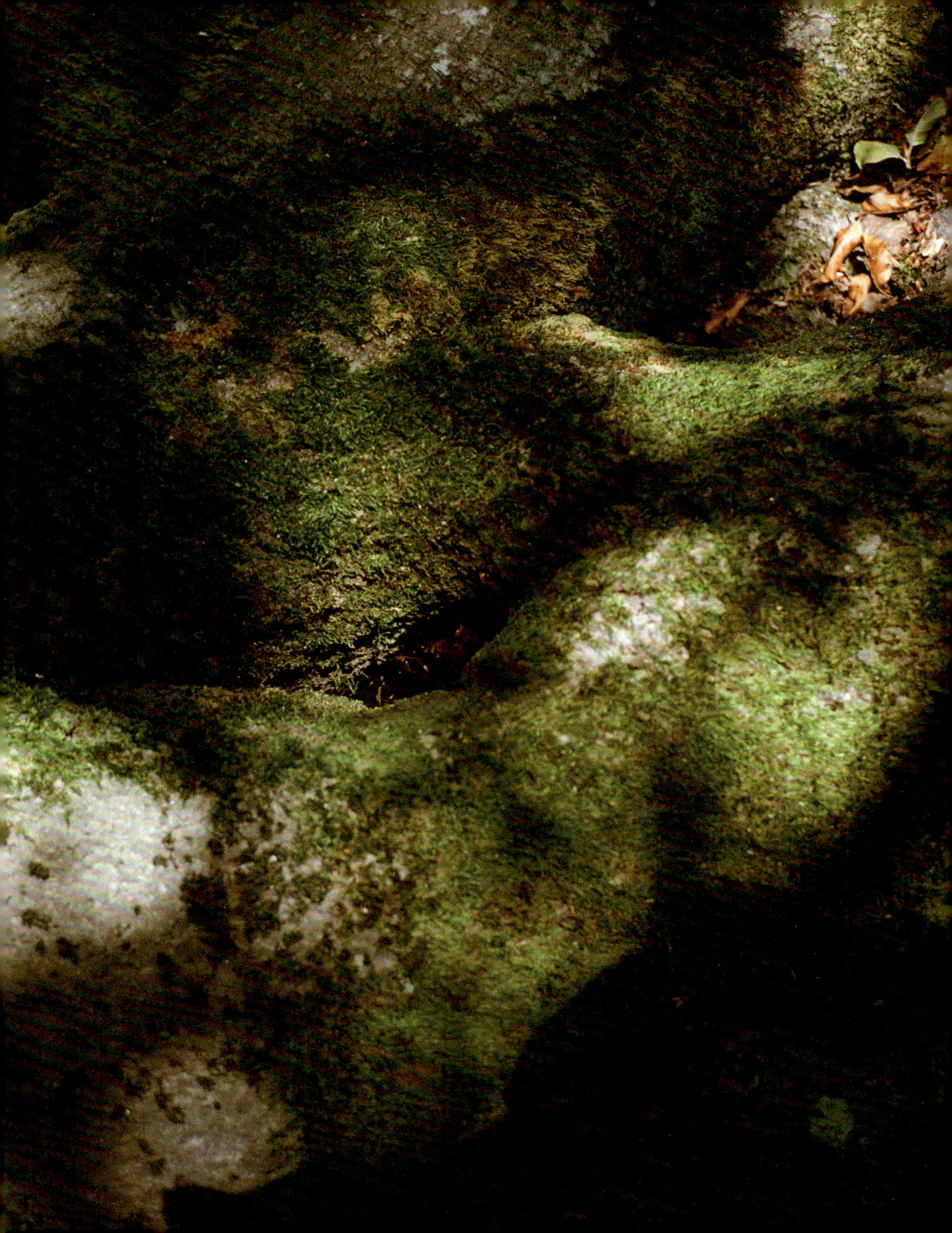

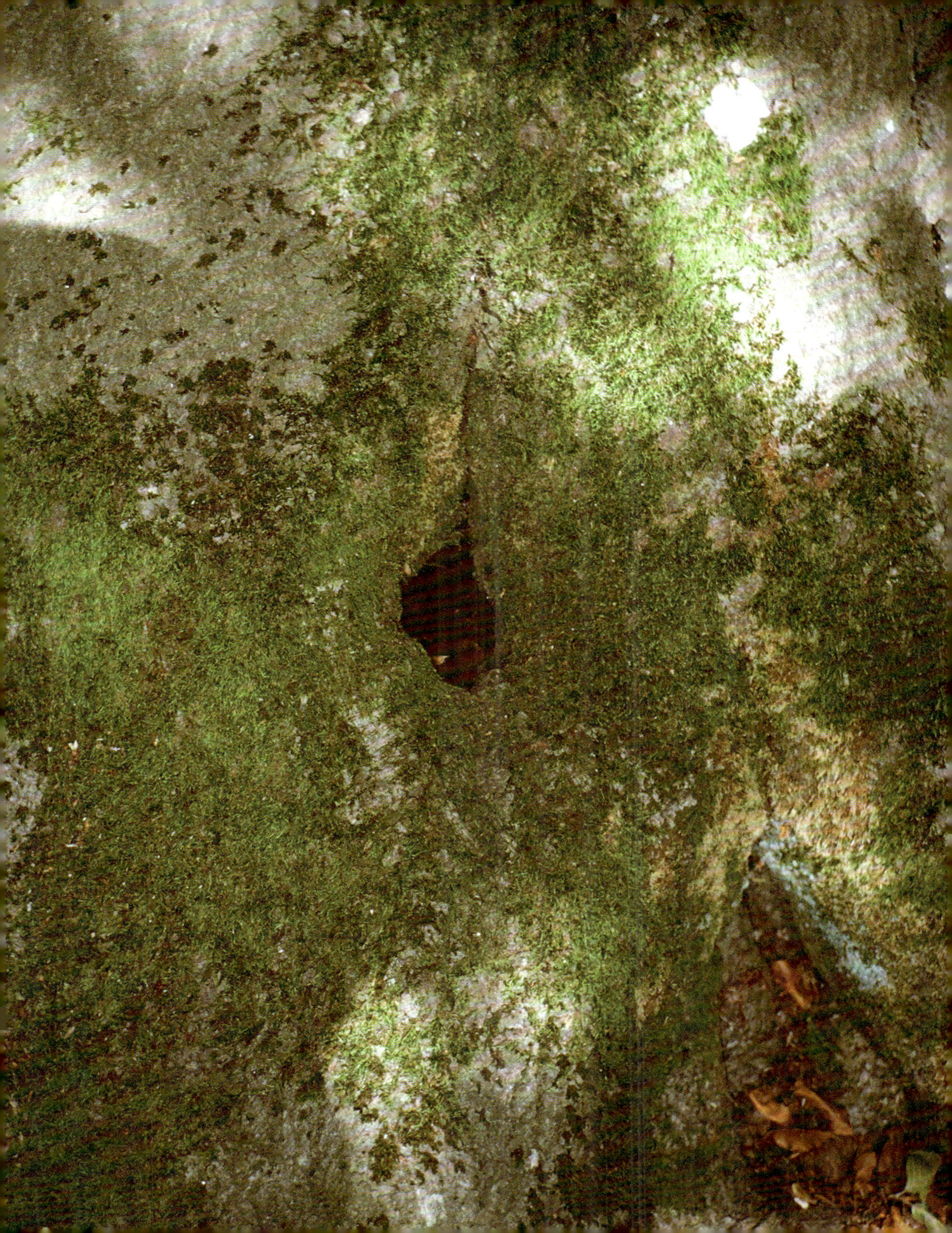

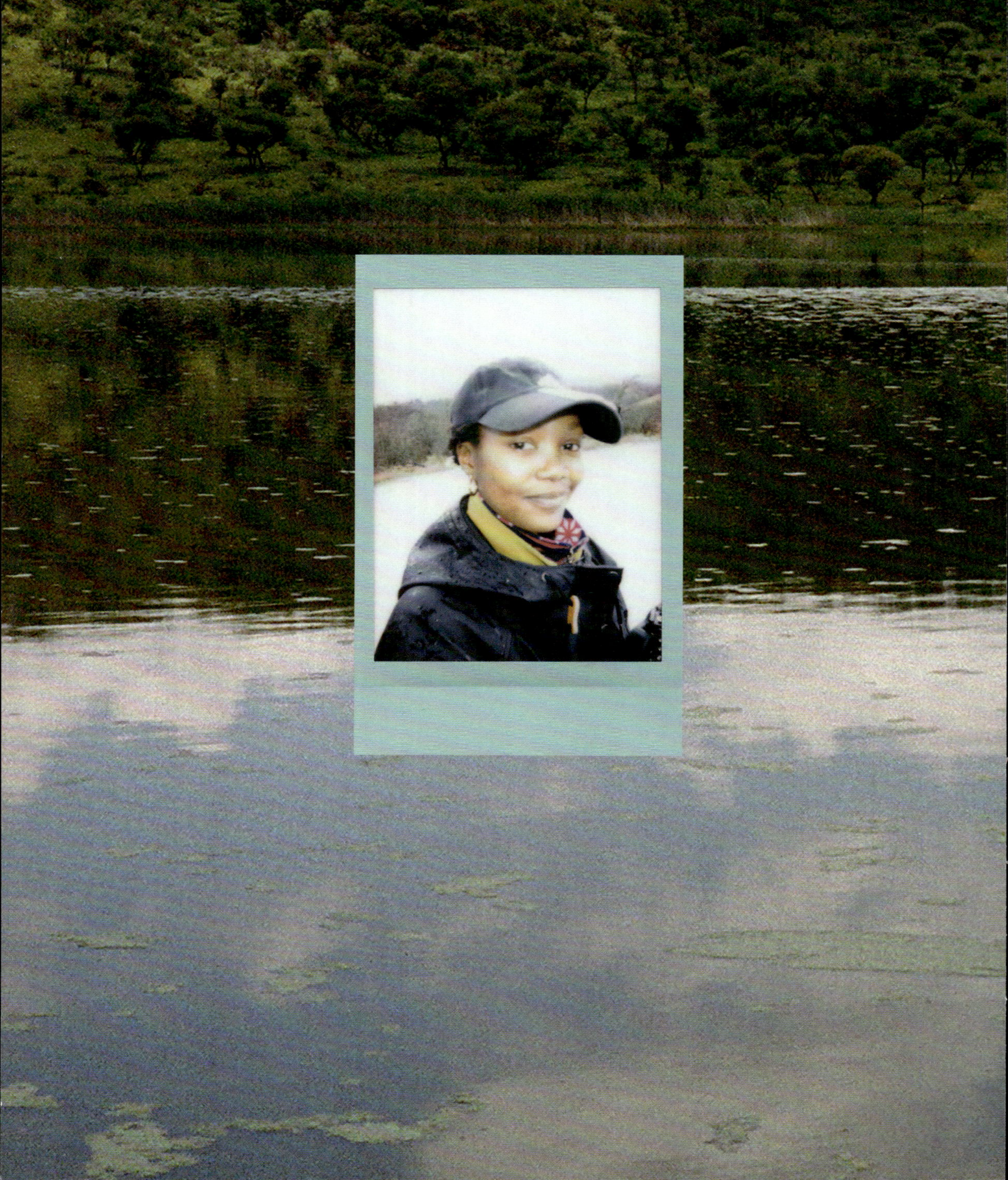

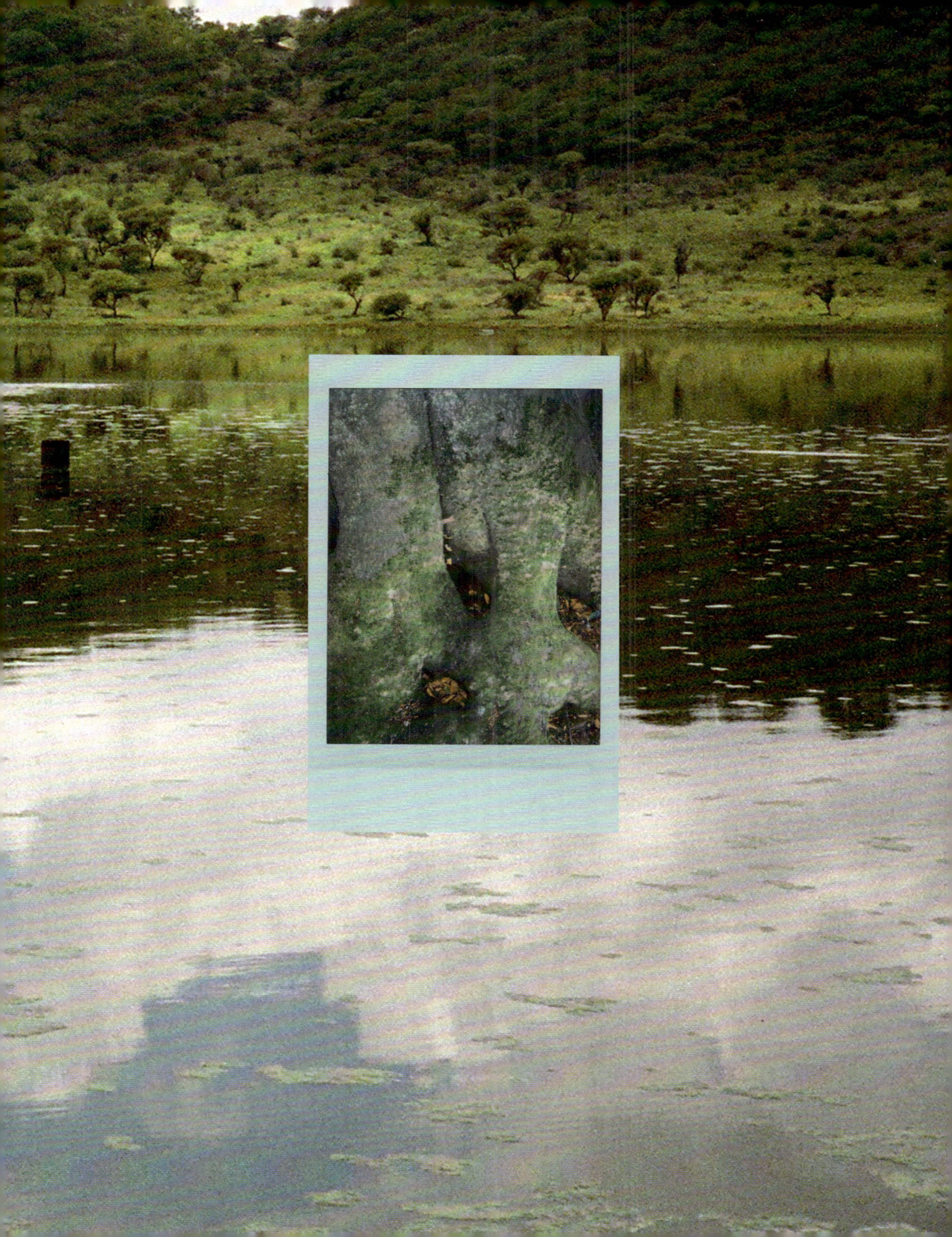

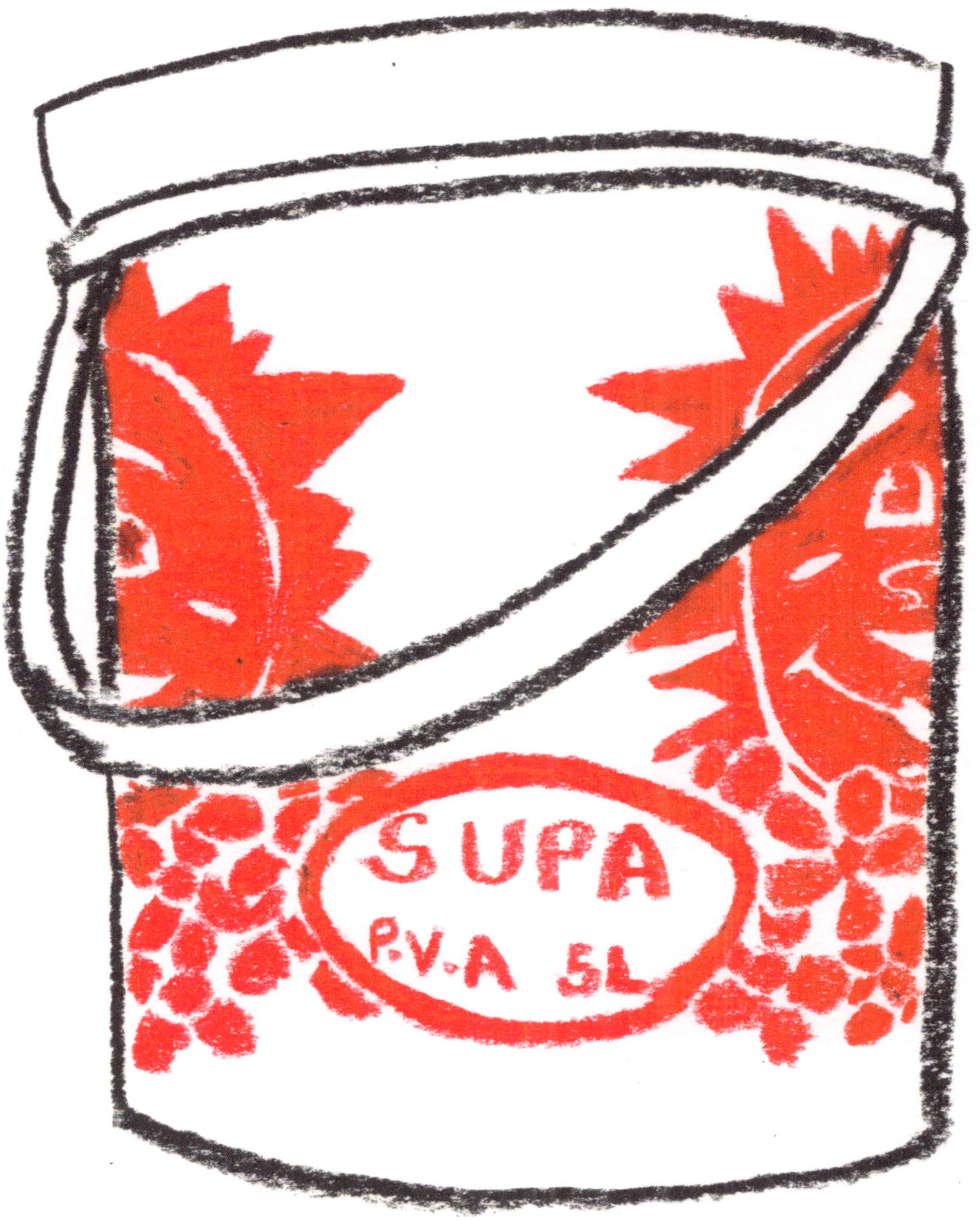
SUPA
P.V.A 5L

Simnikiwe Buhlungu & Riet Wijnen

Simnikiwe → Riet; Riet → Simnikiwe

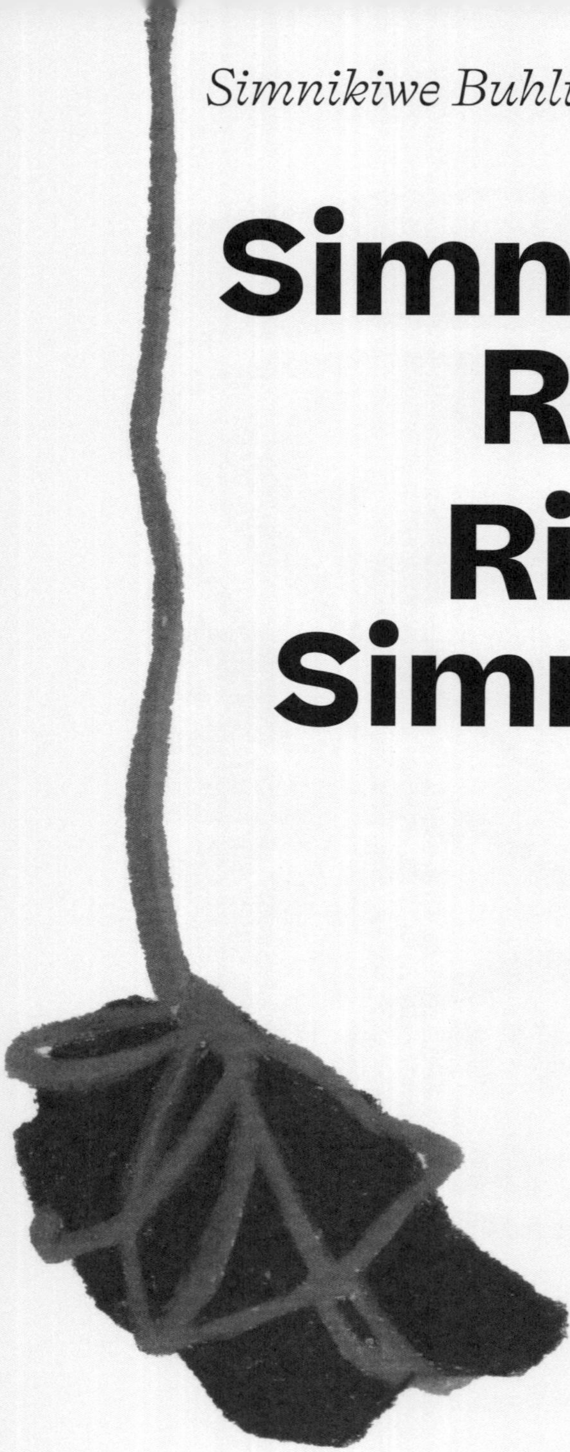

Riet Wijnen is an artist based in Amsterdam, whose practice involves sculpture, photograms, working through texts, woodcuts, and more recently, type design. She is interested in incomplete histories of abstraction, and in what is and who are already there, in ways we might not yet know. To do this she hosts practitioners from the past and present who have been active in the field of art during early modernism, or in science, philosophy, education, and activism. Bringing them together through fictional conversations and sculptures, Riet centres perception, language, and organisational structures, and reconsiders histories to better understand what comes next. This research has come together in the cycle *Sixteen Conversations on Abstraction* (2015) and in publications related to language and alternative biographies of female modernists, providing sources for her practice while functioning independently, such as *Saloua Raouda Choucair* (2025), *Homophone Dictionary* (2019), *Grace Crowley* (2019), and *Marlow Moss* (2013).

BERENSTRAAT 20—1
1016 GH
AMSTERDAM
25 AUGUST 2023

Dearest Riet

How are you?

I hope you are doing fabulousssss and that your summer trips went well. This letter may come as a surprise, hopefully a nice one. (As a head's up this is not a secret induction into an ongoing letter cult…hehe).

I wanted to write you about puddles.

I'm currently working on a project that seeks to…encounter the intrinsic missable-ness of these shallow bodies of water (which, I have found, are deeper than we thought). You're also well versed in the etymology of words, structures…geometries. In what I have observed in you and your work (the stencil rulers come to mind), at least. Forgive me if this outlook is misplaced.

On puddles, I am now into their ability to witness/to exist as evidence, to misbehave, as a subterranean burp, as a pause, as a distraction, as a vessel (transitory)/home (inhabited), as a condition and as a genealogy; the puddle's family tree.

I'm deliberately departing from when we were both in the Rijks CNC workshop (Amsterdam is such a small city/village/concept) and you were in the midst of a project in Italy alongside Falke but I'm not sure how it transpired in the end. →

Anywho, that's the second reason I'm writing to you. I could Google this, but it feels warmer to ask you if there are Dutch words for "puddle"? And not only in Amsterdam's Dutch dialect but in outside-the-randstad-Dutch? Different languages help stretch and complicate how we understand socio-ecological (actually, everything) phenomena.

I struggled to come across a singular word for puddle in ngesiXhosa or ngesiZulu. An array of WhatsApp voicenotes from a contact of an acquaintance of a very good friend landed me on some descriptions/phrases as possibilities of how we understand these sentient beings. The one phrase I'm clinging onto for dear life reads:

AMANZ'AMILEYO

Which roughly translate into 'water that is still'. I understand it more as 'water that is waiting'. Although that would technically be along the lines of 'amanz'alindileyo'. So, you see why I am hanging on for dear life...

Mmmm. So linguistically we can know these phenomena as verbs, spirits, bodies, friends. Which, I think can liberate us from the western hegemonic understanding that 'we' are separate from 'nature'; that 'nature' is to be used/extracted from/done something with; that 'nature' is dependent upon 'us'.

The English word 'puddle' is a shortcut; a government name in an ID book, a 'title' for a phenomena-as-object. It's not even poignant or sexy.

English is a rice cake.

So, I suppose in the Dutch context I'm currently operating from I was wondering if I could escape. The blandness of the rice cake* and enter the terrain of some bitterballen with mustard sauce (I probably wouldn't finish it after I took a bite...).

And my penultimate (no pun intended) prompt/question/gesture is when does a puddle 'start' or 'stop'? When is it a puddle or when is it, say, a pond? Who patrols these definitions and lexicons? I say patrol because the fixed-ness of linguistic definitions, at least in English (and in the west, by extension) feel guarded, static and unimaginative at times.

Enough blergh and though-provoking (or off-putting?) sentences. Please see attached a cute lil' selfie of a puddle and myself on my apartment floor yesterday.

I hope you're good, boo!

Take care and let's hang soon.

Yours,

xxx

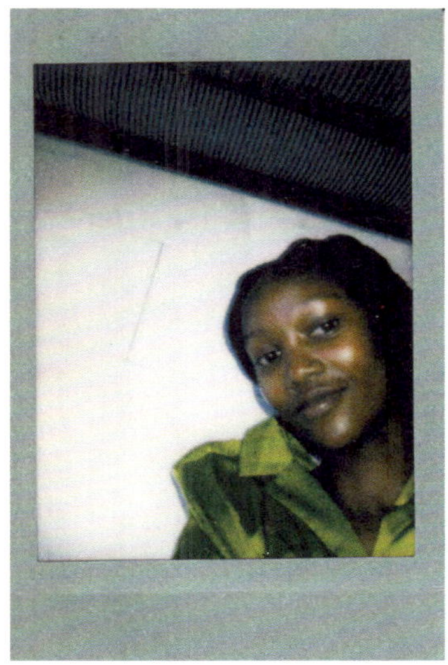

P.S. the puddle in the photo is hiding under the couch.
P.P.S. *I'm actually not sure if rice cakes are a British construct.
So I use it as poetic license.

Van: Riet Wijnen
Verzonden: maandag 29 juli 2024 10:18
Aan: Simnikiwe Buhlungu

Hi dear Simnikiwe,

Thank you for your patience! I've been thinking about your letter; hereby an attempt to bring some of these thoughts together –

At home, a small landlocked town of almost 7,000 inhabitants called Sevenum in the south of the Netherlands, we speak a dialect called Zaerums. I couldn't find a translation in Zaerums for 'puddle' but I did learn a new word, Meuré, which describes the clouding of water by mixing it with sand: to muddle a puddle.

I must have been almost four years old when my father, during one of his manic episodes, had the idea of building a hut with my sister and me in the woods behind our house. He had planned a hut under the ground designed in the shape of a big square. We dug the whole afternoon, and went back the day after to dig even deeper and finish the job. Then my dad lifted me into the hut, which must have been as big as a double bed and almost as deep as the standard height of a doorway. Standing in the hut, a shape-shifting experience overcame me. I suddenly felt ungrounded. This translated into a light panic, which had my dad lifting me out of the hut. Till this day I am not sure if that feeling was a subconscious awareness of his enthusiasm possibly being manic or because a square-shaped puddle had arisen from the bottom of the earth.

The direction from which the water came also reminded me of the Dutch word for puddle, which is 'plas'. 'Plas' also means pee, puddles made from the top down.'

Thinking of possible alternatives to 'plas', I kept hearing the word 'paddenpoel' in my head. A 'paddenpoel' is a shallow body of water, at least one metre deep, where circumstances are optimal for toads, frogs, and salamanders to reproduce. People might refer to 'paddenpoel' as a 'plas' too, since 'plas' also means lake in Dutch. But this translation wasn't why the word 'paddenpoel' had nestled in my head, it was how it sounds when spoken out loud: paahd-en-pool. When repeating the word 'paddenpoel' over and over, in a fast tempo, it starts to sound like puddle-pool. 'Paddenpoelen' were actively made in the area I grew up in, as a way of bringing back some nature. The land was originally wreaked by farms growing bigger and bigger, in part due to governmental policies. Now in turn, these farms are eaten up by vast logistic centres erected by the likes of Amazon. From these centres, products find their way into Europe, as Sevenum is roughly15 kilometers to the German border and 100 kilometers to the Belgium border.

x,

RIET

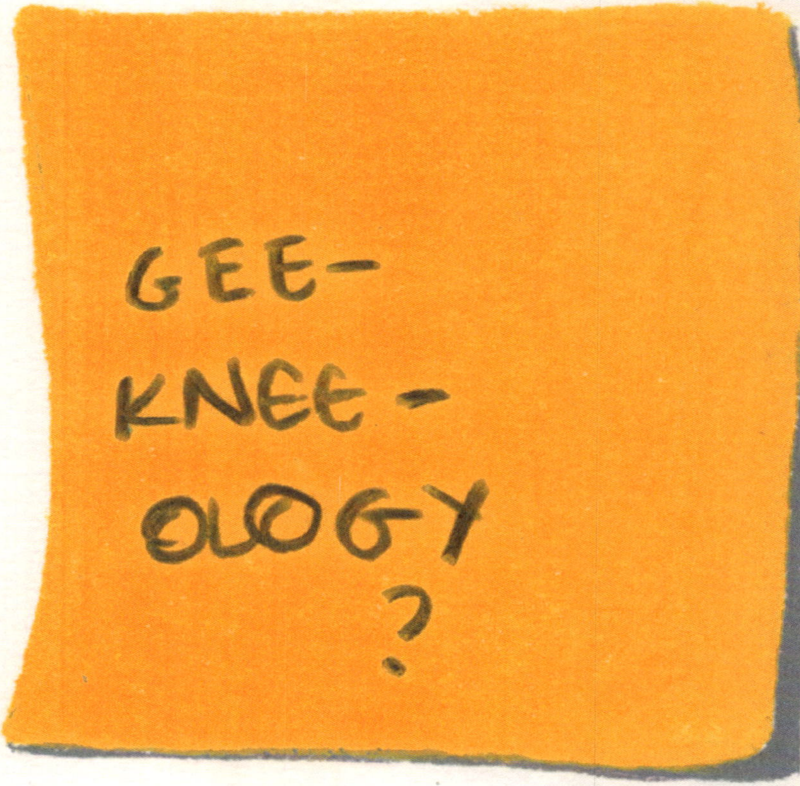
GEE-
KNEE-
OLOGY
?

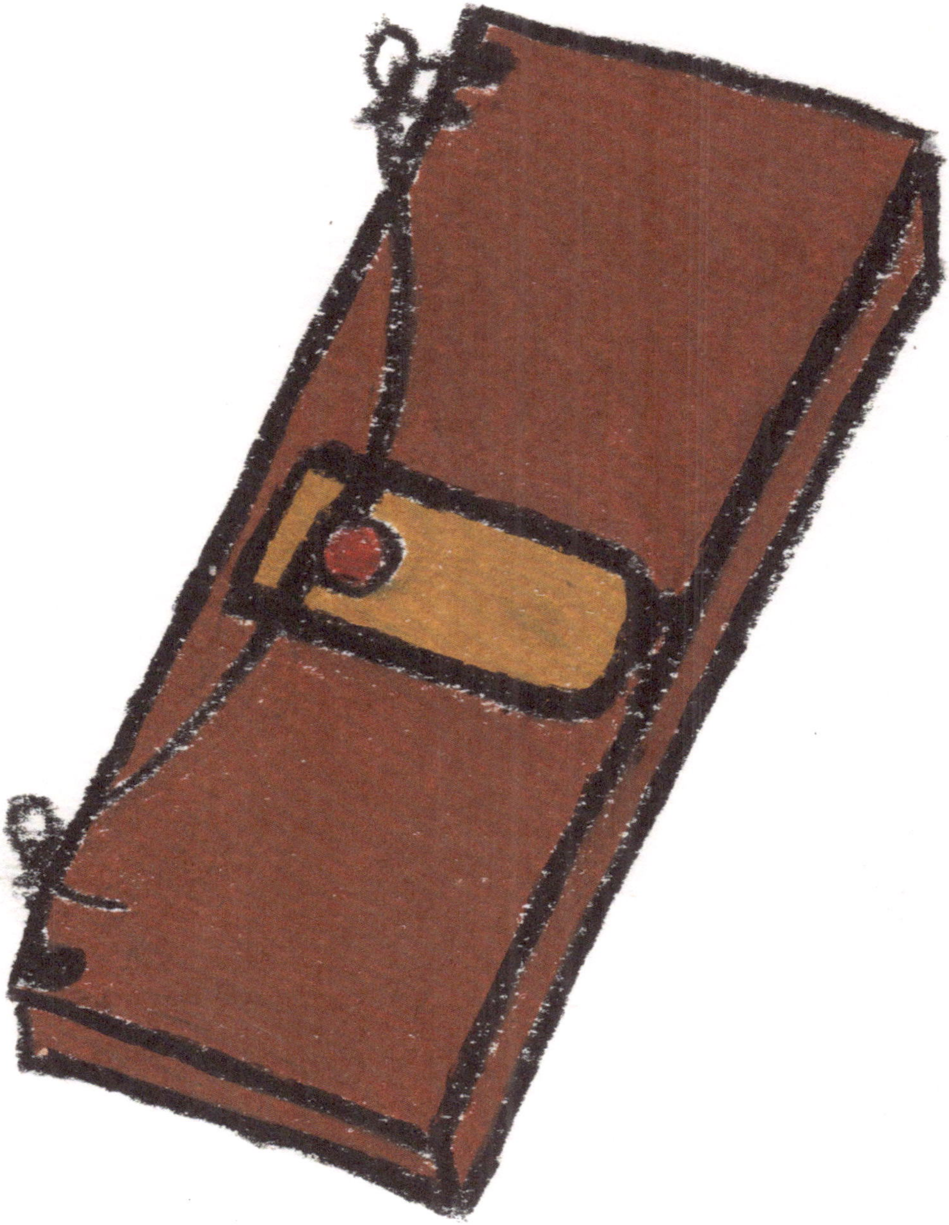

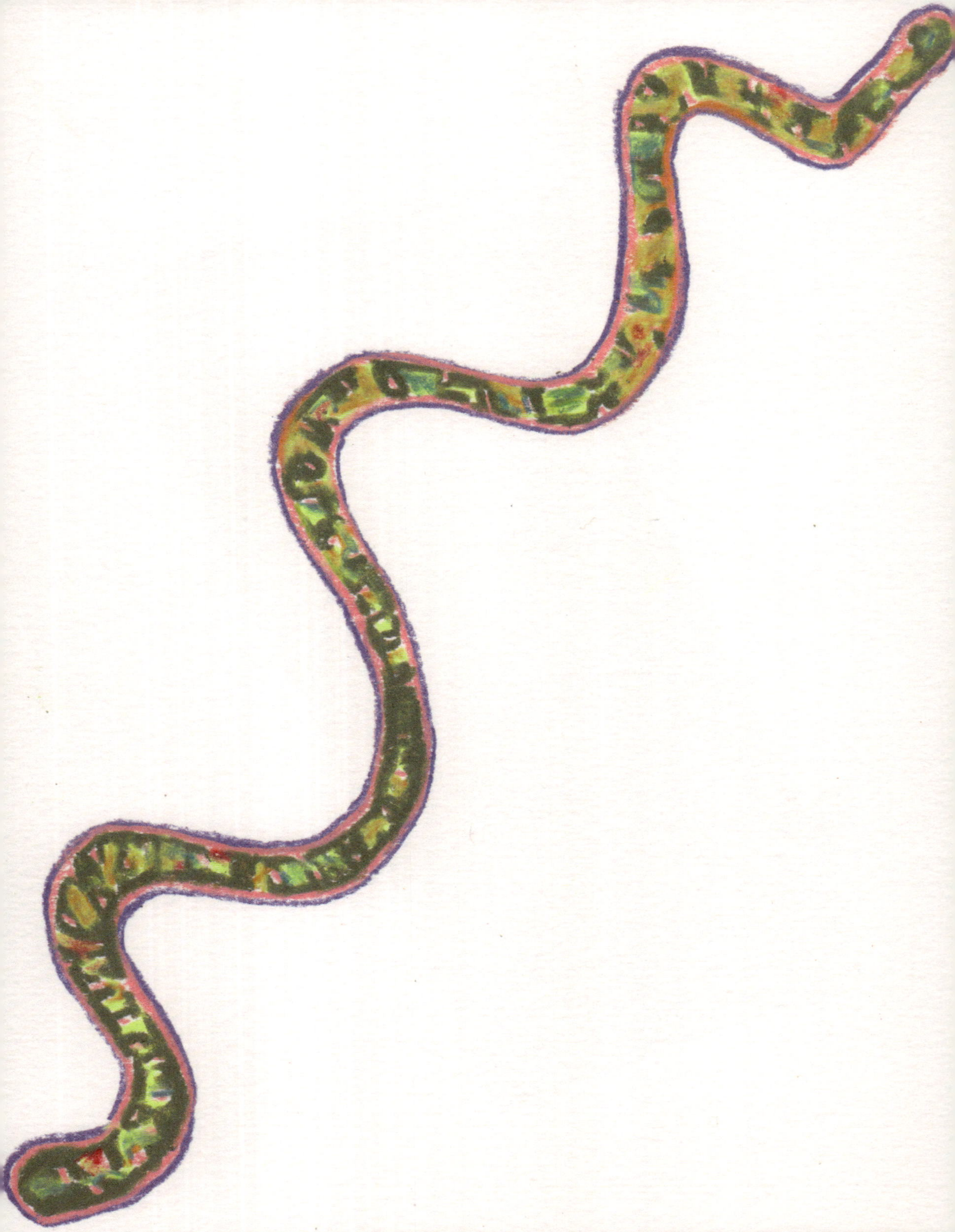

Simnikiwe Buhlungu & Norbert de Ruijter

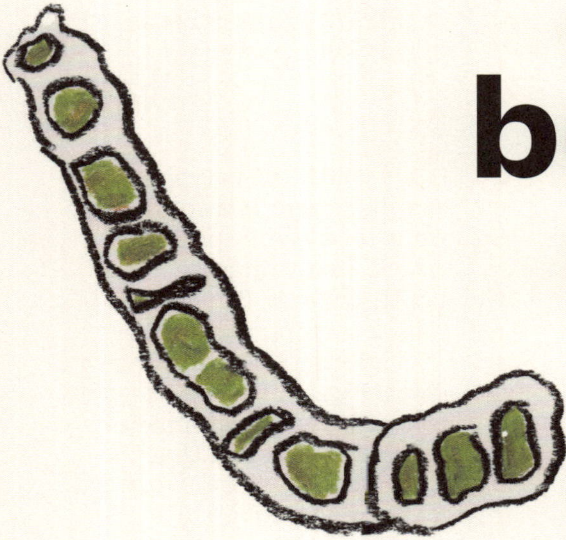

... far beyond what we know, or have seen

During his childhood in Amsterdam, Norbert de Ruijter regularly grew plants and took care of pets. It was no surprise that he pursued life sciences after high school. He graduated first as a biochemical engineer, going on to postgraduate study in genetics and plant biology at Wageningen University, and a doctorate in 1999. As a teacher and researcher in Plant and Developmental Biology at Wageningen University, his broad fascination for biology has resulted in more than 100 scientific publications in the last 25 years. His passion and enthusiasm for the living world makes a perfect fit for teaching (marine) plant biology courses and summer schools. He has established and currently runs the Advanced Imaging Centre for more than 150 users per year at the Wageningen Light Microscopy Centre. In his spare time, he sings as a tenor in classical choirs, and is involved in projects protecting ecosystems and biodiversity on our one and only planet.

SIMNIKIWE BUHLUNGU (SB)

I tend to use the word 'speculate' quite a lot. It's welcome in my field, especially in my role as an artist, to imagine or to propose different possibilities. My work is interested in knowledge(s) production(s), so I'm also afforded the positionality to sit very comfortably in the realm of speculation. For someone who works in microbiology, at what point in your practice does speculation happen for you, if at all?

NORBERT DE RUIJTER (NdR)

I don't feel comfortable with the word 'speculation'. What I do see is that artists and scientists both have creative minds. We like to explore things that we don't know about. The big difference is that I think scientists confine themselves to logical reasoning, and don't allow for pure speculation without solid proof; the stepping stones towards reason. That being said, we need creativity to consider options not yet proven. In practice, any study, any research question, any research proposal, is combined with a hypothesis. That's more the word that I love to hear, in that it needs to be falsified or verified – if you cannot prove it's false, then it's likely possible, but it just hasn't been verified yet. Putting together a proper hypothesis is never just speculation, it's also based on knowledge. Even at its worst,

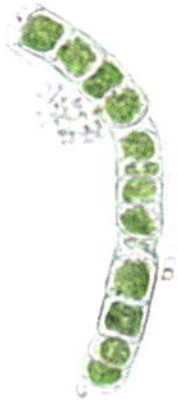

it's an educated guess, but needs to be supported by data. Something that is assumed to be true, and supported by general, 'known' knowledge, is still a *hypothesis* because it hasn't been proven yet.

SB

While the hypothesis is typically never the end stage, it's not the beginning; for me, it happens the other way around. In my practice, I tend to end with, 'what is a hypothesis?' Or the work becomes an open-ended question, without aiming to prove anything. Or, maybe I do, but the methodologies are completely different. It's interesting that the word 'speculation' is like, 'No, we are not trying that'.

NdR

Speculations are tiny, tiny little steps that are taken based on knowledge and what is considered 'proper thinking'. We *do* speculate; when researchers are together, we chat about things that may or may not be true. But as soon as it starts to appear on paper, as a research proposal, it becomes a very clearly defined hypothesis. Of course, we need creativity. We need to think outside of the box, outside of fixed trends. I think that's where artists and scientists overlap, because we like to explore.

SB

It's a calling that comes to us, to wonder and be curious.

NdR

I sometimes envy you because you have the artistic licence to think about everything and anything, and make unexpected correlations. It triggers me. I was hesitating about doing this interview because I was wondering what we were going to talk about. It's a scary, slippery road.

SB

Does that hesitancy have to do with the responsibilities that you have?

NdR

Absolutely.

SB

Ethics, right?

NdR

Yes. Everybody who gets a doctor's title has to promise that they won't mess with science; its ethics. Your statements should always be verified or based on existing knowledge, as opposed to freely chatting about things that we lack knowledge on or are not sure about. One has to be careful with statements and conclusions.

SB

The work that you do proliferates and disseminates, and goes out into the world, and a lot of people take science as fact or as the foundations for decision making.

NdR

That is what it should be. Then again, if you translate scientific results into simple words, as is normally done in popular science writing, often you encounter statements that are too strong, or generalise particular results, since that's what people want to know or read. As a scientist, it is important to share and explain your results to the public but it's difficult to communicate the variations or doubts that always form part of the results, at least in part. Almost nothing is 100% true in all cases. Science always keeps space for analysis from another angle.

SB

Which is how scientists, I guess, can go back to research done 20 years ago and develop it further and keep pushing.

NdR

Of course, we build and grow on existing knowledge, but have to be wary of dogmas.

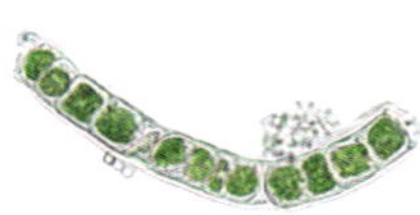

SB

Even as an artist, a lot of times people think we can just do whatever, which we can, but the reality is that a lot of our work also goes into society and we have a sense of responsibility about those positions too.

NdR

Actually, as an artist, your work is probably more widely shared and broadly accessible than the scientific papers written for specialised journals that nobody tends to read outside of the field.

SB

As part of my commission for Chisenhale Gallery and Kunstinstituut Melly, we've been studying various samples of water that I collected. When you and I were together in the light microscopy imaging lab, we were zooming into the diatoms and cyanobacteria. At first, I was like, 'what's going on here?' They're all living in this micro ecosystem. I became curious about their interactions with one another, whether they were navigating in isolation, or together. Is it possible to imagine what microorganisms are meeting about, what they are saying to each other?

NdR

There is definitely a shared interest in being together, but there are also many organisms that coexist next to one another, that provide mutual services but have no direct interaction with one another.

As a human society, we need one another because we are specialised and provide services to each other. There are also multiple types of roles that can be 'copy pasted' and do almost the same thing; they can be exchanged. Their coexistence 'buffers' all the services provided in society. It's an imperfect metaphor, but it is good to have this broad variety in specialised and functional overlapping organisms. Developing and maintaining a broad biodiversity in any society or in any ecosystem is super important, because it increases stability.

SB

One of the puddle samples collected just outside of Chisenhale Gallery in London did not have a lot of biodiversity.

NdR

It's likely still a young or unstable system in itself. The 'pioneers' come first and as succession proceeds, biodiversity rises. High biodiversity is an indicator of older and more stable ecosystems. When an environment goes through changes, brought about by drought or changes in nutrients for instance, the resilience of a biodiverse system is higher. In such a pool, multiple organisms with different lifestyles often have a mutual dependence and can coexist, but organisms with similar lifestyles can potentially take over jobs when required conditions for the predecessor suddenly change.

Self-supporting (autotrophic) phytoplankton, like single-celled algae, create carbohydrates from sunlight and carbon dioxide, but they need minerals and other building blocks to exchange for sugars with bacteria. Zooplankton on the other hand, feed on algae and add to a range of complex life forms in a developing pond ecosystem.

SB

I'm thinking through the notion that some microorganisms dominate certain environments more than their peers...

NdR

It's usually a sign of instability and temporality happening. However, if you look at a complex, stable system, then dominating organisms are counteracted by other impacts, and automatically reduced. If one organism starts to overwhelm the pool, this is a sign of instability, and the beginning of a transition to another stable situation.

SB

Does that ensure the lifespan of everything or...

NdR

Basically, it's a stable status quo that allows all the organisms in that system to thrive. That can also lead to very specific relationships.

It can be the case that one organism can only live if the other one is there. This is preceded by a long evolution towards such a specific interaction. A complete life cycle is based on the life cycle of the others, making it super risky for an organism. It can only exist if you have a stable status quo for prolonged time periods.

SB

It's collective action, in a way.

NdR

It can get more and more complex if it's not disturbed too much.

SB

In terms of the samples I've been collecting, I've been given different kinds of advice on how to dispose of them once I'm done with my research.

I understand that this is because they come from very different geographies and contexts, and *who knows* what they contain, right?

You suggested to me that I boil them in hot water, super-hot water. Another microbiologist told me to dry-dispose them in a dish, through evaporation. Perhaps it's not an inconsistency per se, but I'm assuming there are different ways to do this. It makes me think about after disposing of them, what happens to the microorganisms that were in that sample? Are they dead?

NdR

It depends on the microorganisms. The bulk of them are not heat resistant, drought resistant, or don't have the time to rapidly change into a cyst or into a resting spore that could potentially survive bad conditions. Of course, if you have drought and heat, like we have in the climate, many organisms adapt to become gametes or spores. Slow environmental changes can be slow enough for life forms to wrap themselves in a thick layer. When you have a thick wall, you can resist high UV excitation or heat better. An algae that normally lives in water at 20 degrees, can survive as a spore in 60 degrees in drought or at high UV, to wait for better times.

SB

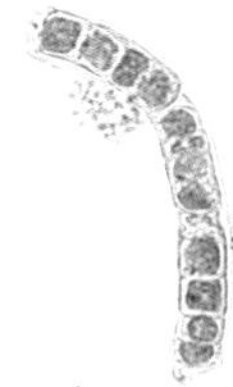

It puts on a little coat.

NdR

Yes, it builds pigments and a thick wall, to become drought and heat resistant. That usually takes time, and how effective it is depends on the organism. Some organisms, called extremophiles, can live in extreme conditions, like hot geysers at 70–80 degrees or acidic pools at pH 2–3.

SB

Is this like a tardigrade? Is that an extremophile?

NdR

Yes. That's actually also a sort of extremophile. They challenge biology, by developing tricks to survive in extreme conditions, also making them harder to get rid of.

SB

Exactly, because then they become resistant to change.

NdR

I think the reason why you have to think about proper disposal, is that we have had historically bad experiences by just bringing samples from one place to another. Introducing a new organism into a place where there are no natural predators or enemies, can allow it to dominate all the other local organisms. Such an introduction can destroy a stable ecosystem by sudden invasion of a new species.

SB

This makes me think of the water hyacinth.

There's a dam in Hartbeespoort in South Africa, in the northwest province where hyacinth were introduced in the early 20th century by colonial settlers.[1] It's said to be indigenous to the Amazon Basin in South America. Now we're stuck with this hyacinth, which at different seasons has completely covered this entire dam, and it's incredibly difficult to get rid of. I'm assuming on a very microscopic level, this is something that could happen with this movement of different geographies.

Tethered to this thought, you mentioned that there needs to be a slow shift or change in environment for these extremophiles to adapt. What about climate change?

NdR

That's an interesting one, because all the organisms will find it challenging to adapt this rapidly. Most of them are not ready. The most developed, the most precious, the most elegant, the most beautiful biological ecosystems are often the most delicate, and also among the first to be completely destroyed. If you have sudden temperature changes, for instance in coral reefs, and the dinoflagellates are the organisms that live in the coral polyps and that support them with sucrose, that's a close symbiotic correlation. This could be lost with a small rise in sea water temperature, and if those organisms don't come back within a short time period to restore their relationship, then a whole coral reef that has been growing for several hundred thousand years, can die off in just a few years.

If stable conditions are not restored to what they once were, it's the end of the story. These are tipping points we study in several ecosystems all over the planet. It's dramatic and extremely worrying to me, and to anybody with a little bit of understanding of how precious and important these relations can be. How it actually took millions of years to get to such phenomenally beautiful ecosystems. Current lack of human responsibility for our own environment leads to climate change and indeed destroys what is too fragile to recover.

SB

It makes me think, if I was, I don't know, a diatom and I'm confronted by this change, this climate change after millions of years of living my best life, and now I'm forced to adapt and change, I'd be pissed!

NdR

Yes, you'd be pissed off. Of course, we've had many fluctuations. This planet will survive, no problem. At the worst point of climate change, 95% of the human population will die and all our knowledge will be gone, but the planet will always survive, and there will be a potential new source for new evolution.

SB

The key is this constant adaptation.

NdR

Yes. Some extremophiles do not need photosynthesis, they can make organic molecules from something other than sunlight. They get energy from chemical connections, chemical structures, and break them down to generate energy, which also potentially carries genetic information, therefore, giving a new path to life.

SB

Say I've thrown out the sample with the extremophile. What happens to it then?

NdR

The extremophile or the spore is still hanging out there in the aerosol, deep in the ground, somewhere high up in the troposphere, and will reappear at some point on planet Earth and start all over again.

SB

It'll come down with the water cycle, with rain, or emerge from the soil?

NdR

Yes. Evolution has taken different roads. Like endemic species that only live on one little isle in the ocean, that have never seen anything else. That also happens with algae and bacteria. Their variable genetic capacities allow them to live all over the planet in their own niche.

They could potentially arise on an isle in the middle of nowhere and get started with a new evolution cycle, and contribute to their own ecosystem.

SB

Create another family branch!

NdR

A family branch that was never there before on Earth, with their own specific genetic modifications.

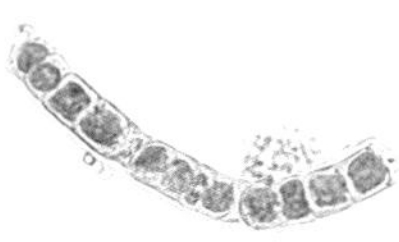

SB

I want to turn to questions of DNA. While water, H_2O, is an inorganic compound, and therefore doesn't contain DNA, some microorganisms inside of the water do...

NdR

All microorganisms contain DNA, otherwise they cannot survive. They have their genetic code, and that encodes how they are built, and what they are. Water is just a solvent. Of course, many of the organisms in the ponds are rich in water. They can even exist as 99% water but for sure have DNA. In the prokaryotes, organisms that do not have a nucleus, they have a single strand of DNA, not enclosed in a nuclear envelope, not as an organelle, but as a free floating genetic code in the solvent of the cell.

SB

With the samples that I brought to the lab for example, one of them was from South Africa,[2] and then the other one was from a clay puddle in Italy.[3] Would it be possible to test two samples and see how they might be related on a genetic level? Like a paternity test, for puddles and water samples?

NdR

That's absolutely doable, and it's done all the time. You can extract or derive from any sample that has even very small amounts of DNA, and that can be traced back to individuals even. You can have different samples of soil from different places on earth and potentially extract the DNA from bacteria and the algae in it, and do a big scan for special analysis, and compare them based on their genetic correlation.

SB

Of course we can make a broad generalisation and say those two soil samples are related because they are both soil from the same planet, but can we be more specific and test to see how exactly they're related, in terms of their genetic sequencing?

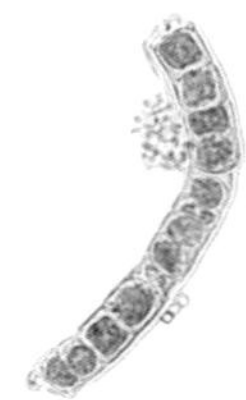

NdR

Yes. But be careful, because how reproducible, how reliable, how statistical, how relevant is that particular soil sample to function as a reliable fingerprint? But in principle, yes, you're right.

SB

Principle is good enough for me! [chuckles] Perhaps this then pivots us towards the type of tools that are being used in microbiology, for example the microscope. Is it possible for us to understand, learn, even see into this microorganism world, without the infrastructure of a microscope as we know it?

NdR

Actually, genetic code tells us more than a microscope. Hundreds and hundreds of bacteria that all are localised, and there can be many, many different types, are all one micron. They don't have any pigment. They don't have any flagella or strange things on the outside. They will all look like tiny little balls or rods of one to three micrometres. The genetic code tells me much more than a microscope can. Sometimes you need morphology. If you want to bring that a level higher, of course, you can go to the electron microscope.

SB

What is an electron microscope?

NdR

We have been doing imaging with a light microscope resolution, which only reads about 200 nanometres. That's the highest detail by which you can still discriminate between two points that are close to one another. If you want to see something in a nanometre scale, then you have to have a completely different sample preparation and analyse that using a completely different microscope, like an electron microscope. Then you are able to see the sub-details of organelles inside cells.

SB

Oh, wow! Okay. That's the full anatomical detail of a cell.

NdR

Then a whole other world opens up. We've been studying the multiple types of organisms in a drop from a pond, but each has their own internal world.

SB

That's crazy.

NdR

Yes, it's amazing to understand the deep extent to which everything is organised. When I was a student, I remember first looking through an electron microscope, zooming and zooming in to see how far I could get. I was looking so far into a nucleus, and I was basically looking at the DNA. I saw the genetic code, not that I could read it, but I could almost see how the chromatin was organised.

I saw how the DNA was densely compacted into different domains inside the nucleus. For me that was an euphoric moment.

SB

Goosebumps!

NdR

It's like a religious experience. It's weird for a scientist who tries to prove everything, and all we do not understand, we waste...

SB

We discard it.

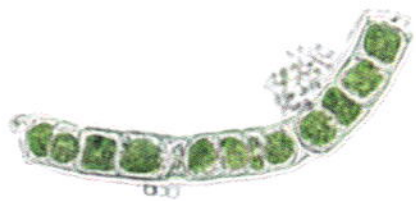

NdR

Life is so beautifully orchestrated and organised down to the smallest details, far beyond what we know, or have seen.

SB

Now, maybe we're returning to hypothesising. It seems there's always a gap between knowing and not knowing; maybe it's a small gap, but it's irrefutable that microscopes can only take us so far.

NdR

We always confront limits.

SB

I find it fascinating that there will always be a threshold of not knowing in this world. It's really important and humbling, in a way.

NdR

Yes... The resolution in microscopy is tremendous, thanks to technological improvements over the years. For organic molecules, we can now look into the scale of these molecules. Molecules are the building blocks of proteins. The building blocks to that level, are in the order of angstroms, which is nine zeros followed by a one after the comma or decimal place in metres. A bacterium is about one micrometre in length, which is a thousandth of a millimetre. Then you divide that 1000 times to get to nanometres, and divide again 1000 times and then get to the size scale of angstroms, of molecules. That is the resolution that we're close to analysing. That's far beyond our scale of thinking. That's the level we reach when we keep zooming in. On the other hand, when we look to outer space, with telescopes, there are endless and endless and endless depths that we cannot resolve.

SB

Yes, and we just have to live with that and that's okay.

NdR

It will never ever resolve.

SB

This is making me think back to the puddle samples, which I've held onto for maybe longer than I should have. I think I've had all of them for over maybe eight months or so; they were taken from a context where they had very specific conditions of life. Certain humidity levels, sunlight, nutrients, I don't know, altitude, et cetera. I put them into vessels, glass bottles, whatever they are. Took them to a completely different context. I tried to keep them alive, but they're still divorced from the context that once kept them thriving. I guess this process of sampling has made me realise what these instabilities of decontextualising can look like. Some of the samples have already changed since we last met.

NdR

> Some organisms will have instantly died and some will just be hanging out in there as sleeping spores; depending on how stress-resilient they are, and this will also determine whether or not they will ever revive if or when they are returned to their ideal conditions. Organic molecules will fall apart, basically, if there is a contaminant from a bacterium that can decompose it, or if they release enzymes on the surface of the little algae and start breaking down peptides. These little organic molecules can be a starting point for something else though, a nutrient in the medium.

SB

One of the samples had a very beautiful green algae. Over time, the algae turned into a fleshy skin-like-substance and then sank to the bottom of the vessel.

NdR

> I guess they were just falling apart. They can start to aggregate or assemble, basically. Then they sink or they form a sticky layer on the glass.

SB

Then that's it.

NdR

> That's already the beginning of the end, yes, already. Then you are just looking at how charges of these proteins and sugars physically interact with one another. That has nothing to do with the life-form anymore.

SB

I think it's also been helping me accept quite a lot of change – change must happen. Death happens, grief happens. Microorganisms need to move on as well.

NdR

> Everything is constantly moving and eventually degrading. If you put your food in the refrigerator and you don't eat it in time, it'll start to form fungi.

SB

Of course.

[laughter]

I want to share a riddle that I wrote:

> *"I'm a puddle, I landed from heavy rainfall at the base of a mountain, nearby is a forest where people forage berries and herbs. I have been here for three days. I'm constantly surrounded by the sun. A few days ago some honey bees were drinking from me. Underneath me is mud and stones, and some leaves are decomposing next to me. There are two earthworms that just drowned in me (oops!). What microorganisms could be living inside me?"*

NdR

Quite a lot.

SB

[laughs]

NdR

You can have all the ingredients for whatever you want. [laughs] Everything is there. The leaves are of course decomposing by bacterial breakdown, their decomposition already giving you many, many, many building blocks for life forms. These life forms are already there to some extent because spores of bacteria and fungi are all over the place. They're there in the mud. Then you have bees, they have their own biofilm of microorganisms. To some extent, they drink and take something, but they also give something back to the puddle.

SB

That's true.

NdR

Bacteria from the insects will be in there. Then you have people passing by, and they have possibly dropped berries in the puddle. I don't know if you put it that way, but there's of course lots of sugars, and lots of lovely ingredients which fungi like to grow on. There is sunlight, which is also *fantastic*! We have all the beginning life forms – we have all the ingredients that you need to make a beautiful party, and to start growing a new environment with its own simple complexity, but a growing complexity which will be biodiverse in time. It is always more interesting than you think in the first instance, when you see that little puddle there, holding entire worlds.

SB

Exactly! And this is the whole point of why this is so fascinating to me. Puddles tend to be completely overlooked, but they are signals of good health, of a good ecosystem. Seemingly inconspicuous, they indicate to us how collaboration occurs even when we cannot see it with the 'naked' eye. Organising is happening, as is deliberation, communication, mourning, multiplying, genealogical links across geographies, visa-free travelling, adaptation, resilience *and* resistance.

One question – spurred by this biological portaling – that I posed to Professor Norbert during the tea break of our microscopy imaging session, required further zooming in. 'If a microorganism had a microscope, what do you think they would see?'

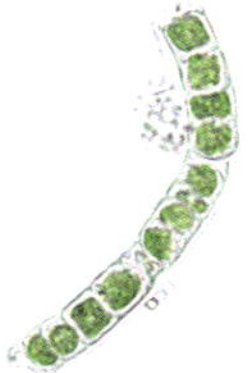

[1] J.M. Kitunda, *A History of the Water Hyacinth in Africa: The Flower of Life and Death* from 1800 to the present (Lexington Books: Lanham, MD, USA, 2018)

[2] Samples taken from the Tswaing Crater lake, in Soshanguve, and a puddle from maize growing in Nokusa Buhlungu's back garden in Johannesburg.

[3] Salse di Nirano Regional Nature Reserve (Municipality of Fiorano Modenese, Italy) is a conservation site of a geologic phenomenon of substrate (consisting of hydrocarbons, salt, petroleum oil, water among other composites) from beneath the surface emerging as burping mud puddles and canonical, cold, clay volcanoes.

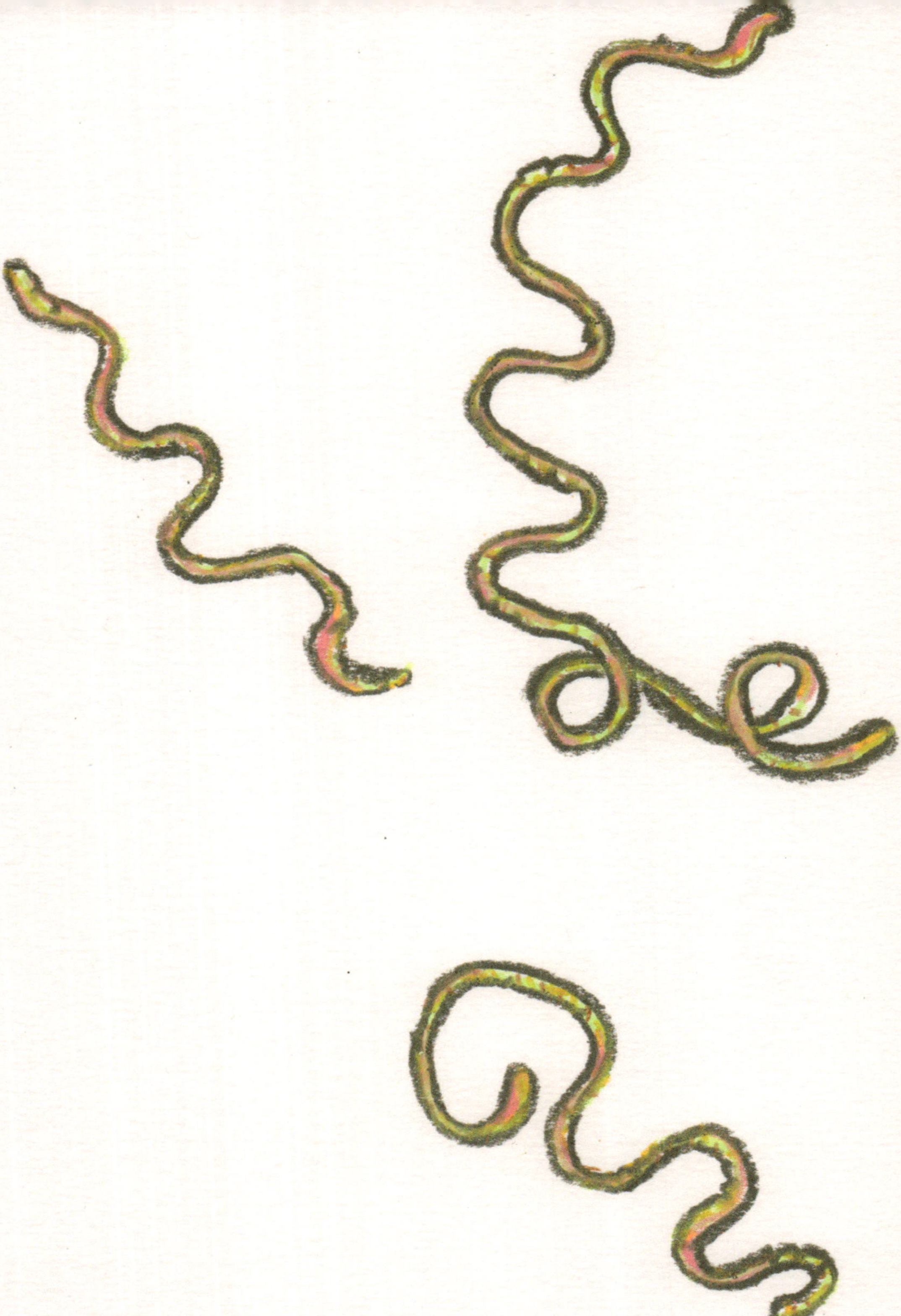

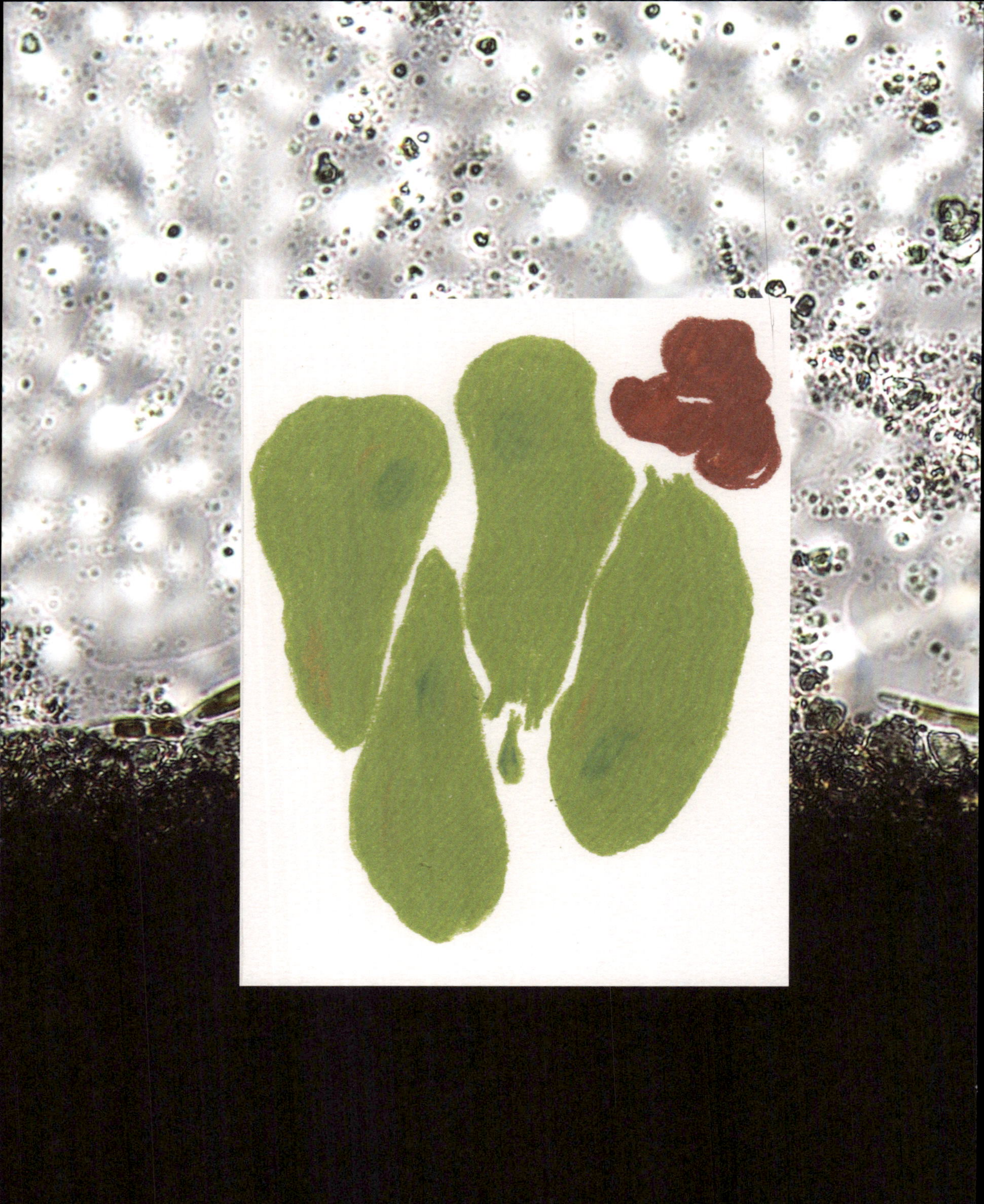

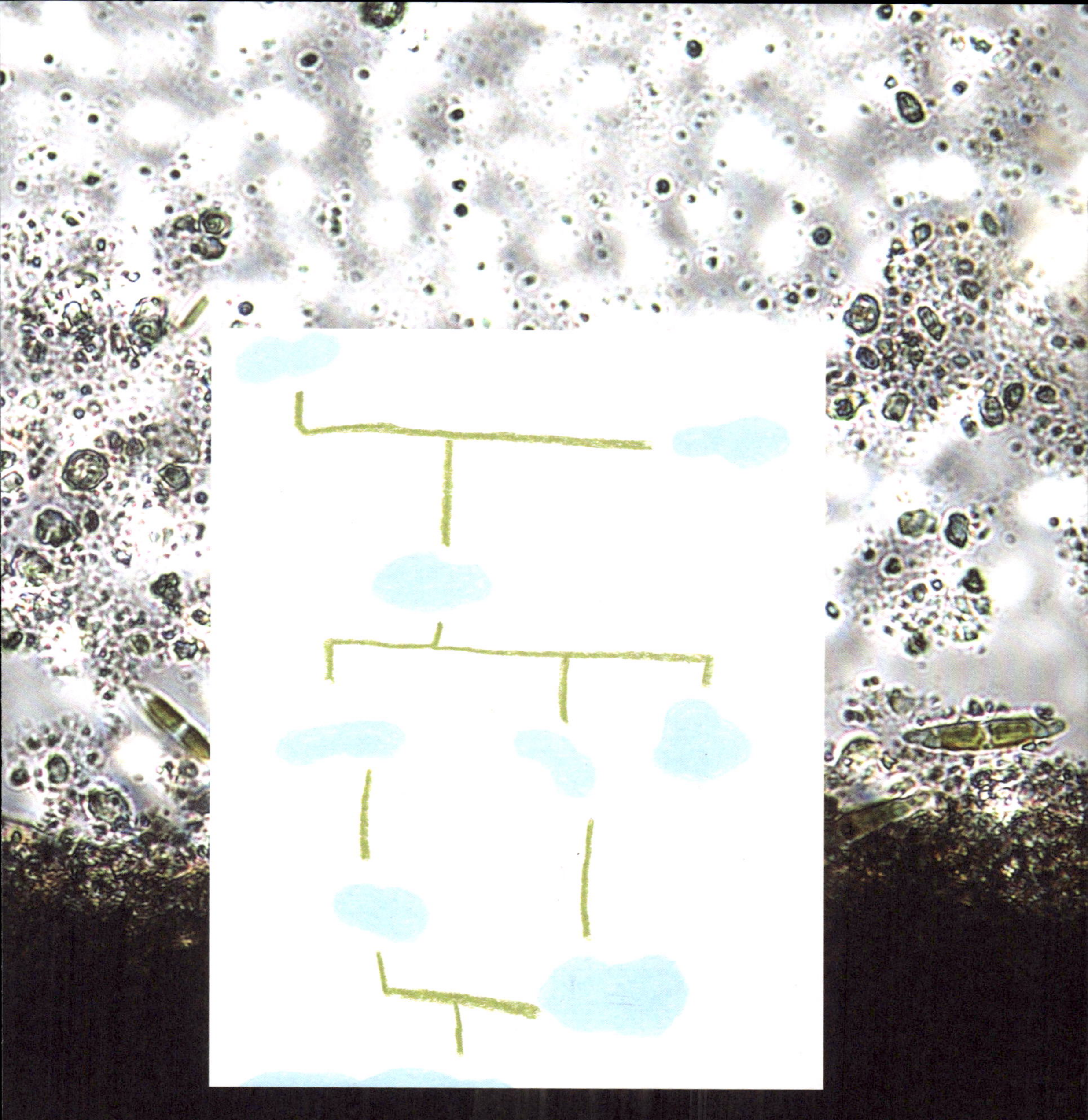

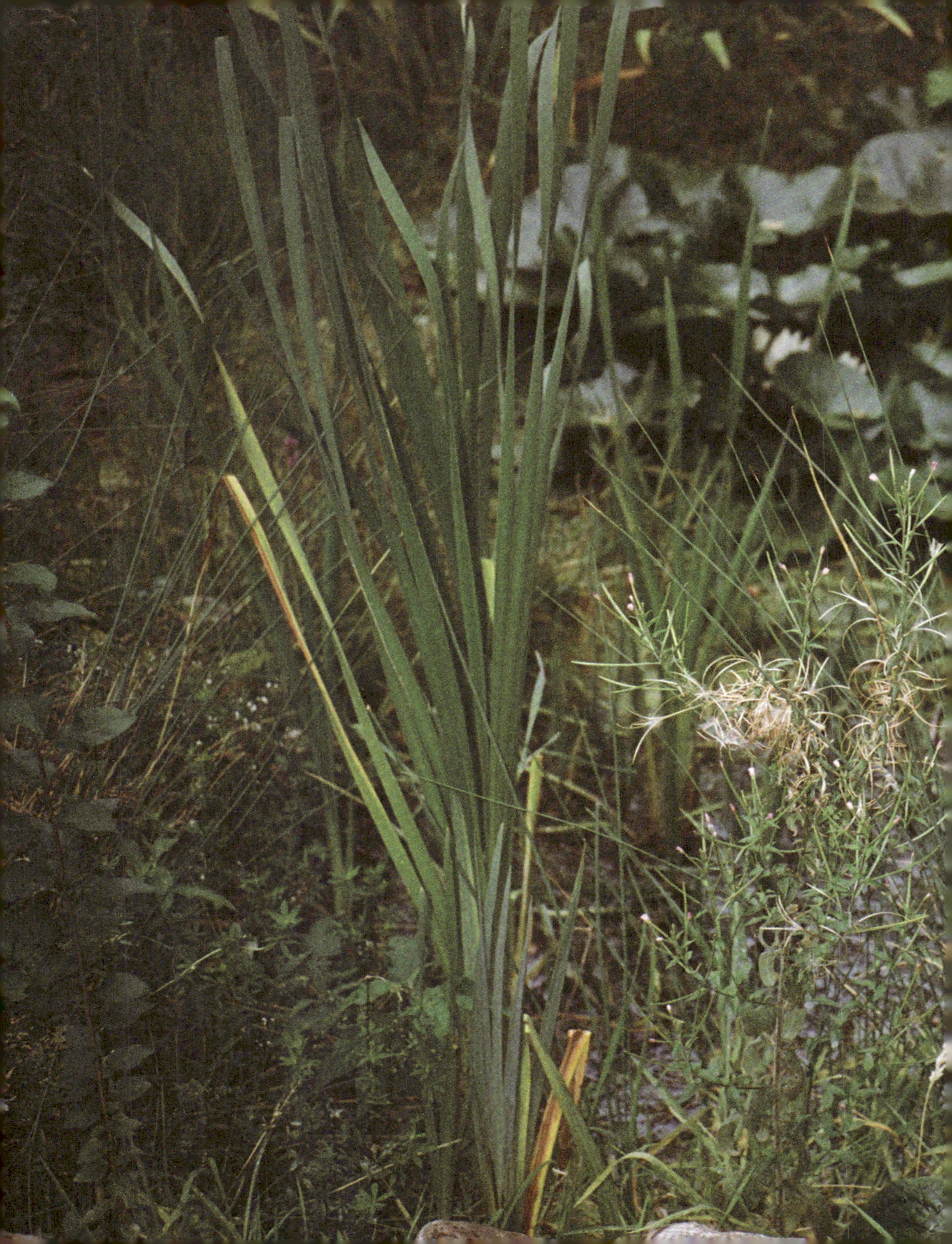

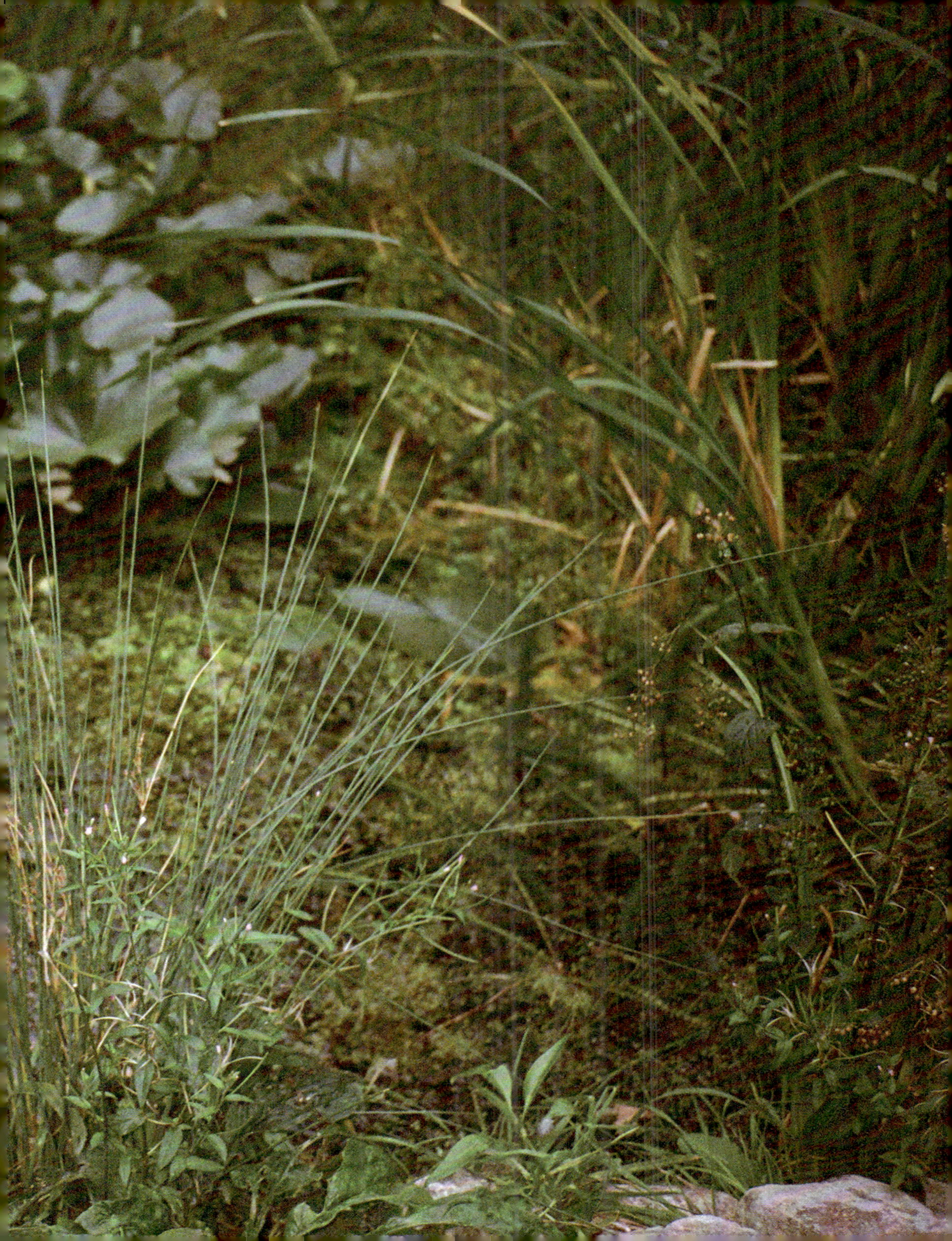

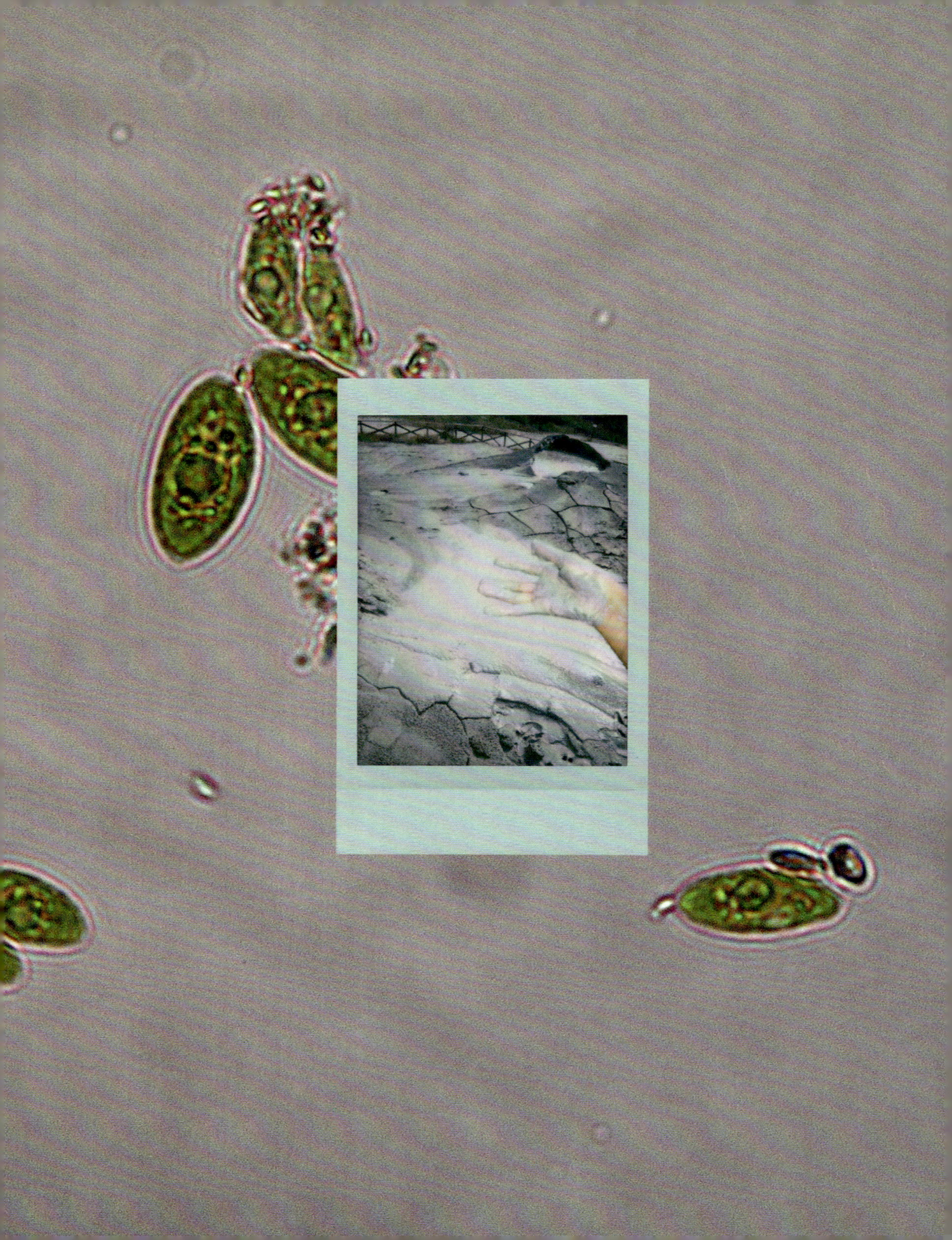

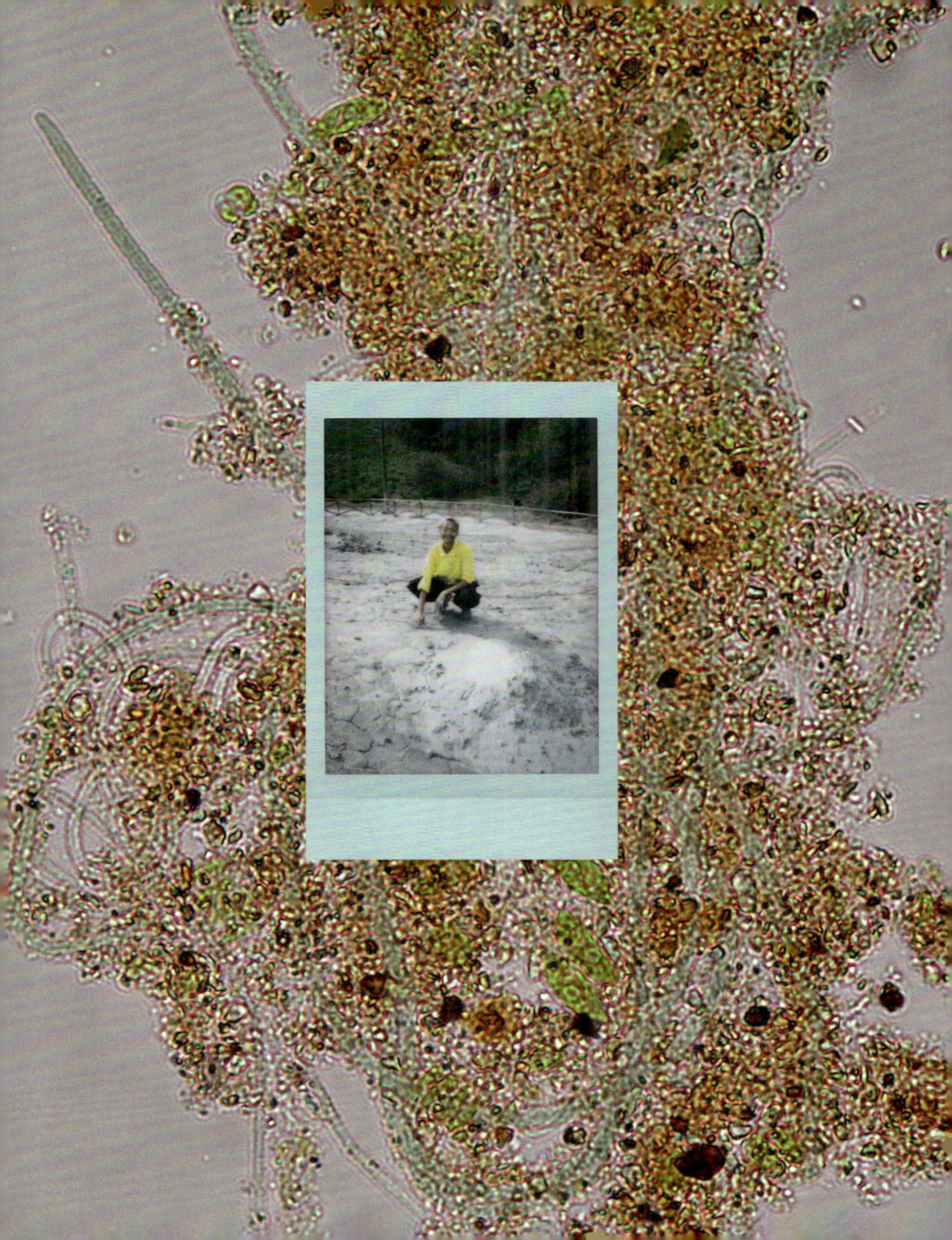

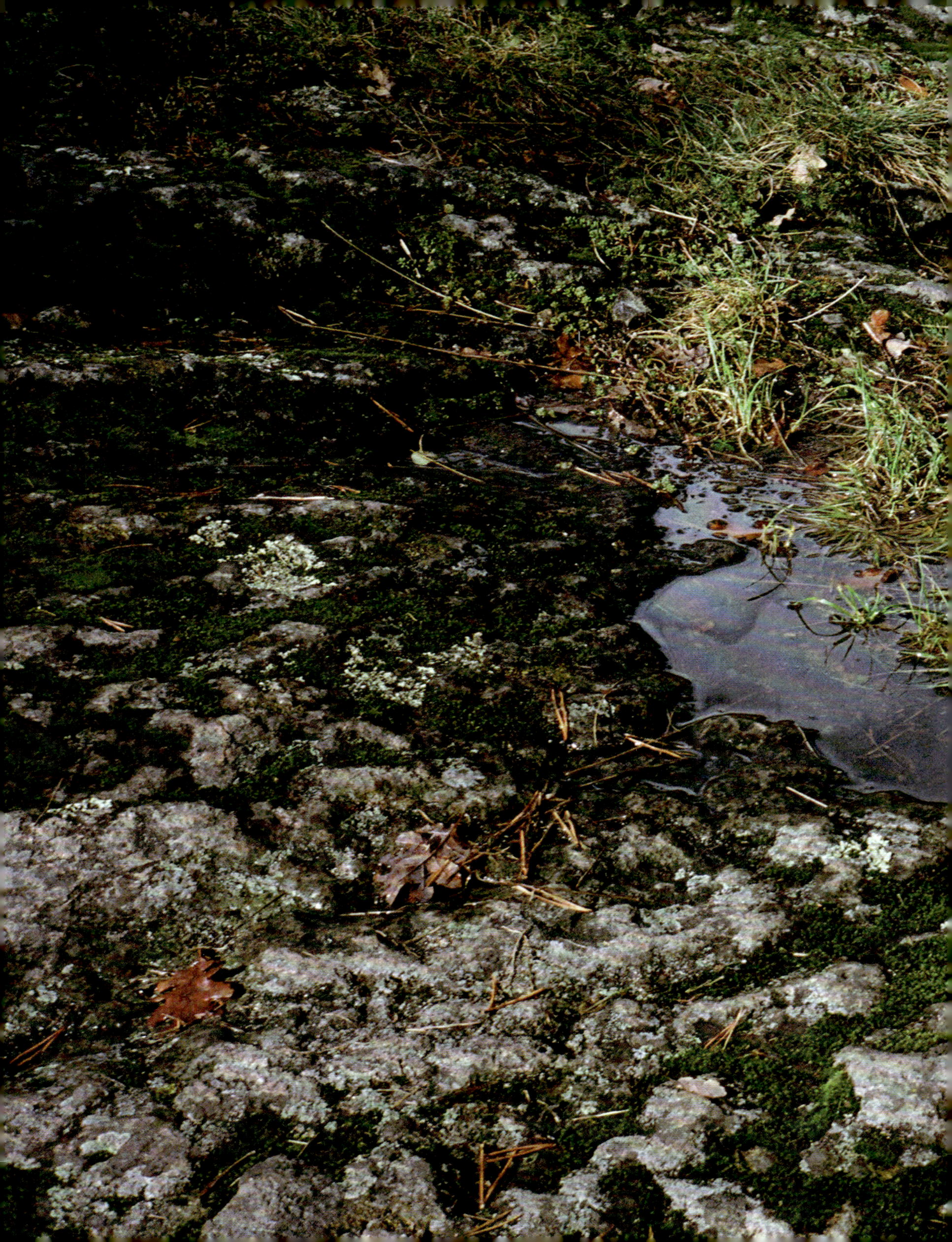

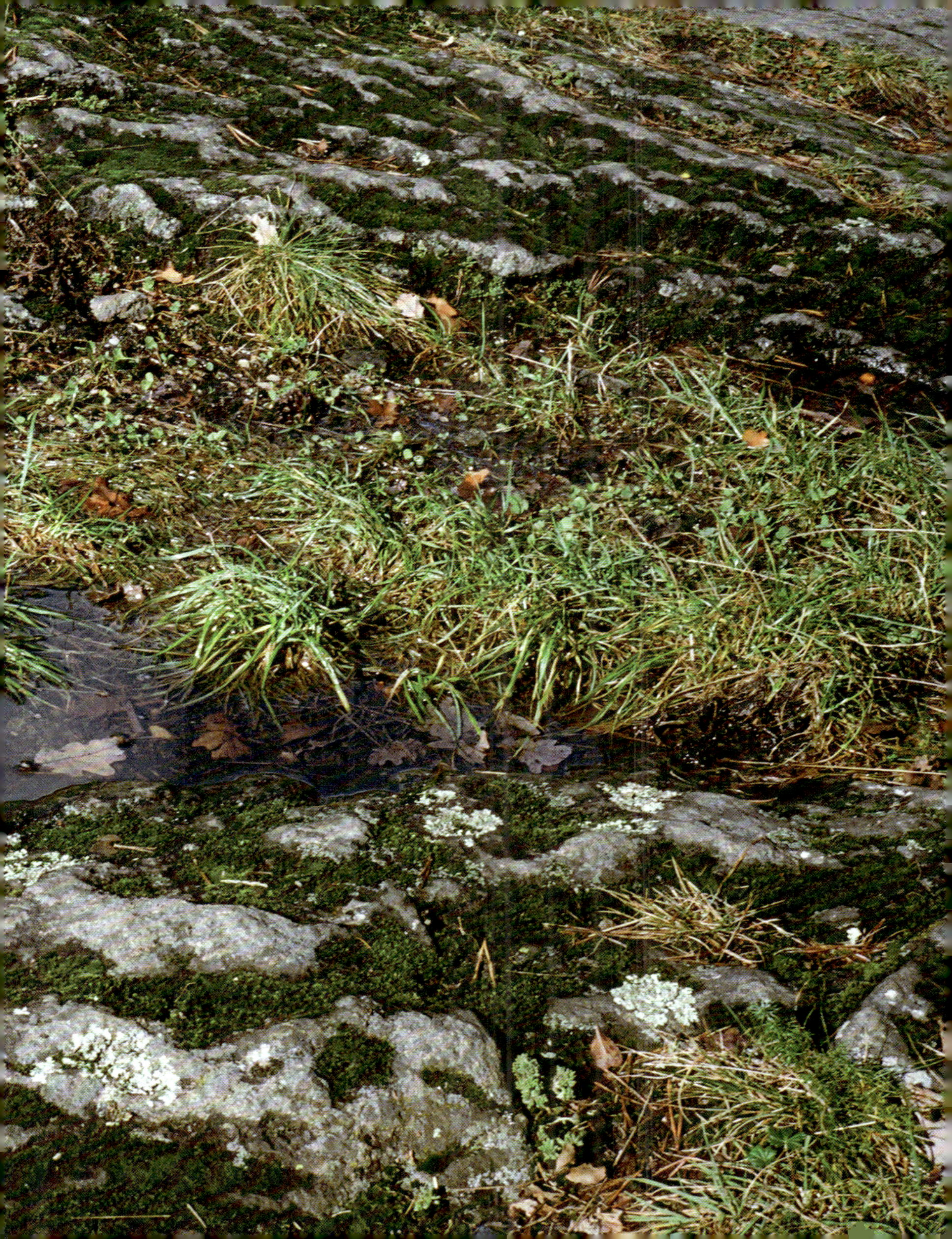

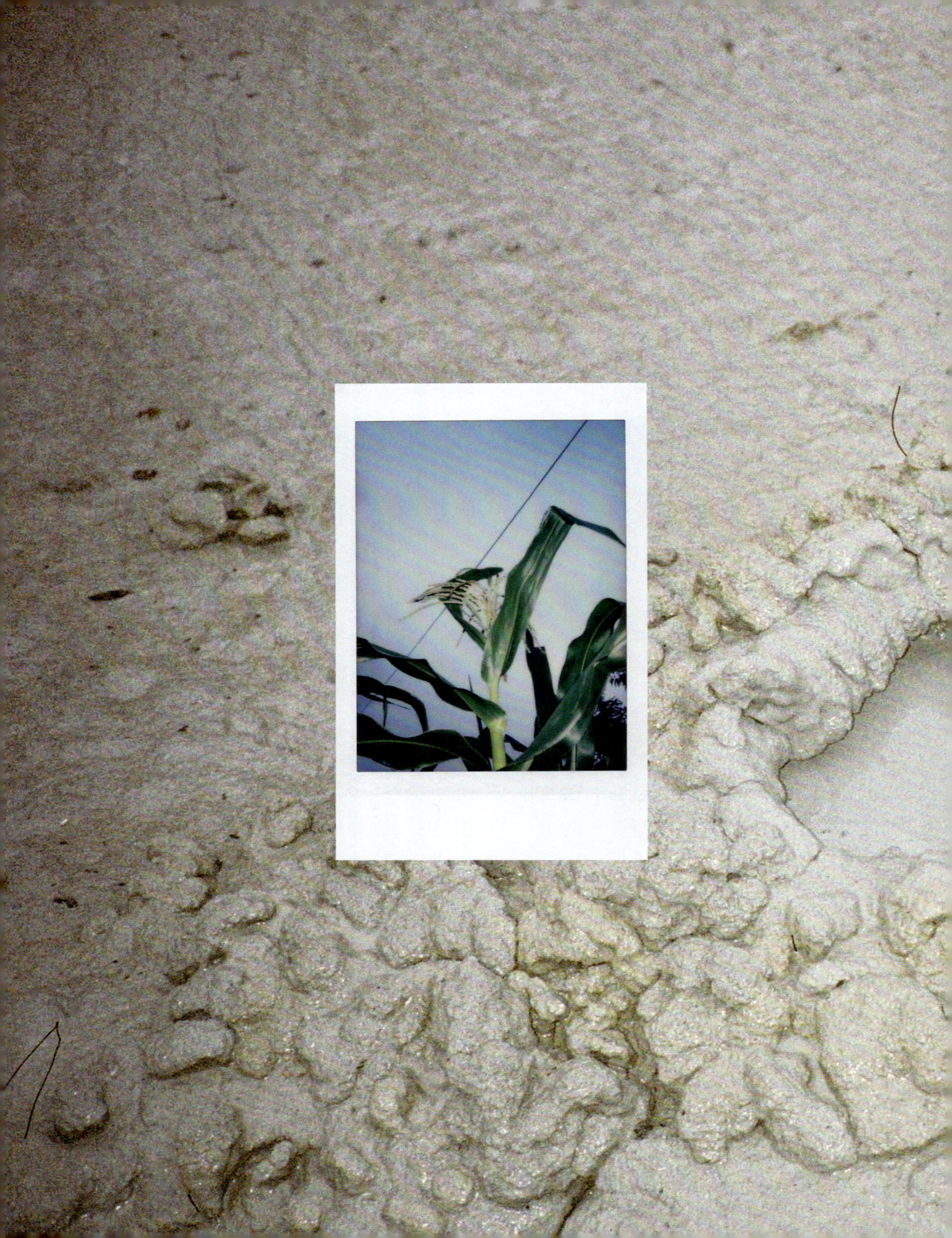

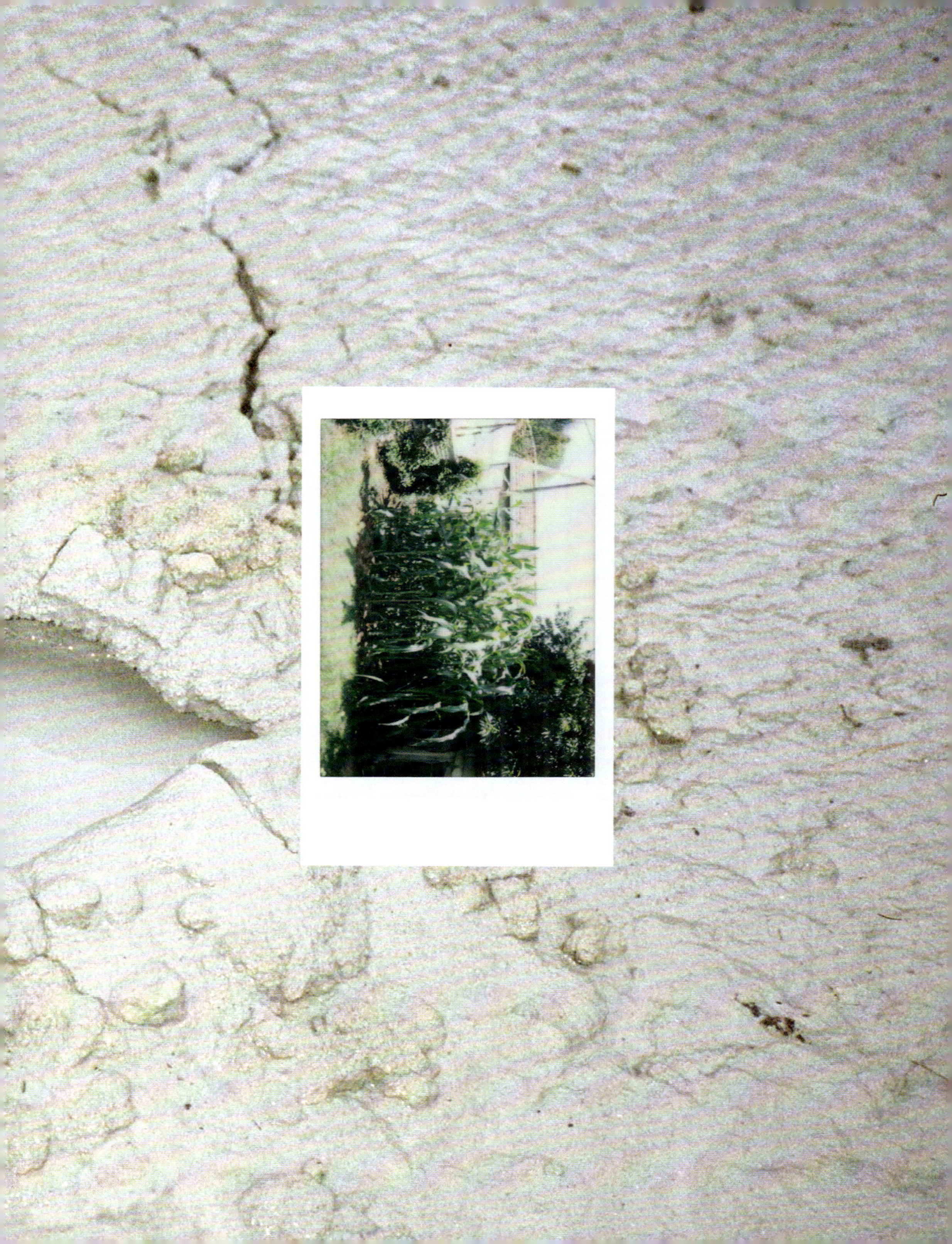

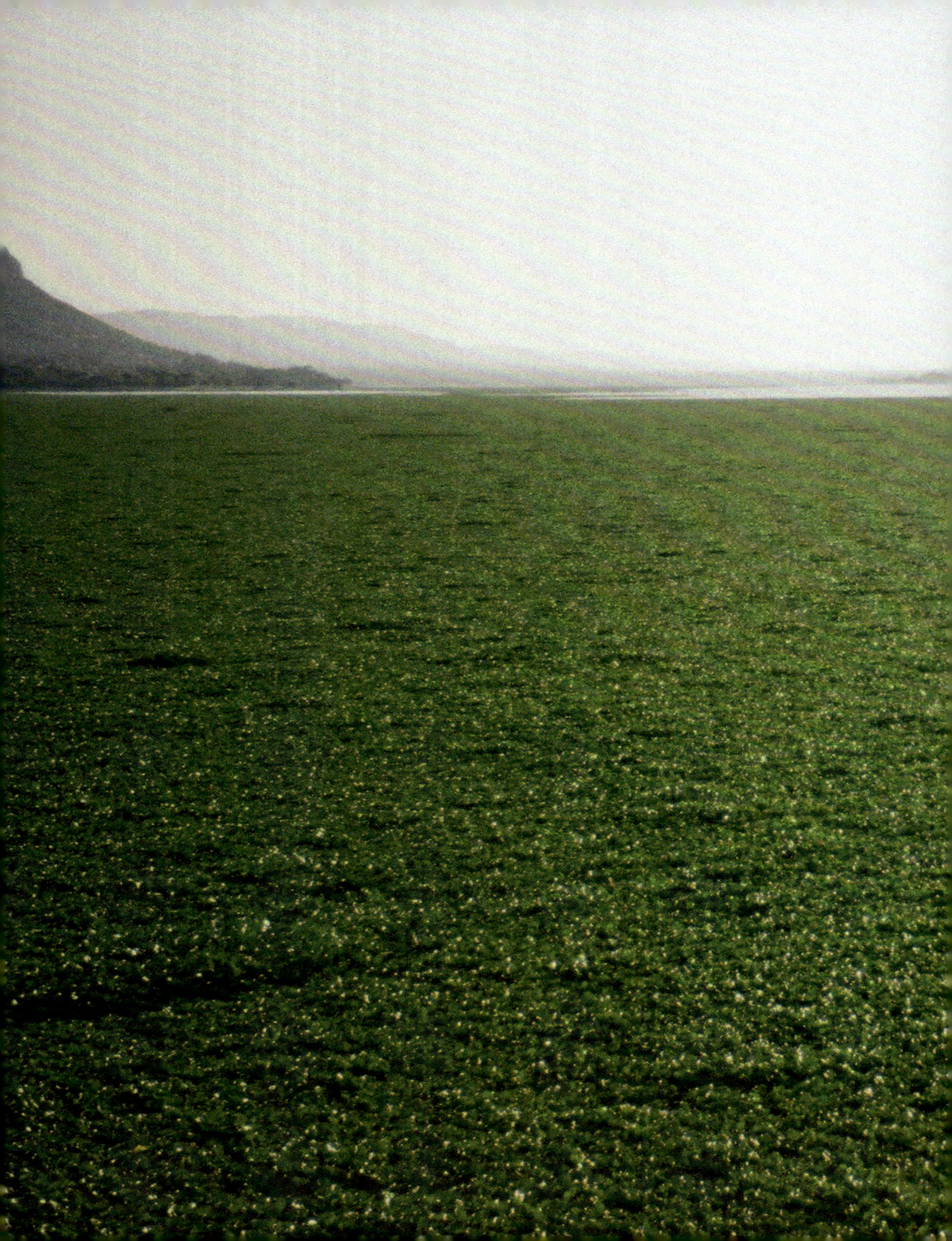

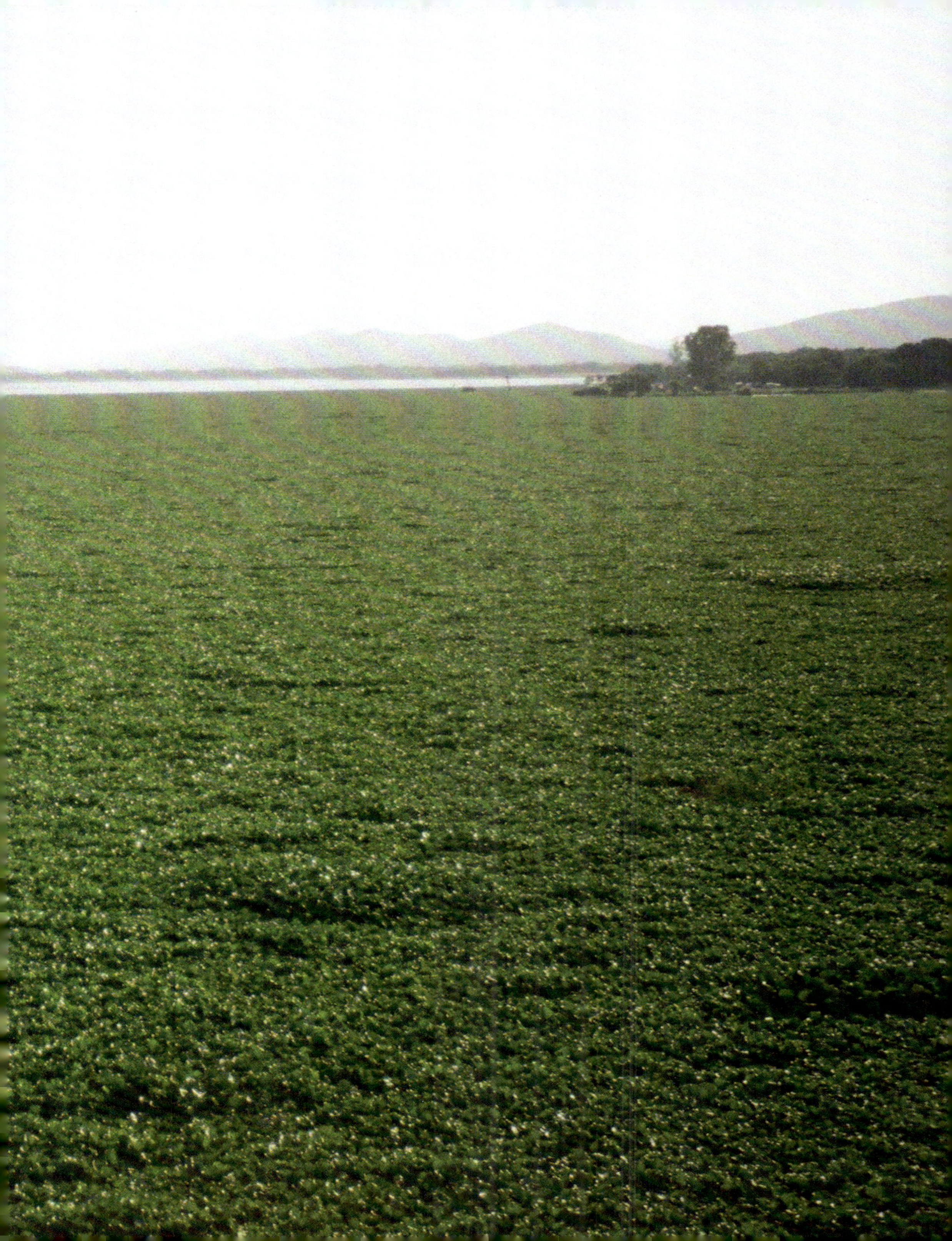

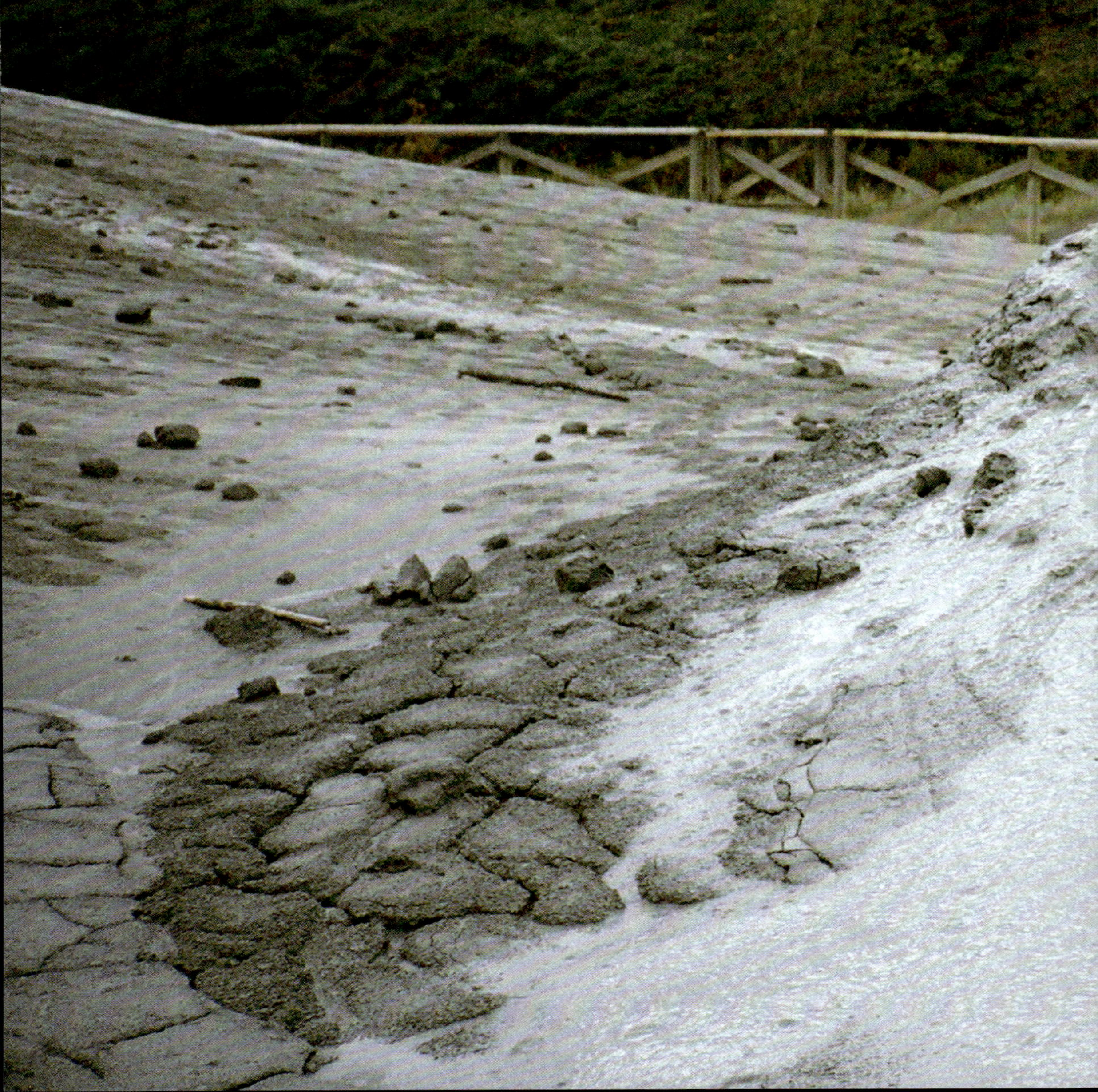

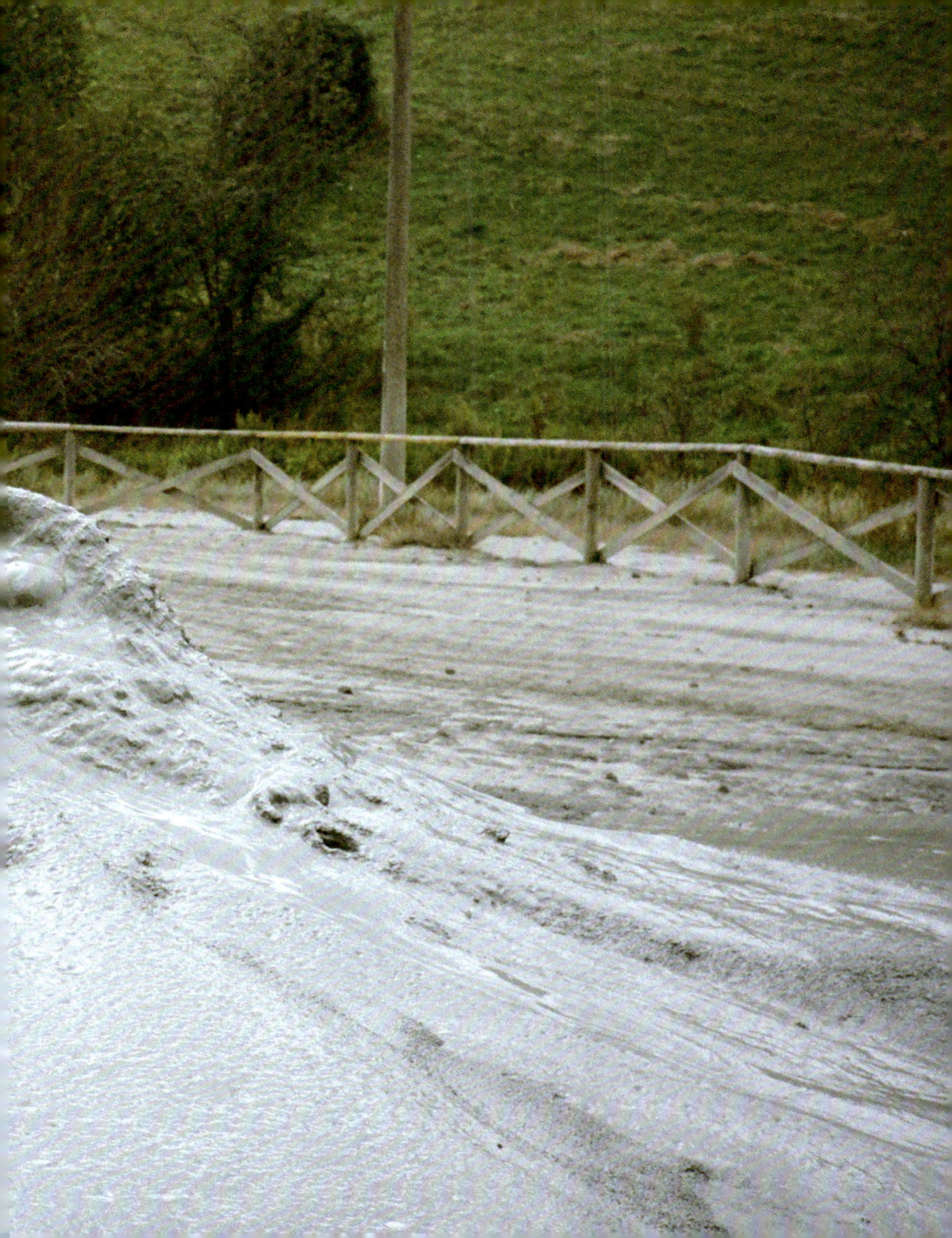

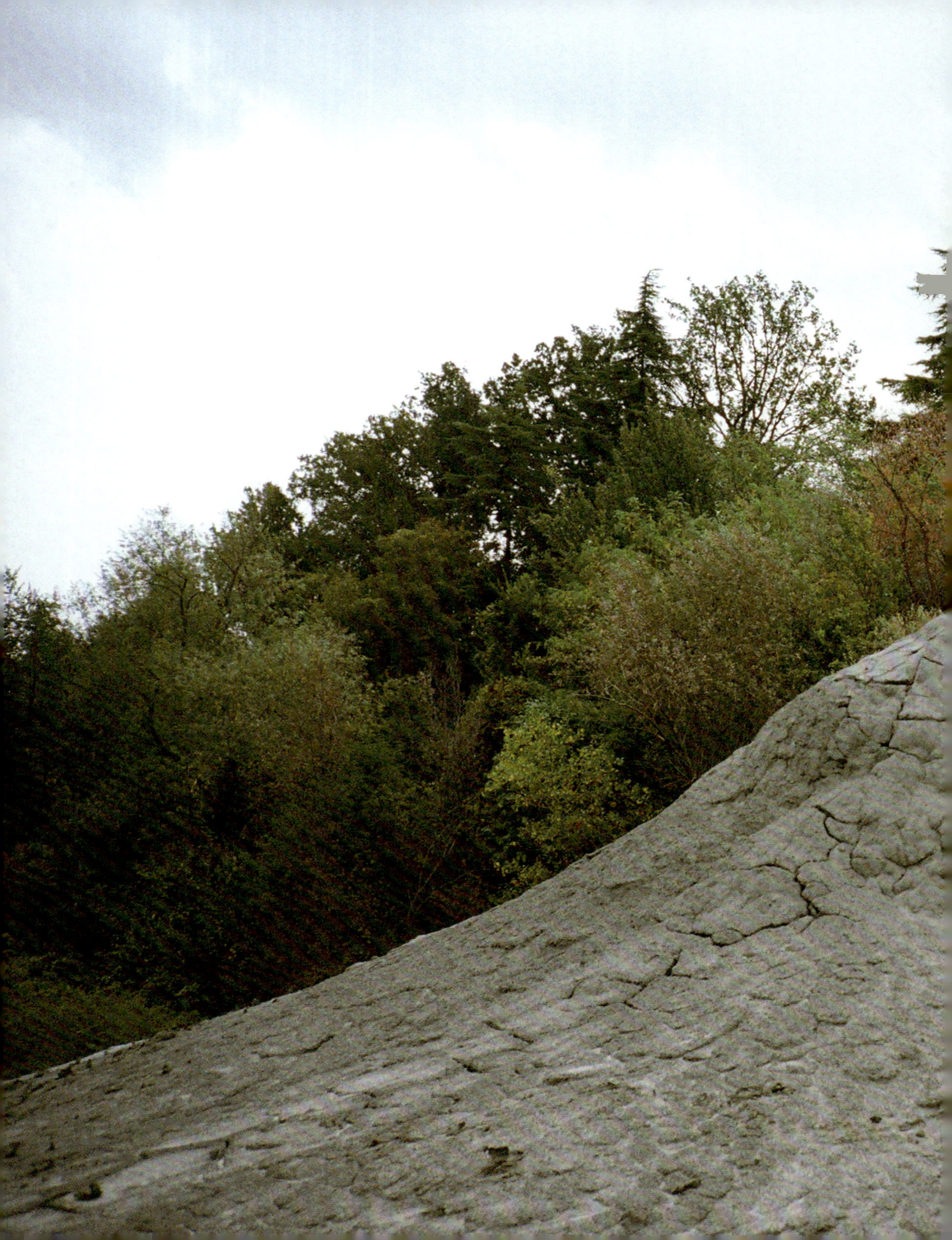

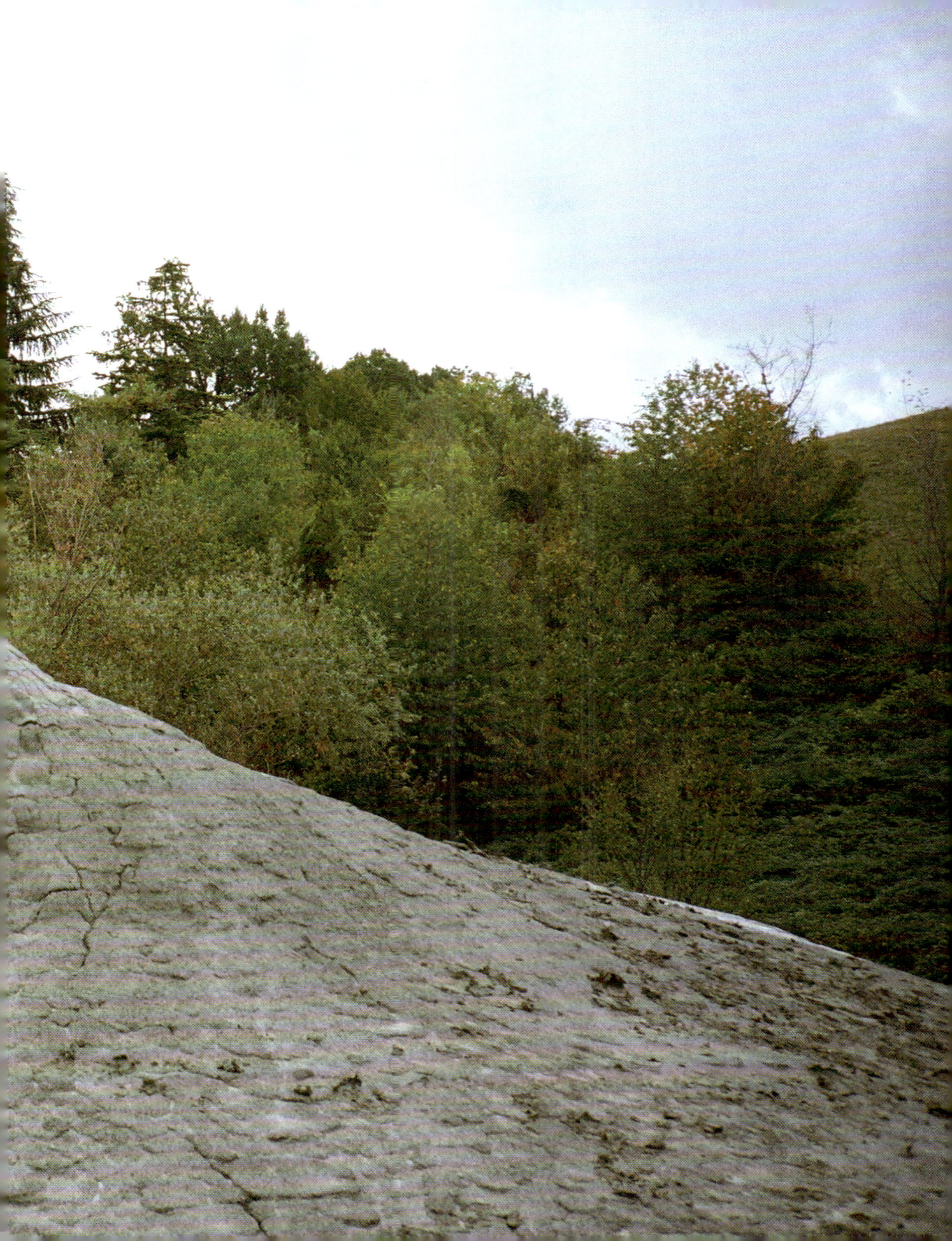

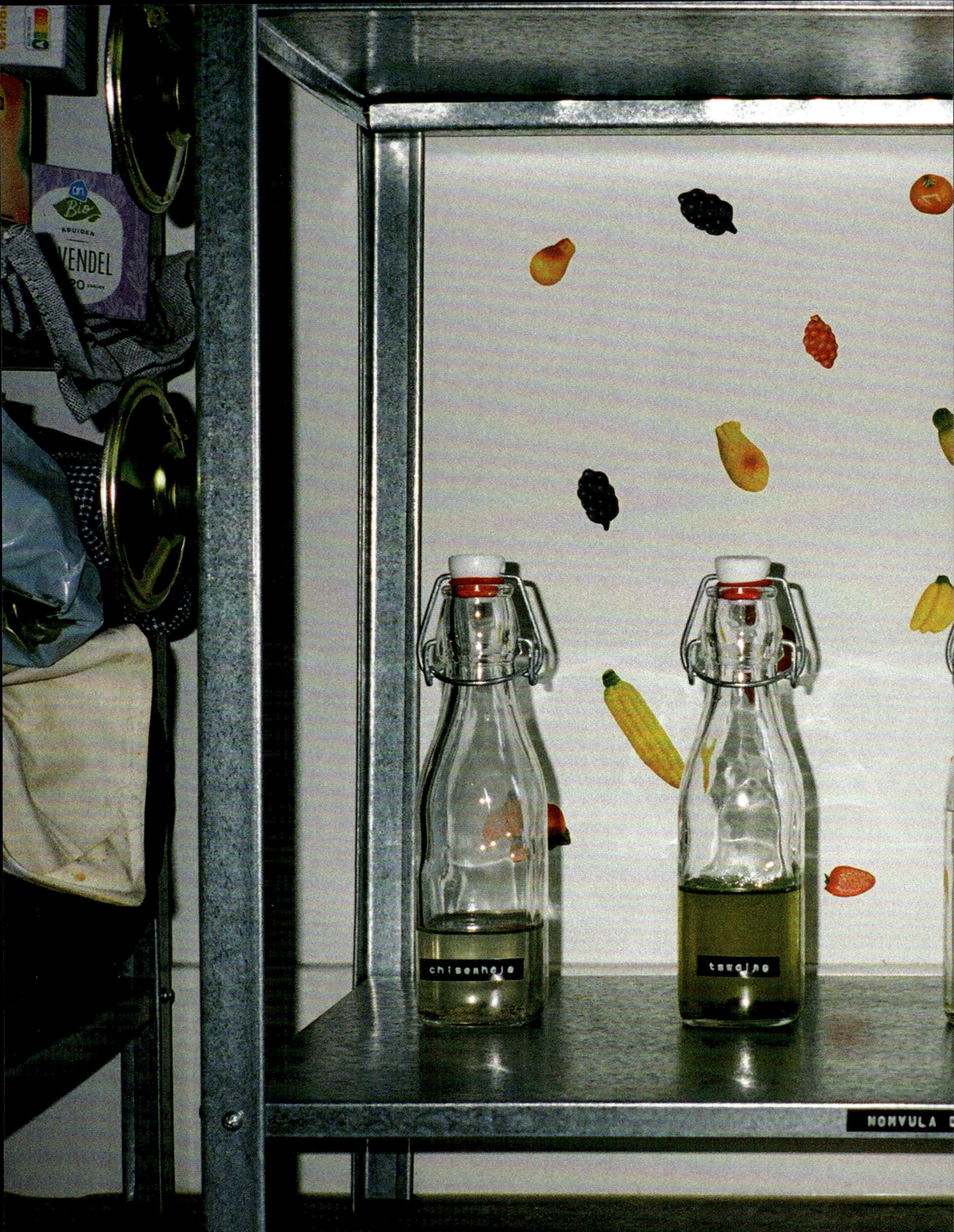
Bio
KRUIDEN

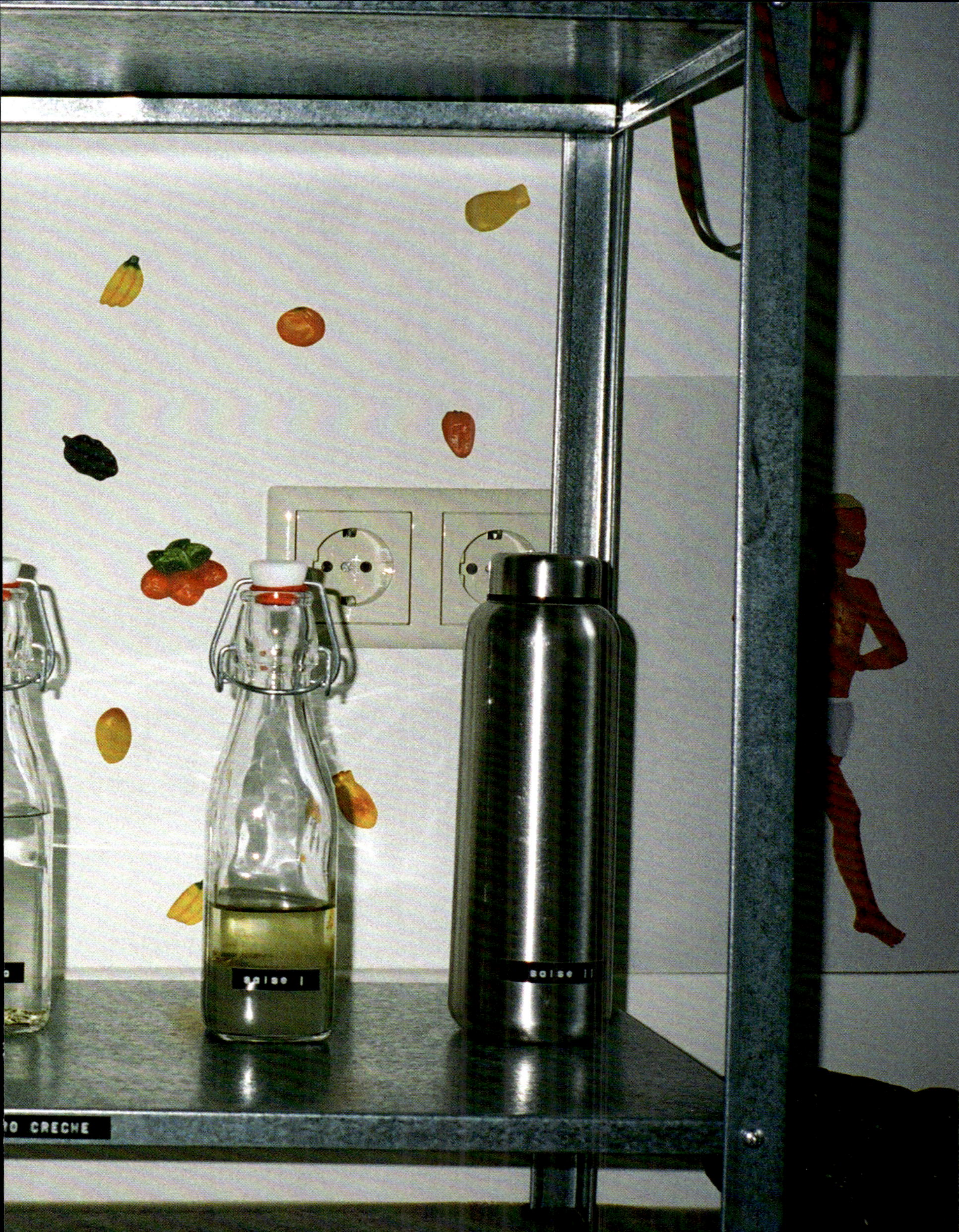
salse I
salse II
CRECHE

Zoé Whitley

to friends and 'yet unknown friends'

Dr. Zoé Whitley is Chisenhale Gallery's Director. An award-winning curator, she co-curated the acclaimed Tate Modern exhibition *Soul of a Nation: Art in the Age of Black Power* and its subsequent international tour (2017–2020). Whitley has distinguished herself working in UK institutions British Pavilion, Venice Biennale (2019); Tate Modern (2014–19); Tate Britain (2013–15); V&A (2003–2013), and also as a writer for all reading ages including children's titles *Meet the Artist: Frank Bowling; Meet the Artist: Sophie Taeuber-Arp;* and consulting for the multiple prize-winning young adult non-fiction reader *Black Artists Shaping the World.* She is a Trustee of the Teiger Foundation and Sir John Soane's Museum, as well as a member of the London Mayor's Commission on Diversity in the Public Realm.

Shadows in the Water

Thomas Traherne
(c. 1637–1674)

In unexperienced infancy
Many a sweet mistake doth lie:
Mistake though false, intending true;
A seeming somewhat more than view;
    That doth instruct the mind
    In things that lie behind,
And many secrets to us show
Which afterwards we come to know.

Thus did I by the water's brink
Another world beneath me think;
And while the lofty spacious skies
Reverséd there, abused mine eyes,
    I fancied other feet
    Came mine to touch or meet;
As by some puddle I did play
Another world within it lay.

Beneath the water people drowned,
Yet with another heaven crowned,
In spacious regions seemed to go
As freely moving to and fro:
    In bright and open space
    I saw their very face;
Eyes, hands and feet they had like mine;
Another sun did with them shine.

'Twas strange that people there
should walk,
And yet I could not hear them talk:
That through a little watery chink,
Which one dry ox or horse might drink,
    We other worlds should see,
    Yet not admitted be;
And other confines there behold
Of light and darkness, heat and cold.

I called them oft, but called in vain;
No speeches we could entertain:
Yet did I there expect to find
Some other world, to please my mind.
I plainly saw by these
  A new antipodes,
Whom, though they were so
plainly seen,
A film kept off that stood between.

By walking men's reverséd feet
I chanced another world to meet;
Though it did not to view exceed
A phantom, 'tis a world indeed,
    Where skies beneath us shine,
    And earth by art divine
Another face presents below,
Where people's feet against ours go.

Within the regions of the air,
Compassed about with heavens fair,
Great tracts of land there may be found
Enriched with fields and fertile ground;
    Where many numerous hosts
    In those far distant coasts,
For other great and glorious ends
Inhabit, my yet unknown friends.

O ye that stand upon the brink,
Whom I so near me through the chink
With wonder see: what faces there,
Whose feet, whose bodies, do ye wear?
    I my companions see
    In you, another me.
They seeméd others, but are we;
Our second selves these shadows be.

'The only curveball I wish to throw is to not think of it as a foreword (I imagine it can land at an unpredictable moment of the publication), so to write the text not as an introduction but something that will happen "in the middle of a sentence"'.

– Simnikiwe Buhlungu, via email

Directors' forewords are commonplace. Simnikiwe Buhlungu's artistic investigations are anything but. So it seems fitting here to deviate from the standard preamble format for the many thanks due.

Nestled among the other contributors – rather than cutting in line to the front of the queue, Simnikiwe made a generous invitation that Gabi Ngcobo and I, as co-commissioning institutional leads, echo one another with our institutional expressions of gratitude. Conversationally, we're not so much finishing one another's sentences as interjecting our thanks to those who have facilitated this ongoing conversation.

My mind immediately went to e e cummings' poem '[in Just-]' where the line 'when the world is puddle-wonderful' anchors the first and second halves of the verses, like a thorax to butterfly wings. Simnikiwe is that rare artist whose research flutters effortlessly between the metaphysical and the concrete which is maybe how I landed upon the puddle-licious words of 17th century metaphysical poet and theologian Thomas Traherne. So much in his 'Shadows in the Water' poem – a willingness to turn inward, a generous questioning of what in the natural world is measurable, how what we observe might constitute the basis of our reality but needn't be the only gauge – resonates with Simnikiwe's project. I marvel at the age of the poem because, bar the odd turn of phrase, it reads as a very contemporary poetic interrogation of different knowledges revealing themselves from below the surface and being absorbed from the surrounding air.

One stanza in particular segues especially fittingly from evocations of palpable humidity to being grounded and earth-bound; Traherne then leads us to a descriptive welling up of greater bodies of water and the formation of new friendships and kinships:

'Within the regions of the air,
Compassed about with heavens fair,
Great tracts of land there
may be found
Enriched with fields and
fertile ground;
Where many
numerous hosts
In those far distant coasts,
For other great and
glorious ends
Inhabit, my yet
unknown friends.'

Numerous friends had faith in this project when it was unseen and unformed, not yet a ripple, including each and every contributor in this volume. Chisenhale Gallery remains grateful to Sir Frank and Lady Rachel

Numerous friends had faith in this project when it was unseen and unformed, not yet a ripple, including each and every contributor in this volume. Chisenhale Gallery remains grateful to Sir Frank and Lady Rachel Bowling for their steadfast support of our publications. Mondriaan Fund and the Embassy of the Kingdom of the Netherlands invest in their artist residents and we are grateful for their funding alongside Arts Council England. This book has benefitted particularly from the early commitment of Mercedes Vilardell, Marcus and Alexa Waley-Cohen alongside Chisenhale's ardent Board of Trustees and Commissions Fund members. To inelegantly belabour my thoracic Cummings reference above, the vital organs of the gallery are Chisenhale's tirelessly dedicated staff, past and present. We aim always to give artists the gift of time to ideate and the gift of critical friendship to hone and realise concepts. To do so with partners as committed and catalysing as Kunstinstituut Melly is a privilege.

The collective effort of individuals pooling their skills, selves, and resources has resulted in this tremendously original project.

DATE	OPENING TIME	CONDITION	CLOSING TIME
19-02-2024	11h39	SEEMS ALL GOOD. BUT WHAT DOES OPENING THE LID / EXPOSURE TO OXYGEN DO?. ARE THESE FOLKS ALIVE ?! I CAN'T TELL. (ROOM TEMP: 12° ; ROOM HUMIDITY: 50 %.)	21h32
20-02-2024	11h25	FINE. IT SEEMS TSWAING'S SEDIMENT IS BECOMING MORE 'SOLID'? I DON'T KNOW IF UMBONA IS DOING WELL. IS IT TOO HOT IN THE STUDIO? (ROOM TEMP: 15° ; ROOM HUMIDITY: 50 %.)	17h36
23-02-2024	18h30	FINE. HOW DOES SEDIMENTATION HAPPEN? (ROOM TEMP: 11° ; ROOM HUMIDITY: 50°) ↳ 'IT FEELS COLDER'.	18h40
29-02-2024	11h22	BEEN GONE SINCE THE 24TH. TSWAING'S ALGAE WASN'T FLOATING ON TOP, BUT ALL THE WATER APPEARED 'GREEN'. UMBONA LOOKS OKAY, IF ALIVE... (ROOM TEMP: 10° ; ROOM HUMIDITY: 50°)	20h45
02-03-2024	15h41	RE-READ NORBERT'S NOTES. THINK THEY NEED SOME SUN. PUT THEM BOTH ON WINDOW SILL AS THERE ARE GLIMMERS OF SUNLIGHT TODAY. UMBONA LOOKS THE SAME. SOME OF TSWAING'S [GREEN] ALGAE IS ALSO BECOMING SEDIMENT. IS THAT MEANT TO HAPPEN?? SIGH. WHAT A RESPONSIBILITY TO RUN THIS CRÈCHE; TO KEEP THESE SAMPLES ALIVE! ANYWHO. (ROOM TEMP: 18° ; ROOM HUMIDITY: 40 %.) → WHERE IS THE CONSISTENCY?	21h25
04-03-2024	11h11	ALL SEEMS THE SAME. SALSE DI NIRANO SAMPLE STILL IN METAL BOTTLE! A BIT OF SUNLIGHT TODAY. MAYBE THEY (↳ TSWAING & UMBONA) NEED THE VITAMIN D LIKE I DO. (ROOM TEMP: 19° ; ROOM HUMIDITY: 45 %.). ↳ HEATERS AREN'T ON. SPRING IS COMING!	16h30
05-03-2024	12h43	FINE. THE ALGAE LAYER IN TSWAING SEEMS TO BE GETTING THINNER. WHY? WHEN TO TRANSFER SALSE'S SAMPLE INTO CLEAR PLASTIC BOTTLE? (ROOM TEMP: 15° ; ROOM HUMIDITY: 50 %.)	16h54
06-03-2024	11h48	SAME, SAME. SUN IS OUT TODAY. (ROOM TEMP: 17° ; ROOM HUMIDITY: 45 %.)	16h50
11-03-2024	11h16	CALM. IT IS RAINING OUTSIDE. UMBONA IS QUIET. THE ALGAE (?) IN TSWAING SEEMS TO BE GETTING THINNER AND SEDIMENTING / CLUSTERING INTO CHUNKS. MAYBE TOO MUCH LIGHT / SUN?. GOOD NEWS THOUGH: SALSE DI NIRANO'S SAMPLES HAVE OFFICIALLY JOINED THE CRÈCHE! ONE IN TRANSPARENT BOTTLE, THE OTHER IN A METAL WATER BOTTLE. NAME TAGS HAVE ARRIVED ☺ (ROOM TEMP: 15° ; ROOM HUMIDITY: 50 %.).	18h32

DATE	OPENING TIME	CONDITION	CLOSING TIME
12-03-2024	13h37	VERY SOFT/LIGHT SUN. ALL GOOD. BUT. SALSE (I) HAS SEPARATED INTO WATER AND SEDIMENT! I WISH YOU COULD SEE IT. I WONDER IF THERE ARE GASSES (LIKE METHANE) SOMEHOW IN THIS SAMPLE. HOW TO TEST FOR THAT? (ASK SAÏD!). EVERYONE ELSE IS GOOD. TSWAING'S ALGAE IS STILL IN CLUMPS... DOES TSWAING HAVE A HIGH SALT CONTENT? HOW TO TEST FOR THAT? (ASK SAÏD!). (ROOM TEMP: 16°, ROOM HUMIDITY: 45%.)	18h50
13-03-2024	10h43	WE'RE GOOD. TSWAING IS A BIT STINKY. THE SEDIMENT OF SALSE (I) LOOKS LIKE THE SURFACE OF [WHAT WE HAVE BEEN TOLD AS] A PLANET. UMBONA IS UMBONA. (ROOM TEMP: 15°; ROOM HUMIDITY: 50%.)	17h44
19-03-2024	9:23	OVERCAST TODAY (NO SUN :( ). Everyone looks good... I think. Tswaing needed air, their bottle was alittle sucked in, but their algae looks good and seems to be growing??. (ROOM T°: 15°, ROOM HUMIDITY: 50%	17:05
20-03-2024	9:50	(Room T°: 15°, Room HUMIDITY: 50%) Tswaing's water looks a little yellower? Algae is forming smaller clumps concentrated at the Centre of the bottle. Salse I's water is quite milky today.	18:22
21-03-2024	12:34	(Room T°: 13°, ROOM HUMIDITY: 50%) Really cold today, Low light (very over cast) Tswaing's algae has concentrated at the edges again, forming a ring. Salse I's water has cleared. Umbona stays chilling.	17:48
23-03-2024	11:37	(Room T°: 14°, Room HUMIDITY: 50%) Its Sunny today. Tswaing's algae looks thick and gel-like, still concentrated along the edges. Everyone else looks the same... all chilling.	18:00
25-03-2024	09:19	(Room T°: 13°, Room Humidity: 50%) The "gel" layer under Tswaing's algae has concentrated on the surface and has begun to grow new algae "strings"? like this → 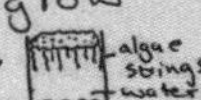 looks pretty cool so I took a photo. Umbona is still chilling, nothing to report. Salse I's clay sediment looks like the full moon. ps.. It was full moon last night.	16:50.
27-03-2024	09:23	(Room T°: 14°, Room Humidity: 45%) More or less the same as above.	17:48
29-03-2024	11:38	(Room T°: 15°, Room Humidity: 45%) Tswaing's water looks more yellow-green. algae is thick and transporent green. Some late afternoon sunlight for the Children...	

DATE	OPENING TIME	CONDITION	CLOSING TIME
30-03-2024	13:42	(Room T°: 13°, Room Humidity: 50%) Very Cold, Grey and Rainy today. Tswaing's Algae gel layer has reduced and become stringy again.	19:30
31-03-2024	12:23	(Room T°: 14°, Room Humidity: 50%) Tswaing's water looks less yellow today. Much more Clear. Algae is concentrated to the water surface, very stringy.	18:53
01-04-2024	09:53	(Room T°: 14°, Room Humidity: 50%) Same Same. Everyone is getting along.	16:12
04-04-2024	10:47	(Room T°: 12°, Room Humidity: 55%) Tswaing's algae is alot less concentrated to the ~~top~~ water surface, less algae altogether. Perhaps more consistent opening times are needed? P.S. It's cold and rainy and grey....	18:37
05-04-2024	14:27	(Room T°: 18°, Room Humidity: 45%) Sunny and warm today. It rained earlier. Have given the babies some time in the sun.	18:52.
08-04-2024	10h20	TSWAING IS SO... SLENDER NOW. LESS OF THE ALGAE LAYER AND MUCH MORE COLLECTIVE SEDIMENT. KEEPING SALSE II CLOSED. EVERYONE ELSE IS SUPERBLY ~~BEHAVIG~~ BEHAVED. (ROOM TEMP: 17°; ROOM HUMIDITY: 50%.)	16h50
09-04-2024	10h53	BAYAFANA. (TSWAING ISN'T STINKY ANYMORE) (ROOM TEMP: 19°; ROOM HUMIDITY: 50%.)	18h28
10-04-2024	10h43	I HAVEN'T ACCOUNTED FOR EVAPORATION AND HOW THIS DECREASES SAMPLE LEVELS. ALL GOOD. UMBONA MUST BE ... GONE. IT'S JUST DOING NOTHING. (ROOM TEMP: 18°; ROOM HUMIDITY: 55%.)	17h10
11-04-2024	15h08	I HAVE DECIDED TO KEEP THEM ALL CLOSED TODAY. TSWAING IS GETTING STRINGY AGAIN. (THE ALGAE). ALGAE ACCUMULATED ON THE EDGE OF THE BOTTLE, SO MAYBE IT WAS LOST THERE (OWING TO EVAPORATION). I THINK I GIVE PREFERENTIAL TREATMENT TO TSWAING. NOT GOOD. I ALSO GET THE SENSE THAT I AM FORGETTING GRAMMAR & SPELLING. WORSE. UMBONA IS GOOD (PROBS DEAD) AND SALSE IS AS CELESTIAL AS EVER. WHAT KIND OF CRÈCHE AM I RUNNING?! (ROOM TEMP: 20°; ROOM HUMIDITY: 50%.)	15h08

DATE	OPENING TIME	CONDITION	CLOSING TIME
15-04-2024	13h54	TODAY I'LL OPEN THEM FOR A BIT. AT THE END OF THIS MONTH/EARLY MAY WE WILL GO TO PROF. NORBERT IN WAGENINGEN FOR MICROSCOPIC IMAGING. WHAT AN EXCITING FIELD TRIP AHEAD! TSWAING IS GETTING STRINGY. THE WATER ABOVE THE SEDIMENT OF SALSE I IS GETTING MORE BROWN. IT'S RAINY AND WINDY OUTSIDE (ROOM TEMP: 16° ; ROOM HUMIDITY: 45%.)	15h56
20-04-2024	13h32	I HAVE KEPT THEM CLOSED FOR THE PAST 15 DAYS. TSWAING'S ALGAE IS FLOATING AGAIN. THEY'RE ALL BROWN. SOME SUN TODAY. (ROOM TEMP: 18° ; ROOM HUMIDITY: 44-15H%.)	—
	17h15	I FORGOT TO OPEN THEM! AH. SO ~~GA~~ GIVING THEM SOME AIR NOW. MISSED OPPORTUNITY AS THERE WAS SUN. PITY... (ROOM TEMP: 21° ; ROOM HUMIDITY: 41-15H%.)	± 20h26
22-04-2024	11h14	WOW! I CAME IN TO FIND UMBONA'S SEDIMENT FLOATING. THEY'RE ALL TURNING YELLOW → BROWN. IS IT A VITAMIN D DEFICIENCY? SHOULD I HAVE USED GLASS BOTTLES? SHIT! MICRO PLASTICS... I'LL KEEP TSWAING CLOSED FOR A BIT TO LET THE ALGAE DO ITS THING. DAMN... MICROPLASTICS! (ROOM TEMP: 14° ; ROOM HUMIDITY: 45%.) (NOW PUT THEM IN THE SUN)	18h10
26-04-2024	21h05	TSWAING THRIVES (THE ALGAE) WHEN THE BOTTLE LID IS CLOSED FOR A FEW DAYS. AFRAID OF OXYGEN? I'LL CLOSE AFTER AN HOUR OR SO. WILL KEEP UMBONA AND SALSE I OPEN FOR A BIT LONGER. OH! A NEW SAMPLE WILL JOIN US SOON: CHISENHALE'S FRONT ENTRANCE PUDDLE! I NEED TO LIAISE WITH TAYLOR (LE MELLE) TO CO-ORDINATE A DROP OFF AND FIRST DAY OF CRÈCHE. I HAVE ORDERED FOUR GLASS BOTTLES TO TRANSFER THE SAMPLES FOR THE FIELD TRIP TO WAGENINGEN FOR MICROSCOPY IMAGING WITH PROF. NORBERT AND FOR AFTER. A BIT SCARED OF POTENTIAL MICROPLASTIC INVITATIONS. I THINK I'LL ORDER TWO MORE GLASS BOTTLES. NEED TO ADD LABELS. ALSO NEED TO BUY DEMINERALISED WATER TO TOP UP THE SAMPLES; THEIR LEVELS HAVE REDUCED AND NEED TO BE REPLENISHED. I NEED TO WORK ON THE CRÈCHE WALLPAPER... (ROOM TEMP: 18° ; ROOM HUMIDITY: 45%.)	22h01 (TSWAING) 00h40 (EVERYONE ELSE)
〃	〃	I FORGOT TO MENTION I FOUND A DEAD MACRO-ORGANISM/PUDDLE/WATER INSECT WORM IN TSWAING EARLIER THIS WEEK!! MAYBE THAT'S WHY IT WAS STINKY?	〃

DATE	OPENING TIME	CONDITION	CLOSING TIME
27-04-2024	13h03	ALL OKAY. UMBONA'S SEDIMENT HAS A LIGHT BROWN TONE IN ADDITION TO THE DARKER SOIL-Y SEDIMENT. SALSE I ALSO HAS THIS LIGHT BROWN SEDIMENT ON TOP OF IT'S MOON-LIKE-CLAY SEDIMENT SURFACE. I WILL KEEP TSWAING OPEN FOR 1 HR. GOING TO GET DEMINERALISED WATER THIS AFTERNOON. (ROOM TEMP: 20°; ROOM HUMIDITY: 50%.)	17h26
28-04-2024	17h38	GIVING THEM SHORTER BREAKS OF OXYGEN. UMBONA'S SEDIMENT IS SO BEAUTIFUL; LIKE COPPER. TSWAING'S ALGAE IS FLOURISHING (NO SIGN OF THE DEAD WORM/WATER INSECT, PROBABLY WOUND UP IN THE SEDIMENT). SALSE I'S SEDIMENT IS BECOMING THE PLANETARY SURFACE AGAIN. THEY REALLY NEEDED A TOP UP OF THAT DEMINERALISED WATER, HEY. AG, SHAME MAN. ALL GOOD GOOD! (ROOM TEMP: 18°; ROOM HUMIDITY: 45%.)	19h21
29-04-2024	10h43	SALSE I'S WATER: SEDIMENT RATIO IS MORE APPARENT. TSWAING IS THRIVING (ALGAE-WISE). UMBONA IS... UMBONA. I FEEL SO CLOSE TO THEM ALL! (ROOM TEMP: 16°; ROOM HUMIDITY: 45%.)	12h48
30-04-2024	11h39	SALSE I'S WATER: SEDIMENT RATIO IS EVEN MORE DRASTIC TODAY. 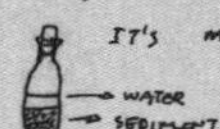 IT'S MORE COMPACTED. GRAVITY... AND TIME. THIS MORNING AS I APPROACHED THE CRÈCHE, I NOTICED A FLYING INSECT, WHICH I'M FAIRLY CERTAIN WAS A MOSQUITO. THINKING ABOUT THE OPEN SAMPLE BOTTLES, I WAS CONCERNED THAT THIS MOSQUITO WOULD - IF IT COULD - LAY EGGS IN THE SAMPLES. SO... FA. I... TOOK CARE OF IT. IT'S SUNNY TODAY AND I HAVE OPENED A WINDOW FOR FRESH AIR BUT CLOSELY MONITORING ANY MORE EGG-LAYING OPPORTUNISTS WHO MIGHT PULL THROUGH... (ROOM TEMP: 20°; ROOM HUMIDITY: 45%.)	16h33
01-05-2024	11h31	IT'S SUNNY OUTSIDE TODAY. 20°C. AT 17h00 IT IS ESTIMATED TO BE 25°C. WINDOWS OPEN. PEOPLE JOYOUS. TSWAING'S ALGAE SEEMS VERY, VERY HAPPY. ALL AROUND, SIGNS OF CONTENTMENT. (ROOM TEMP: 20°; ROOM HUMIDITY: 48%) JUST BEFORE CLOSING, I NOTICED 3 (!) WORM-WATER-INSECTS IN SALSE I. I TOOK CARE OF IT.	14h53
02-05-2024	11h47	CUE NICK HOLDER'S "SUMMER DAZE". IT IS 21°C OUTSIDE. SUN IS OUT. WINDOWS OPEN. PEOPLE CONTINUE TO BE JOYOUS. I'VE JUST (11h46) RECIEVED A TEXT FROM TAYLOR THAT THE CHISENHALE SAMPLES HAVE ARRIVED! I'M GOING TO PICK THEM UP TOMORROW. THE CRÈCHE IS GROWING. SAMPLES ALL GOOD. I'M ALERT FOR ANY CURIOUS WORMS/FLIES/INSECTS THAT MIGHT JUMP INTO THE SAMPLES BECAUSE THE WINDOWS ARE OPEN. (ROOM TEMP: 20°; ROOM HUMIDITY: 48%.)	16h08

DATE	OPENING TIME	CONDITION	CLOSING TIME
03-05-2024	14h26	SALSE I'S WATER : SEDIMENT RATIO IS ABOUT 50%., I WOULD SAY. CHISENHALE HAS ARRIVED! DID AN AFTERNOON PICK UP FROM TAYLOR (VIA IMA, AS TAYLOR IS ILL) AND NOW PREPARING CHISENHALE'S GLASS BOTTLE AND WILL DO TRANSFER. TSWAING'S ALGAE IS HAVING A PARTY; UMBONA IS RESERVED (LIKE ME). CRÈCHE WALLPAPERS SHOULD BE COMING IN THE NEXT DAYS. TODAY IT'S A BIT CHILLY, WITH SOME DRIZZLE. (ROOM TEMP: 18°C; ROOM HUMIDITY: 45%) [JEEZ! CHISENHALE STINKS!] → THE SAMPLE, NOT THE GALLERY! :)	16h22
06-05-2024	11h30	INTERESTING POST-WEEKEND DEEE-VEH-LOPE-MENT; CHISENHALE NO LONGER STINKS. THE SULPHUR SMELL HAS BEEN 'NEUTRALISED'. IT ALSO HAD SOME BUBBLES SO I WAS EXPECTING A SERIOUS SULPHURIC SITUATION BUT IT SEEMS TO HAVE RELAXED. WAS IT THE PLASTIC CARRIER/TRAVEL BOTTLE? HEAT? TIME? TRANSFER TO GLASS BOTTLE? CURIOUS... TSWAING IS ALGAE-ING. UMBONA IS RESERVED (I ASSUME). SALSE I'S SEDIMENT (THE TOP LAYER, AT LEAST) IS TURNING A KIND OF COPPER-BROWN COLOUR. WHY??? - IT'S WARM AND SUNNY OUTSIDE. THE CRÈCHE'S 'WALLPAPER' SHOULD BE INSTALLED TODAY. WAGENINGEN IN EXACTLY ONE WEEK. THE KIDS ARE ALRIGHT. (ROOM TEMP: 18.5°C; ROOM HUMIDITY: 45%)	14h50
07-05-2024	11h16	THE TOP LAYER OF SALSE I LOOKS LIKE IT IS CRACKING AND PEELING. LIKE WHEN YOU HAVE A FACE MASK ON AND IT GETS DRY. AT MOST, CHISENHALE HAS A STALE SMELL BUT STILL QUITE 'NEUTRAL' - NOT LIKE OUR FIRST ENCOUNTER. WONDERING WHEN TO GIVE THEM A DROP OR TWO OF DEMINERALISED WATER. TSWAING'S ALGAE IS STICKING TO THE SIDES OF THE BOTTLE. UMBONA IS CHILLED. (BEHAVIOUR, NOT TEMPERATURE). (ROOM TEMP.: 19°C; ROOM HUMIDITY: 48%)	14h35
08-05-2024	10h23	EVERYONE SEEMS OKAY. IT'S COLD OUTSIDE. I THINK I'LL GIVE THEM ALL A DROP OF DEMINERALISED WATER BEFORE CLOSING. SAME-SAME. (ROOM TEMP: 19°C; ROOM HUMIDITY: 50%)	13h35
09-05-2024	10h46	YESTERDAY BEFORE CLOSING, I ADDED A SMALL AMOUNT OF DEMINERALISED WATER TO REPLENISH EVERYONE. TSWAING'S ALGAE IS BOTH STRINGY (FLOATING) AND CLUMPING UP NEAR THE SURFACE OF THE WATER. SALSE I'S SEDIMENT THAT IS STICKING TO THE SIDES OF THE GLASS BOTTLE IS PEELING LIKE A FACE MASK, TOO. UMBONA'S GENERAL WATER LEVEL IS MORE THAN 50%. (BECAUSE IT'S BEEN THE LARGEST SAMPLE SIZE). CHISENHALE IS GOOD; SMELLS 'STALE'. (AND DEMINERALISED WATER REFILL!) (ROOM TEMP: 19°C; ROOM HUMIDITY: 50%)	14h53

DATE	OPENING TIME	CONDITION	CLOSING TIME
11-05-2024	13h50	TSWAING & SALSE I ARE BOTH FEELING (ALGAE AND CLAY, RESPECTIVELY. CHISENHALE ALSO DOESN'T SMELL TOO STALE TODAY, AND UMBONA IS QUIET. EVERYONE IS FINE. IT'S HOT OUTSIDE! IT'S THE LAST WEEKEND BEFORE SEEING PROF NORBERT ON MONDAY! FEELING GOOD! :) (ROOM TEMP: 21°C; ROOM HUMIDITY: 45%)	18h24
12-05-2024	—	PACKING. WE'RE GOING TO WAGENINGEN! WOOOO! (BACK TOMORROW AFTERNOON) (ROOM TEMP: 21°C; ROOM HUMIDITY 45%)	—
13-05-2024	17h38	WOW. WHAT A DAY. WE'RE BACK FROM WAGENINGEN. PROF. NORBERT HAS BEEN ABSOLUTELY AMAZING. I WASN'T ABLE TO TAKE MANY PHOTOS, BECAUSE THIS LAB/MICROSCOPIC WORK IS A DIFFERENT ENVIRONMENT. AFTER OUR 1h40min TRAIN RIDE TO WAGENINGEN, AND BUS TO THE MICROSCOPY CENTRE, WE HAD A TEA WITH NORBERT AND I EXPLAINED THE PROJECT. LA LA LA. OK, I WILL GIVE A <u>BRIEF</u> REPORT ON WHAT WE SAW! TSWAING: WE SPOTTED THREE DIFFERENT KINDS OF MICRO-ORGANISMS THERE WAS A SQUIGGLY ONE LIKE THIS: ~~~ WHICH WAS A 'COLONY' (I'D CALL IT A COMMUNITY, BUT SHUP, KE). THE SECOND WAS A LOOOOOOOOOOOOONG CYANOBACTERIA THAT WAS MOVING LIKE A SNAKE AND IT ATTEMPTED TO STRANGLE ITSELF. IT WAS LIKE: [A 'COLONY' WORKING TOGETHER.] THE THIRD WAS A DIATOM. WELL, MANY OF THEM. VERY BEAUTIFUL. THEY LIVE IN GLASS HOUSES. KIND OF LIKE THOSE NEW-BUILD GLASS PSEUDO-SKYSCRAPER APARTMENTS IN ROSEBANK OR SANDTON. THESE ARE THE DIATOMS: . THE ALGAE AND CYANOBACTERIA SHOW COLLECTIVE ACTION! THE DIATOM MOVES LIKE A MILITARY TANK (...OH!) AND SPITS OUT SUGARS FROM ITS 'MOUTH' AND REABSORBS THEM FROM THE OPPOSITE ... SIDE. DIATOMS TEND TO HAVE SYMMETRICAL SHAPES (?). SALSE I: IT WAS A DENSE SAMPLE BECAUSE OF THE CLAY. WE SPOTTED SOME DIATOMS (WHICH HELPED SEEING THEM IN TSWAING) WHICH WERE OCCASIONALLY MOVING. WE HAVE SOME NICE FOOTAGE OF THEM WIGGLING OUT OF THE CLAY INTO THE WATER, BECKONED BY THE SUN-LIKE ILLUSION OF THE MICROSCOPE'S LIGHT. CHISENHALE: THIS SAMPLE, ALBEIT THE "FRESHEST" OF THEM ALL, HAD THE LEAST AMOUNT OF MICROORGANISM DIVERSITY AND LOW DENSITY. ALTHOUGH A HUMBLE SAMPLE OF A PUDDLE FROM THE STREETS, WE SPOTTED SOME EUGLENAS, ORGANIC WASTE, AND SOME SPIROGYRA (WE FOUND 12 CELLS COMMUNED TOGETHER LIKE →).	~~17h50~~ 20h43

DATE	OPENING TIME	CONDITION	CLOSING TIME
		~~[struck out]~~ ... PROF NORBERT SUSPECTS THAT – IF THERE ARE 12 CELLS PRESENT, AND ± 2 CELLS GROW/ARE BORN EVERY 2 HOURS, – THEN THIS SPIROGYRA (AND THE SAMPLE ITSELF – WAS ABOUT 15 HOURS MINIMUM (AT THE TIME THE SAMPLE WAS TAKEN). A MATHEMATICAL MOUTHFUL! (NOT REALLY..) UMBONA – I JUST FEEL SO INSPIRED BY THIS SAMPLE. VERY QUIET AND UNASSUMING BUT WE SPOTTED SOME CYSTS, BIG CHLOROPLASTS, POSSIBLE CYANOBACTERIA 'COLONY' STRINGIES. A FUN FACT ABOUT CYANOBACTERIA, IT IS MORE LIKELY TO BE PRESENT WHEN THE SAMPLE SOURCE IS RICH IN NUTRIENTS (E.G. NITROGEN), SOIL AND SLIGHTLY OLDER/LESS FRESH SAMPLES. UMBONA IS QUIET BECAUSE THEY ARE WISE! JUST LIKE A MAKHULU. LAST COMMENTS FROM PROF NORBERT: THERE IS 'NO' SPECULATION WITHIN SCIENCE IN GENERAL. KUTHIWA IT IS DANGEROUS AND UNETHICAL; IT IS PREFERRED FOR ONE TO HYPOTHESISE (→ ISN'T THIS SPECULATION?), TEST THOROUGHLY ~~AND~~ AND MAKE A STRONG ARGUMENT. TODAY, WE CELEBRATE LIFE – MORESO ON A MICROSCOPIC LEVEL – AND THAT THESE SAMPLES BETWEEN THE AGES OF 1 – 6 MONTHS CONTAIN AND DISSEMINATE KNOWLEDGE ~~AWAY~~ BEYOND THE LIMITATION OF THE "NAKED HUMAN EYE". WE CELEBRATE THE LIFE WE DO NOT KNOW, THAT CONTINUES TO THRIVE ON ITS OWN TERMS. WE CELEBRATE WHAT WE DO NOT KNOW AT ALL, WE CELEBRATE THE COMMUNAL ~~SESN~~ SENSIBILITIES OF THE ECOLOGICAL COSM. TODAY, WE CELEBRATE NOMVULA DIPHORORO CRÈCHE (A 5-STAR INSTITUTION) FOR ~~KEEPING~~ TAKING CARE OF THESE SAMPLES, HISTORIES, KINSHIPS, GEOGRAPHIES, GEOLOGIES, GENEALOGIES AND ECOLOGIES. PHAMBILI! (ROOM TEMP: I FORGOT, ROOM HUMIDITY: I FORGOT)	
14-05-2024	15h44	THEY'RE GOOD. STILL IN EUPHORIA FROM YESTERDAY'S ADVENTURE. REALISING THAT I SHOULD'VE GIVEN THEM MORE ACCESS TO LIGHT (SUNLIGHT) SO THAT THEY COULD PHOTOSYNTHESISE (CONVERT THE LIGHT INTO SUGAR/FOOD). I ALSO REALISE I HAVEN'T BEEN FEEDING THE SAMPLES... WHEN "IN" LIGHT, THE ALGAE 'SEDIMENT' (→ DEBRIS, SOIL) RISES TO THE TOP, LIKE PROF NORBERT SAID. AND KENI BURKE. HOW TO KEEP THEM ALIVE UNTIL SEPTEMBER? WHY IS THERE NO SIGNIFICANT ALGAE GROWING IN UMBONA? (ROOM TEMP: 24°C; ROOM HUMIDITY: 45%.)	17h52
15-05-2024	14h37	SOME AIR AND LIGHT AND WINDOW SILL CHILLING. SALSE I'S BOTTLE IS SLOWLY SETTLING INTO ITS SEDIMENTATION. TSWAING'S ALGAE CLUMPS ARE AT THE SURFACE. CHISENHALE AND UMBONA ARE CHILLING. (ROOM TEMP: 23°C; ROOM HUMIDITY: 45%.)	16h51

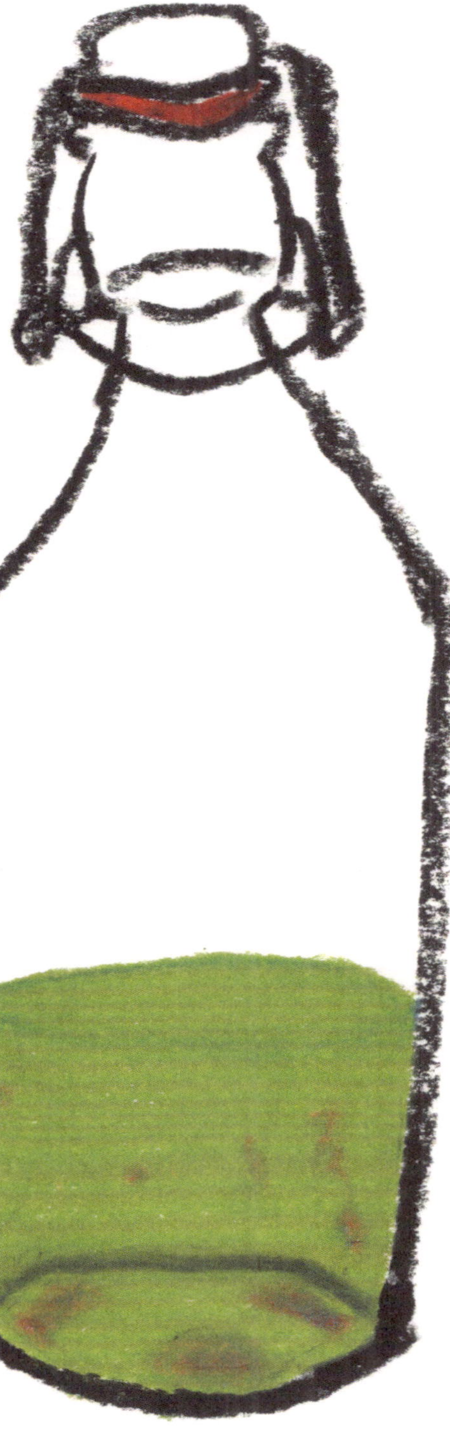

DATE	OPENING TIME	CONDITION	CLOSING TIME
16-05-2024	13h41	A MILD DAY. TSWAING'S ALGAE AND DEBRIS IS CHILLING AT THE SURFACE. SALSE I'S WATER : CLAY RATIO IS SETTLING IN AGAIN. UMBONA & CHISENHALE ARE OKAY. MIGHT PUT THEM ON THE WINDOW SILL LATER FOR SOME LIGHT. (ROOM TEMPERATURE : 22°C ; ROOM HUMIDITY : 48 %.)	15h51
27-05-2024	11h17	OH OH... SOME CONCERNS. I TOOK A WEEK-LONG LEAVE OF ABSENCE. I WASN'T PHYSICALLY AT THE CRÈCHE. THEY LOOK EXHAUSTED AND BLASÉ. AFTER THE VISIT WITH PROF. NORBERT AND THINKING OF HOW THEY HAVEN'T BEEN EATING, I LEFT THEM ON MY WINDOW SILL. BUT I FEEL DEEP REGRET. TSWAING HAS LOST ITS ETHEREAL GREEN ALGAE SPIRIT AND IS NOW A LIGHT BROWN SOUP OF DEBRIS AND THE ALGAE HAS COAGULATED INTO A DISTANT RELATIVE OF A KOMBUCHA SCOBY. SALSE I FOLLOWS - IF IT WASN'T FOR ITS DENSE CLAY CONTENT IT WOULD BE UNCANNILY SIMILAR TO TSWAING. UMBONA SEEMS TO BE DEVELOPING SMALL ALGAE 'DOTS' (?) AT THE BASE OF ITS BOTTLE. CHISENHALE IS STREET SMART, AS IT HAS ALWAYS BEEN. LET'S GET BACK ON SCHEDULE. GAVE THEM ALL A SIP OF DEMINERALISED WATER TODAY. THOUGHTS AND PRAYERS ABOUND! (ROOM TEMP : 19°C ; ROOM HUMIDITY : 48 %.)	16h28
29-05-2024	11h39	WOW! CHISENHALE IS DEVELOPING ALGAE AT THE BOTTOM OF ITS BOTTLE. AND UMBONA, TOO! I GUESS LEAVING THEM IN THE SUN WASN'T THE WORST DECISION OF MY CRÈCHE CARE-TAKING CAREER! TSWAING IS COMPLETELY BROWN WITH NO VISIBLE (WITH THE NAKED EYE) SIGNS OF NEW ALGAE. SALSE IS MOODY BUT STILL. (ROOM TEMP : 18°C ; ROOM HUMIDITY : 50%.)	18h55
02-06-2024	18h03	CHISENHALE IS THE NEW TSWAING! I SAY THIS WITH A HEAVY HEART, NOT A JOYOUS LEAP. CAN DNA, THAT IS ALREADY EMBODIED WITHIN A GENEALOGY, DIE? HAS MY CARELESS CARE-TAKING KILLED TSWAING (MY DEAR GOLDEN CHILD! OH! WHAT A TRAVESTY! I DON'T CARE ABOUT CRITIQUE OR ACCUSATIONS OF FAVOURITISM AND BIAS! OH! TSWAING!!). WHAT DOES A FUNERAL FOR A SAMPLE LOOK LIKE? I MISS TSWAING'S ALGAE. THE CONDITIONS FOR SUCH, HAVE PASSED. UMBONA IS OKAY. SALSE'S WATER : SEDIMENT RATIO LOOKS LIKE 1:1. (ROOM TEMP : 19°C ; ROOM HUMIDITY : 45%) OH! TSWAING!	20h55

DATE	OPENING TIME	CONDITION	CLOSING TIME
03-06-2024	17h08	FEELING ON TRACK AGAIN. I HAVE ACCEPTED THAT TSWAING HAS CHANGED. CHISENHALE'S ALGAE HAS FORMED A THIN LAYER AROUND SOME OF ITS DEBRIS. UMBONA HAD A MOMENT OF PROMISING ALGAE PRESENCE BUT IT HAS NOT MADE MUCH CHANGES SINCE THOSE OBSERVATIONS. SALSE I IS THE MOON. ALL CHILLED. WEATHER OUTSIDE IS CHILLY. KANTHI WHERE IS THE SUN? (ROOM TEMP: 18°C; ROOM HUMIDITY: 50%)	19h59
04-06-2024	12h27	SO, I LEARNED THAT TSWAING'S ALGAE TURNED INTO AN ALGAL BIOFILM. I'M STILL NOT SURE WHAT THAT MEANS OR WHY IT HAPPENS. THE KIDS ARE ALL GOOD. NO MAJOR UPDATES. CHISENHALE IS LOOKING VERY... GREEN. MAYBE I SHOULD PLAY SOME ELECTRONIC ORGAN FOR THEM? ALSO THINKING TO INDIRECTLY SHINE SOME ORANGE-FILTERED LIGHT CLOSE TO THEM AS THE SUN HAS BEEN RARE THESE DAYS. (ROOM TEMP: 18°C; ROOM HUMIDITY: 50%)	22h22
05-06-2024	11h55	TODAY I'LL GIVE THEM A BIT OF DEMINERALISED WATER TO QUENCH THEIR THIRST. NOTHING MAJOR TO REPORT; THEY SEEM THE SAME AS YESTERDAY. (ROOM TEMP.: 18°C; ROOM HUMIDITY: 50%)	22h45
06-06-2024	11h21	YESTERDAY I GAVE THEM DEMINERALISED WATER. TODAY, THEY'RE ALL QUIET. SAME CONDITION AS YESTERDAY. PROCESSING CHANGE... THE WEATHER IS MEDIOCRE TODAY. THE SUN REALLY DOESN'T WANT TO BE HERE. (ROOM TEMP: 19°C; ROOM HUMIDITY: 45%)	21h04
08-06-2024	17h21	ALL CALM. SALSE I'S SEDIMENT IS LEVELLING OUT AGAIN. UMBONA'S WATER LEVEL IS QUITE HIGH, ALTHOUGH I KNOW THAT I HAVE BEEN CAREFUL WITH THE DEMINERALISED WATER AMOUNTS. TSWAING ISN'T MAKING MORE ALGAE AND HAS LOST ITS BRIGHT GREEN COLOUR. ITS ALGAL BIOFILM IS ALSO NOT... VISIBLY DOING ANYTHING NEW; IT MAY HAVE DECOMPOSED. I CAN SEE CHISENHALE'S BRIGHT GREEN ALGAL FLOOR FROM HERE (I'M ABOUT 1 2 METRES AWAY). MAYBE THEY'RE A BIT BORED AND NEED AN ACTIVITY. PERHAPS A FIELD TRIP IS NEEDED - MAYBE TO THE PORT OF ROTTERDAM? FOR SOME AIR. I'M AFRAID THESE GLASS BOTTLES MIGHT BE KILLING THEM AND I SHOULD JUST LET THEM GO? GIVING THEM AN ORANGE SPOTLIGHT - THERE IS "NO" SUN OUTSIDE. IT'S SUCH A FUCKING GLOOMY LIFE HERE! (ROOM TEMP: 19°C; ROOM HUMIDITY: 48%)	22h45

DATE	OPENING TIME	CONDITION	CLOSING TIME
09-06-2024	15h00	VISIBLY, THEY LOOK THE SAME AS YESTERDAY. SO, THEY'RE ... FINE. THEY PROBABLY NEED FRESH AIR. LEAVING THEM ON THE WINDOW SILL AS THERE IS INTERMITTENT, SOFT, SUN. (ROOM TEMP: 19°C; ROOM HUMIDITY: 45%.)	20h56
10-06-2024	10h49	IT'S RAINING AND POURING OUTSIDE - THE EXPECTED FORECAST FOR THE WHOLE DAY. MOODY. I NOTICED THE ALGAL BIOFILM OF TSWAING (WELL, SOME OF IT AT ~~[illegible]~~ LEAST) WAS FLOATING AT THE SURFACE. THERE WAS ALSO A BORDER OF BUBBLES SURROUNDING THE BIOFILM / ALONG THE EDGE OF THE BOTTLE. I THINK IT'S A BYPRODUCT OF PHOTOSYNTHESIS. CHISENHALE IS GLOWING GREEN LIKE THE "GO" SIGNAL ON A ROBOT. UMBONA IS TRANQUIL. SALSE I'S WATER : SEDIMENT RATIO APPEARS TO HAVE SETTLED INTO 1:1. GIVING THEM A SOFT ORANGE-FILTERED LED LIGHT - NOT BECAUSE IT WILL DO ANYTHING, BUT JUST TO MAKE THE CRÈCHE "WARM" TODAY. (ROOM TEMP: 17°C; ROOM HUMIDITY: 50%.)	20h49
12-06-2024	15h43	BOTH THE ~~[illegible]~~ ALGAE-COVERED DEBRIS AND ALGAL BIOFILM OF TSWAING WERE FLOATING WHEN I ~~[illegible]~~ ~~[illegible]~~ CAME IN. UMBONA AND SALSE I ARE CHILLED ξ. ~~SOF~~ SO MANY "TYPOS" TODAY. LISTENING TO A PODCAST, SO A BIT DISTRACTED. (ROOM TEMP: 17°C; ROOM HUMIDITY: 48%.)	21h49
13-06-2024	11h27	CHISENHALE HAS ALGAL-LIKE (?) SPORE (?) GROWTHS (?) ON THE SIDES OF THE GLASS BOTTLE. AS THE YOUNGEST ATTENDEE OF THE CRÈCHE, PERHAPS IT HAS OFFERED MORE OPPORTUNITIES FOR MICRO-ORGANISMS TO GROW; FRESHER PUDDLE SAMPLE, ACCOUNTING FOR TIME? I WONDER WHY THE CRÈCHE IS SO PREMISED ON CHANGE, AND MAYBE A FOCUS AND ACCEPTANCE OF INERTIA IS MISSING: UMBONA AND SALSE I ARE ~~WAITING~~ STILL... IN WAITING. MAYBE THEY ARE WAITING TO BE "PICKED UP" FROM CRÈCHE <u>OR</u> LEAVE ON THEIR OWN ACCORD? BWAING, I THINK, HAS REACHED A STAGE OF WAITING. ESPECIALLY AFTER MAKING VISIBLE ITS PHYSICAL CHANGE [FOR THE CRÈCHE] FOR A LITTLE OVER 6 MONTHS. IT MUST BE EXHAUSTING TO CHANGE ALL THE TIME. IT'S IMPORTANT, BUT THIS IS ~~TOT~~ ONE EXAMPLE OF WHEN THAT IMPORTANCE BECOMES EXHAUSTING. ~~B~~ NAP TIME, FOR EVERYONE, MAYBE? BWAING'S ALGAL BIOFILM IS... MAKING BUBBLES AS USUAL. (ROOM TEMP: 18°C; ROOM HUMIDITY: 50%.)	20h18
15-06-2024	14h10	SUN IS OUT (RIGHT NOW)! I'VE OPENED THEM ALL UP AND PLACED THEM ON THE WINDOW SILL. EVEN OPENED THE WINDOWS TODAY. I WAS LIKE, "YOU KNOW WHAT, WE NEED SOME CROSS-VENTILATION CONVERSATIONS TODAY!". MAYBE I'M FEELING EMPATHETIC TOWARDS ANY MACRO-AND-MICRO-ORGANISMS WHO MIGHT BE CURIOUS TO ENGAGE WITH THE SAMPLES. I CAN'T SMOTHER THEM; IT'S NOT HEALTHY. THEIR CONDITION IS THE SAME AS THURSDAY THE 13TH. I NOTICE THE ALGAE IN CHISENHALE IS TAKING OVER. THERE IS ALWAYS CONDENSATION IN THAT BOTTLE - FROM THE PHOTOSYNTHESIS, PERHAPS? (ROOM TEMP: 18°C; ROOM HUMIDITY: 50%.)	22h45

DATE	OPENING TIME	CONDITION	CLOSING TIME
16-06-2024	14h16	UMBONA IS THE TALLEST CRÈCHE MEMBER (WATER CONTENT). JUST SOME TRIVIA I THOUGHT I SHOULD NOTE DOWN. THEY ARE THE SAME AS YESTERDAY. MAYBE THEY'RE BORED? OR MAYBE I AM? (ROOM TEMP: 18°C, ROOM HUMIDITY: 50%.)	21h23
17-06-2024	10h22	A BIT OF SUN TODAY; I WILL LEAVE THEM ON THE WINDOW SILL FOR SOME FOOD – NYANA. WINDOW WILL BE A BIT OPEN TOO. CHISENHALE IS GROWING AN ALGAL GARDEN. TSWAING IS DORMANT AND THE WATER SEEMS... NOT SLIMEY BUT THERE IS A THIN FILM LAYER. SALSE I IS CHILLED. UMBONA ALSO. SOMETIMES, I HAVE VERY LITTLE TO REPORT. (ROOM TEMP: 18°C; ROOM HUMIDITY: 50%.)	22h23
18-06-2024	11h18	ONE THING THE SAMPLES HAVE HARDLY DEMONSTRATED – AS FAR AS THEIR CHANGE IN CONDITION GOES – IS ANY DISTINCT SMELLS / ODOURS THAT LAST FOR A CONSIDERABLE LENGTH OF TIME. ASIDE FROM CHISENHALE'S INITIAL SULPHRIC-STREET DRAIN SMELL AND THAT ONE TIME TSWAING HAD A RAW EGG ODOUR GOING ON, IT'S PRETTY CALM IN THE OLFACTORY DEPARTMENT. PERHAPS AN INDICATOR OF A LACK OF BACTERIA LIVING IN THEM? WHAT'S GOING ON? CHISENHALE'S ALGAE LOOKS LIKE FUR. PLACED ALL OF THEM ON THE WINDOW-SILL. IT'S MID-JUNE AND STILL NO SUN. WHERE IS IT? WHAT'S GOING ON? — CLIMATE CHANGE (ROOM TEMP: 19°C; ROOM HUMIDITY: 50%.)	20h23
24-06-2024	11h19	JUST REALISING THE OPENING AND CLOSING TIMES ARE SO... SERENDIPITOUSLY (?) ALIGNED. ANYWHO. GAVE THE SAMPLES A TOP UP OF DEMINERALISED WATER. THE SUN HAS FINALLY ARRIVED, AFTER BEING STUCK IN METEOROLOGICAL TRAFFIC (OR WHATEVER REASON THAT APPLIES FOR THE SLOW ARRIVAL OF A CONDITION AKIN TO "SUMMER"). IT'S WARM, SUNNY AND NOT TOO DEPRESSING. JOYOUS. WINDOWS OPEN. SAMPLES ARE THE SAME-ISH. ALL GOOD. CHISENHALE, IN PARTICULAR, SEEMS SUPER HAPPY. UMBONA AND TSWAING SEEM HOMESICK. (ROOM TEMP: 20°C; ROOM HUMIDITY: 50%.)	20h29
25-06-2024	14h59	NOTICING SOME SPOTS ON CHISENHALE'S ALGAE; THEY REMIND ME OF MOLD SPORES. TSWAING IS LIKE "I JUST CAN'T! I'M DONE!". UMBONA ACTUALLY HAS SOME GLARES OF ... A VERY SOFT, ALMOST-IMPERCEPTIBLE ALGAE STRING THING. IT LOOKS LIKE A WAVE – SO A LOT IS GOING ON IN UMBONA AND I FEEL LIKE IT'S THE SAMPLE THAT CHALLENGES MY EXPECTATIONS OF MICROBIOLOGY/WATER AND WHAT I MAY EXPECT TO BE VISIBLE. VISIBILITY IS A SCAM! ANYWHO, WINDOWS OPEN AND IT'S SUNNY. MUST PLAN A FIELD TRIP TO ROTTERDAM SOON! ALSO, I HAVEN'T DROPPED THE NEWS TO THE SAMPLES ABOUT THEIR DEPARTURE DATE IN LONDON CIRCA JULY – AUGUST. *LOOKS FOR NEW PEN* *FOUND NEW PEN* JA. SO, FIELD TRIP AND DEPARTURE SOON!	22h14

DATE	OPENING TIME	CONDITION	CLOSING TIME
26-06-2024	13h28	TODAY, I PUT THEM ON ~~T~~ THE WINDOW SILL FOR A BIT OF SUN SO THEY CAN PHOTOSYNTHESISE. PERHAPS THE SUNLIGHT IS TOO DIRECT? I NOTICE WHEN THEY'RE PHOTOSYNTHESISING, NOT ONLY DOES THE ALGAE / ALGAL-MATTER RISE TO THE SURFACE, BUT BUBBLES APPEAR. WHO IS MAKING THESE BUBBLES? IS IT CO_2? IN TERMS OF HOW THEY VISIBLY LOOK, THEY'RE THE SAME AS YESTERDAY. I THINK HAVING THE WINDOWS OPEN ALLOWS FOR THEM TO HAVE IMPORTANT EXCHANGES. WHAT IS 'CONTAMINATION' AT THIS POINT, WHEN PUDDLES ARE RECEPTIVE TO WHOMEVER WALKS, SPITS, SPLASHES, LIVES, DROWNS OR DIES IN THEM? MAYBE THE CONCEPT OF 'CONTAMINATION' DOESN'T QUITE LAND HERE. AAAAND THAT'S OKAY. (ROOM TEMP: 23°C; ROOM HUMIDITY: 50%.)	21h39
27-06-2024	14h34	SUN? OUT. WINDOWS? OPEN. AIR QUALITY? I THINK THERE IS A HIGH POLLEN COUNT TODAY. UMBONA'S SEDIMENT IS PLAYFULLY FLOATING AROUND; A CRYSTAL CLEAR SAMPLE! SALSE I SEEMS TO BE STRUGGLING TO GROUND ITS WATER: SEDIMENT RATIO. OR ~~TOO~~ MAYBE IT'S TOO MUCH DEMINERALISED WATER? *SWEATS* TSWAING IS CLOUDY. SWAMPY. MOODY (?) CHISENHALE IS CHILLED. ~~ALGAE~~ ALGAE IS PHOTOSYNTHESISING. TRACK OF THE DAY? 'AGLAONEMA PICTUM TRICOLOR' BY CIAO CIAO MARIGOLD. (ROOM TEMP: 25°C; ROOM HUMIDITY: 45%.)	22h38
28-06-2024	10h03	THE EARLIEST OPENING IN A WHILE. SUN IS OUT, WINDOWS OPEN, POLLEN COUNT <u>SEEMS</u> LESS INTENSE THUS FAR (?). I'VE PLACED THEM ON THE WINDOW SILL. THERE IS A PIECE OF ALGAL-COVERED DEBRIS IN CHISENHALE THAT IS STUCK TO THE BOTTOM OF THE GLASS BOTTLE. BECAUSE OF THE SUN, IT WANTS TO RISE TO THE TOP (SHOUT OUT TO KENI BURKE!) ~~BUT, IT IS STUCK~~ SO IT LOOKS LIKE IT IS MOVING, WAVING, DANCING. LIKE THIS: 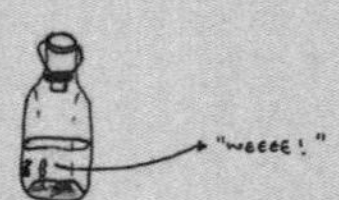 ALL OTHER SAMPLES ARE CHILLED. (ROOM TEMP: 21°C; ROOM HUMIDITY: 45%.)	23h27
01-07-2024	11h07	ARGH! WHAT A DULL DAY! HOW IS ANYTHING MEANT TO GROW, FLOURISH AND PROSPER IN THIS WEATHER? SAMPLES' CONDITION IS THE SAME; NOT MUCH CHANGE. SALSE I'S WATER: SEDIMENT RATIO IS ~~T~~ 2:1 (MORE OR LESS). TSWAING IS A HOTSPOT FOR DECAYING ALGAL MATTER. CHISENHALE'S BOTTLE HAS [INTERNAL] CONDENSATION. UMBONA STILL SEEMS TO HAVE A SLIGHT ALGAL ~~T~~ PRESENCE, BUT I CAN'T BE SURE. HAPPY [DULL] JULY. (ROOM TEMP: 20°C; ROOM HUMIDITY: 45%)	18h48

DATE	OPENING TIME	CONDITION	CLOSING TIME
02-07-2024	10h59	THE SAMPLES' WATER IS GENERALLY YELLOWING ~~IN ALL OF THEM~~. IT MUST BE THE ACCESS TO MORE LIGHT (WINDOW SILL) AND OCCASIONAL SUN (WHEN IT DECIDES TO PULL THROUGH). INTERESTINGLY ENOUGH, I'VE NOW SPOTTED A THIN ALGAL RING AT THE BOTTOM OF UMBONA'S GLASS BOTTLE. PERHAPS I WASN'T PAYING AS MUCH ATTENTION AS I THOUGHT YESTERDAY. CHISENHALE'S ALGAE IS ALSO DEVELOPING BROWN SPOTS (SUN SPOTS?!). SALSE I'S WATER IS YELLOWING (AS AFOREMENTIONED). TSWAING MAKES ME WONDER ABOUT DECAY, LIFE <u>FROM</u> DECAY AND LIFE <u>AFTER</u> DECAY. WEATHER OUTSIDE IS UTTERLY DEPRESSING. I MISS SOUTHA. (ROOM TEMP: 20°C; ROOM HUMIDITY: 50%.)	22h38
03-07-2024	13h37	THE USUAL. THE USUAL. SAMPLES OPEN. OCCASSIONAL SUN GLARES (THIS MORNING WAS SO DEPRESSING!). BUT, WINDOWS CLOSED. I CLEANED THE SIDES (INSIDE) OF SALSE I'S BOTTLE AS IT HAD SOME DRIED CLAY (FROM THE MICROSCOPIC IMAGING SESSION WITH PROF. NORBERT) WHICH MADE IT TRICKY TO NOTE CHANGES AND UPDATES. SO, SALSE I IS — ONCE AGAIN — SETTLING IN TO ITS WATER : SEDIMENT RATIO (STILL ABOUT 2:1). UMBONA IS LIKE A NETBALL PLAYER (GOAL KEEPER). UMBONA IS TALL. TSWAING SEEMS SO AGITATED BUT JADED AT THE SAME TIME. LIKE A TEENAGER ON A FAMILY FUNCTION WHO HAS NO ONE ELSE TO HANG OUT THAT IS THEIR AGE. CHISENHALE IS CHILLING. (ROOM TEMP: 20°C; ROOM HUMIDITY: 50%.)	20h14
04-07-2024	10h44	IS THIS A FLY-BY-NIGHT CRÈCHE? (ROOM TEMP: 19°C; ROOM HUMIDITY [WATER ?!]: 50%.)	23h03
05-07-2024	11h28	I SHOOK UP TSWAING BECAUSE I NOTICED THERE WAS A THIN BIOFILM(?) LAYER DEVELOPING ON THE SIDES OF THE BOTTLE. LIKE A <u>VERY</u> THIN AND LIGHT YELLOW-BROWN LAYER. SO, NOW IT FEELS ALIVE. THE PRESENCE OF THIS BIOFILM (?) MAKES ME BELIEVE THERE IS ONGOING MICROBIAL LIFE PROCESSES IN TSWAING. IT ALSO MAKES ME SUSPECT THAT TSWAING IS NOT BORED OR DEAD, BUT THAT IT IS MOVING IN SILENCE. SALSE I AND UMBONA ARE OKAY. THE BIGGEST PIECE OF FLOATING DEBRIS IN CHISENHALE IS COVERED IN AN ALGAL FILM, TOO. NO SUN. CLOUDY. WINDOWS CLOSED. WHEN TO TOP OFF WITH SOME DEMINERALISED WATER? (ROOM TEMP: 19°C; ROOM HUMIDITY: 50%.)	15h47
08-07-2024	10h52	GAVE EVERYONE A SIP OF DEMINERALISED WATER. UMBONA IS ALMOST FULL. OTHERWISE? THEY'RE ALL THE SAME AS FRIDAY (THE 5TH). THE PEAK(S) OF CHANGE MIGHT ALREADY BE OVER. (ROOM TEMP: 18°C; ROOM HUMIDITY: 50%.)	22h44
09-07-2024	11h32	THEY'RE BASKING IN THE AMBIANCE OF SOME SUN, FRESH AIR, STREET-LEVEL VIEW... UMBONA HAS A SLIGHTLY THICKER ALGAL RING AT THE BOTTOM OF ITS GLASS BOTTLE. EVERYONE ELSE IS GOOD. (ROOM TEMP: 20°C; ROOM HUMIDITY: 50%.)	18h20

DATE	OPENING TIME	CONDITION	CLOSING TIME
10-07-2024	10h00	ALL THE SAME. THE FURRY ALGAL FILM AT THE BOTTOM OF CHISENHALE'S ~~BOTTLE~~ BOTTLE, IS ~~[illegible]~~ PEELING OFF SLOWLY. LIKE A FACE MASK. ALL THE OTHER SAMPLES ARE LIKE :  GREY SKIES. NOTHING TO REPORT. WHAT DO PUDDLES THINK OF LAND? LAND DISPOSSESSION? ECOCIDE? (ROOM TEMP: 20°C ; ROOM HUMIDITY: 50%.)	21h07
11-07-2024	10h01	NOTHING I CAN SEE WITH MY NAKED EYES IS ABLE TO REPORT ANY SIGNIFICANT CHANGES IN THE LAST 24 HOURS. IT'S CLOUDY TODAY. THE SUN IS ON STRIKE. CHISENHALE'S ALGAE HAS TURNED MORE BROWN. REMINDS ME OF TSWAING A FEW MONTHS AGO. IT'S AS IF ~~[illegible]~~ CHISENHALE LOOKS UP TO TSWAING. CUTE. UMBONA AND SALSE I ARE CHILLED. ~~[illegible]~~ (ROOM TEMP: 20°C ; ROOM HUMIDITY: 50%.)	19h48
12-07-2024	10h30	HAVE TO RUSH TO DEN HAAG! — WATER, AGAIN!	——
15-07-2024	——	I FORGOT TO CLOSE THEM. THEY'VE BEEN OPEN SINCE MONDAY MORNING! I DID, HOWEVER, JUST NOTICE THAT TSWAING'S ALGAL BIOFILM (?) IS DEVELOPING A BRIGHT GREEN OUTER LAYER / OUTLINE! ~~[illegible]~~ CHANGE IS ALWAYS POSSIBLE. ITS WATER IS ALSO ~~LESS CLEAR~~ CLOUDY / MURKY. I UNDERESTIMATED THE NEED FOR OXYGEN ; THE NEED TO BREATHE. EVERYONE ELSE IS CHILLED. SUN IS OUT TODAY. (ROOM TEMP: 19°C ; ROOM HUMIDITY: 50%.)	——
16-07-2024	——	I DECIDED TO LEAVE THEM OPEN. I'M NOT SURE IF THE FIELD TRIP TO ROTTERDAM WILL HAPPEN IN TIME. I'LL LEAVE THEM OPEN FOR THE NEXT TWO WEEKS, OR SO. THINKING ABOUT CONDITIONS... SAMPLES ARE THE SAME AS YESTERDAY. (ROOM TEMP: 20°C ; ROOM HUMIDITY: 50%.)	——
17-07-2024	——	ALL GOOD. EVERYONE IS STILL OPEN. SCHOOL HOLIDAYS ARE COMING UP. AND IT'S POSSIBLE THAT THE FIELD TRIP TO ROTTERDAM MIGHT NOT HAPPEN (TIME CLASH). HOW TO TELL THEM? ~~[illegible]~~ ALGAE WRAPS ITSELF AROUND WHATEVER FINDS ITSELF IN WATER (AND WET SURFACE, I SUSPECT). ALGAE IS A COMMITMENT. (ROOM TEMP: 20,5°C ; ROOM HUMIDITY: 50%)	——
18-07-2024	——	THEY SEEM TO BE RESPONDING ~~[illegible]~~ POSITIVELY TO THE WHOLE OPEN-AIR SITUATION, (UNDER-THE-TREE LEARNING...). I DO WONDER WHAT THEY WOULD HAVE GROWN TO BE. TSWAING IS TURNING SLIGHTLY MORE GREEN. MAYBE THE WINDOW SILL WAS TOO MUCH. OVERALL, THEY SEEM OKAY. BUT THEY NEED TO GO! (ROOM TEMP: ~~[illegible]~~ 20°C ; ROOM HUMIDITY: 50%.)	——

DATE	OPENING TIME	CONDITION	CLOSING TIME
19-07-2024	—	THIS IS NOT A FLY-BY-NIGHT CRÈCHE. THIS IS NOT A FLY-BY-NIGHT CRÈCHE. THIS IS NOT A FLY-BY-NIGHT CRÈCHE. DAILY AFFIRMATIONS. ANYWHO, THEY'RE ALL GOOD. THINKING ABOUT THIS ROTTERDAM TRIP AND REALISING THAT THEY CAN ACTUALLY TAKE THEMSELVES THERE. ONE ETHOS OF THIS CRÈCHE IS ALSO FOSTERING GROWTH AND ALLOW FOR DEPARTURES, AGENCY, SLOW ESCAPES ETC. ETC. SO, I TRUST I WILL MEET TSWAING, UMBONA, SALSE I AND CHISENHALE ON THE OTHER SIDE, AT ANOTHER TIME, ON ANOTHER GROUND, INVARIABLY, INVISIBLY, ANNOYINGLY. THE CRÈCHE WILL CLOSE AT THE END OF THIS MONTH FOR SUMMER/WINTER/RAINY/DRY SEASON BREAK. (ROOM TEMP: 21°C; ROOM HUMIDITY: 50%.)	—
21-07-2024	—	THIS OPEN AIR SITUATION SEEMS TO BE TREATING THE SAMPLES RATHER WELL. TSWAING'S ALGAE SITUATION HAS PIVOTED TO THE GREEN SIDE OF THINGS. A LITTLE BIT THE SAME FOR CHISENHALE. SALSE I IS CALM. WHAT I DON'T UNDERSTAND ABOUT UMBONA IS WHY THE ALGAE AT THE BOTTOM OF ITS BOTTLE HASN'T... "BLOOMED"? ASIDE FROM THE CONTINUOUSLY FLOATING SOIL/DEBRIS, UMBONA IS CHILLED. (ROOM TEMP: 24°C; ROOM HUMIDITY: 50%.)	—
23-07-2024	—	ALL GOOD. I'M SURPRISED I HAVEN'T SPOTTED ANY SMALL FRIENDS THAT HAVE MADE HOMES IN THE SAMPLES (WORMS, FLIES, SPIDERS, MOSQUITOES ETC.). SUN IS OUT. VERY SOFT. IT'S CALM ALL AROUND. 8 DAYS UNTIL CRÈCHE CLOSES... (ROOM TEMP: 21°C; ROOM HUMIDITY: 50%.)	—
24-07-2024	—	SUN IS HERE. HOLIDAYS SOON. SO STRANGE; I STILL ASSOCIATE THIS TIME OF YEAR WITH NOVEMBER – JANUARY. IN SALSE I, I SPOTTED SOME SMALL BROWN DOTS LIKE FRECKLES. OR, HYPERPIGMENTATION. UMBONA IS CHILLED. I WAS ON A CALL WITH PROF. NORBERT YESTERDAY AND MY DESCRIPTION OF WHAT I SUSPECTED WAS AN 'ALGAL BIOFILM' DIDN'T SEEM TO REGISTER. IT MIGHT JUST BE A CHANGE IN THE ALGAE AFTER A PERIOD OF DISINTEGRATING AND BECOMING A DORMANT... THING. OMG! I SPOTTED A BUBBLE TRAPPED UNDER SOME ALGAE IN THE CHISENHALE SAMPLE. IT LOOKS AS THOUGH THE BUBBLE IS WEARING A COAT MADE FROM ALGAE. OR MAYBE THIS IS HOW WE KNOW THAT CHISENHALE IS READY FOR THE SCHOOL HOLIDAYS. TIME TO COME HOME! 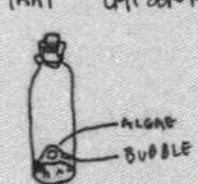 (ROOM TEMP: 23°C; ROOM HUMIDITY: 45%.) 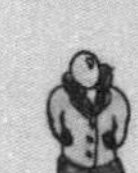	—

Alunamda Buhlungu

Drawings for Dabsie

Alunamda Buhlungu is a curious, confident, and intelligent five-year old. The endearing daughter of Siyabulela and Simthandile Buhlungu – and the niece of artist Simnikiwe Buhlungu – her recent activities include drawing on 'everything and everywhere', sliding into swimming pools, playing with her friends and building with Lego. She is an ardent fan of the TV show, Peppa Pig, and highly recommends the film, *Under The Boardwalk* (2023). Her favourite colours are currently purple and pink, and her most cherished doll toys are named Cairo and Kelly. Alunamda is fond of mermaids and unicorns. She is undecided on what she wants to be when she grows up, but has previously expressed interest in becoming a doctor or a 'police girl'.

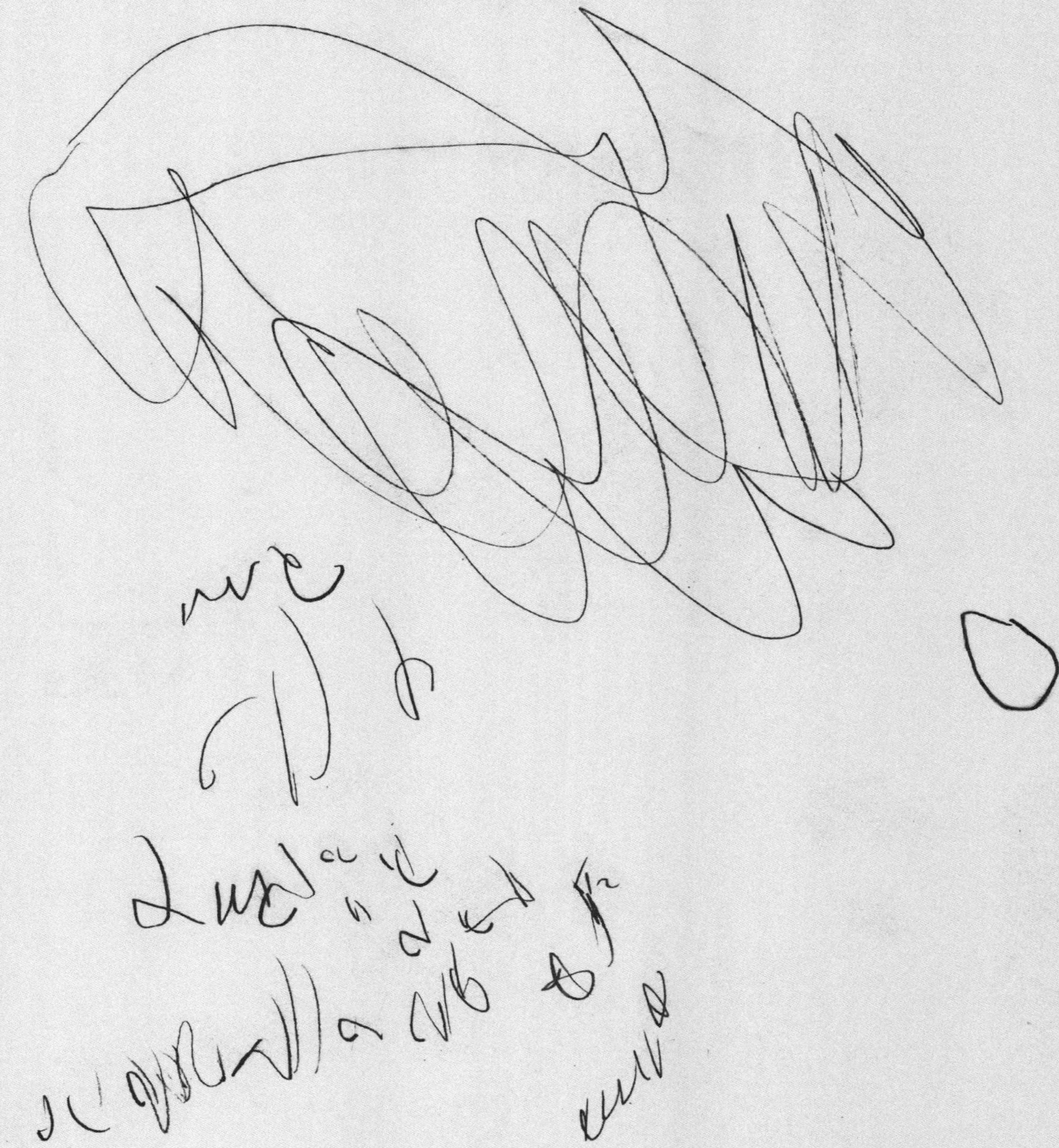

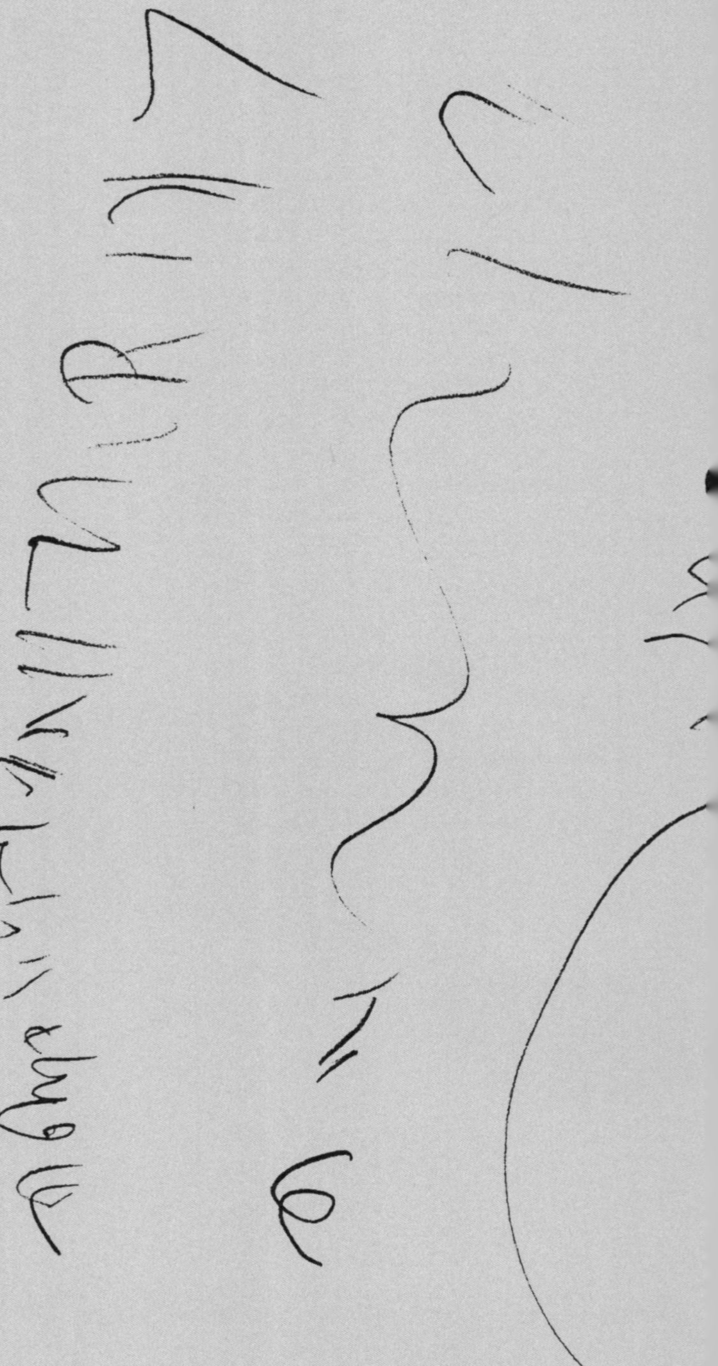

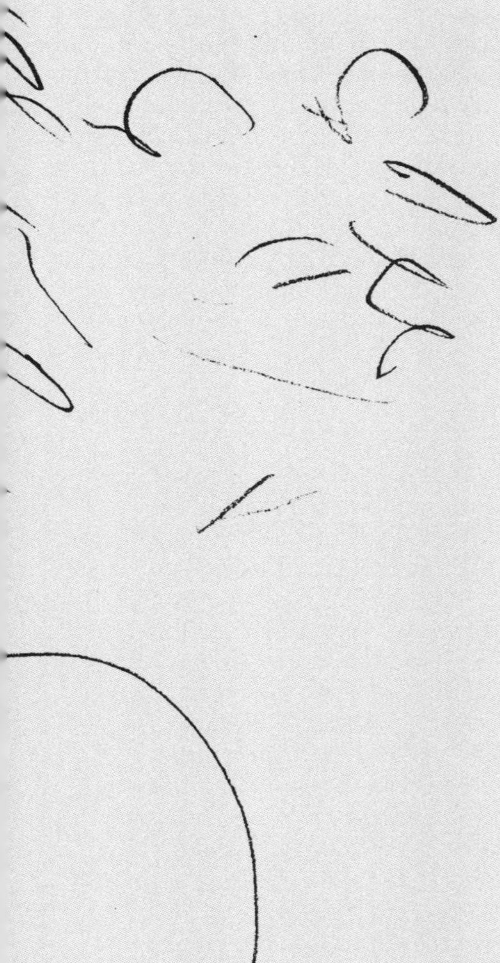

Gabi Ngcobo

Staying afloat 010

Gabi Ngcobo is the Director of Kunstinstituut Melly, Rotterdam, the Netherlands. Between 2020 and 2023 she was Curatorial Director at the Javett Art Centre at the University of Pretoria (Javett-UP) where she curated *Handle with Care* (2021), *SCENORAMA* (2022) and *Frequencies*, a project by Oscar Murillo and *Specifications for a Reverse Archaeology* (2023) with artist Nolan Oswald Dennis. She curated *The Show is Over* at the South London Gallery and co-curated *The 't' is Silent* at the Museum Dhondt-Dhaenes in Deurle, Belgium (both 2022). In addition to lecturing at the Wits School of Arts in Johannesburg, she was also the curator of the 10th Berlin Biennale: *We Don't Need Another Hero* (2018) and was one of the co-curators of the 32nd São Paulo Biennial: *Incerteza Viva* (Live *Uncertainty*) (2016). She is a founding member of the Johannesburg based collaborative platforms NGO – Nothing Gets Organised (2016–) and the Center for Historical Reenactments (2010–14).

Where water once stood, it will stand there again. This is true for navigating being-ness and our ability to constantly renew 'our' collective consciousness. It's easy to forget how to float, how to keep our feet dry... As adults, we do not see oTikoloshe, the mischievous water spirit. We must be our higher selves to see uTikoloshe, not as an inconvenience nor an evil force, but rather as a friend, a visitor from a place that is both beyond and not yet. Fugitives refuse to stand still; they change form as they dissolve into themselves, only to reappear. To give an account of fugitivity, one needs to be able to see inside it, or at least try.

Simnikiwe Buhlungu's new commission will manifest twice, in London then Rotterdam, with more than 25 metres of sea levels separating the two. As a collaboration between Chisenhale Gallery, London and Kunstinstituut Melly, Rotterdam, the travelling commission locates itself in conversation with both contexts. In Rotterdam where the city is at varying levels below the sea, the project will arrive to a place where everything seems controllable around water; a place with wet socks.

Kunstinstituut Melly is supported by the city of Rotterdam and the Ministry of Education, Culture, and Science in the Netherlands. Our activities are also supported through foundation grants, private funds, project sponsorships, individual donations, and income from admission tickets, sales, and events.

Simnikiwe Buhlungu's experiment forms part of the *Call and Response* exhibition program supported by Ammodo. Thank you to team Melly who work tirelessly to bring to life critically exciting content to our visitors, whilst ensuring that each project runs side-by-side with education and public program events of knowledge.

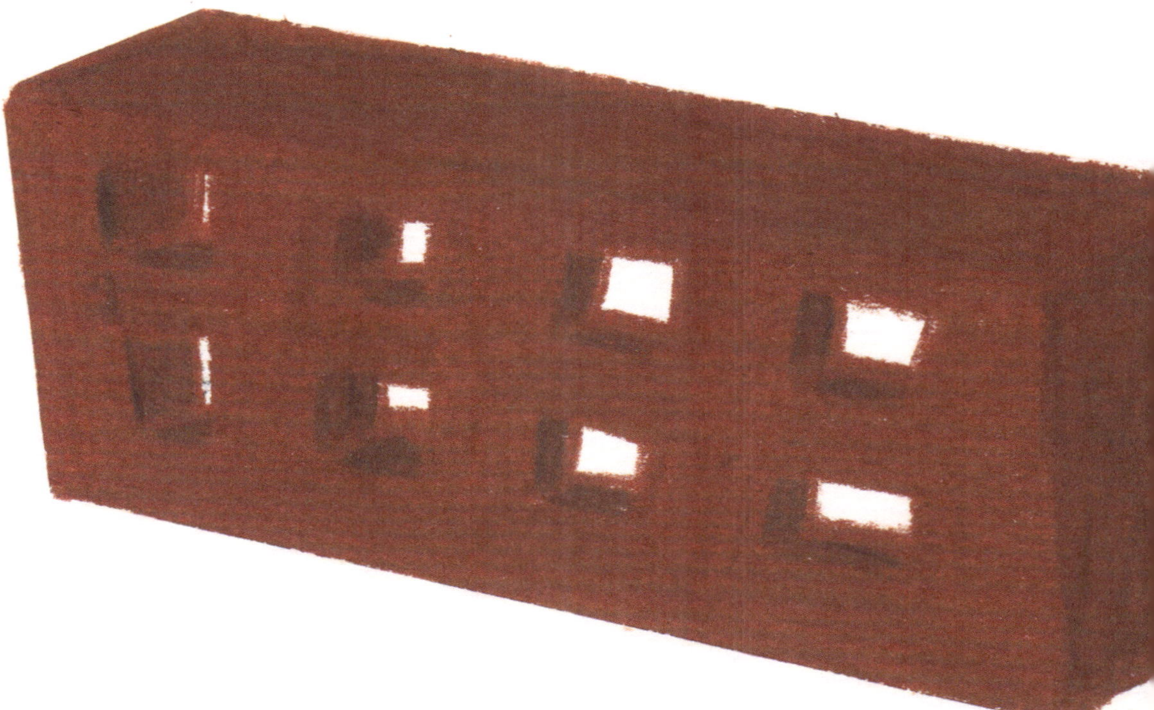

Saïd Rosales

The most abundant: on hydrogen, feelings and ubiquity

Saïd Rosales, a.k.a. Momias in the Mictlan underworld, was born in the Valley of Anahuac, México, in 1993. After spending his early years surrounded by cumbias, tlacoyos, and other spells of the Anahuac, life took him to the flat but effervescent Yucatan Peninsula.

Following many unexpected events, far too many to tell here, Saïd ended up pursuing a PhD in the field of magic, which some might call 'chemistry', and where he seeks the hidden spell to turn hydrogen into a Jaguar (the animal, not the car). Life has been kind, gifting Saïd with many good friends in the, also magical, field of art. These magical interactions continue to lead to more unpredictable events.

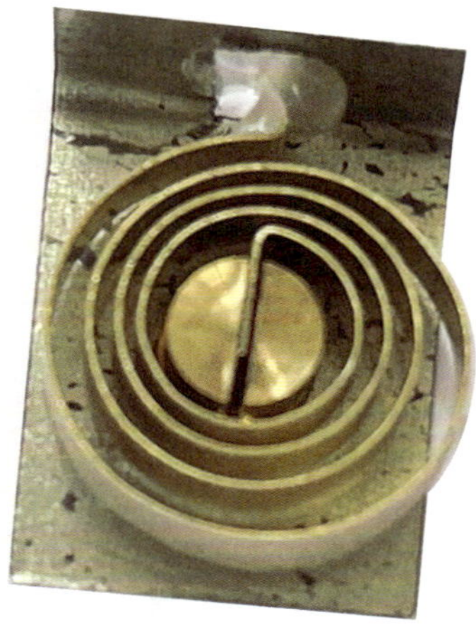

SIMNIKIWE BUHLUNGU (SB)

When we last met, you told me, 'Hydrogen is in everything; it's in the stars, it's in water, it's in everything'. It left me curious about gases, their persistence in the world, how we sense them and know that they are present, with us. Am I sitting next to hydrogen right now?

SAÏD ROSALES (SR)

It's hard to know, because hydrogen is colourless, and it's odourless, while also being highly flammable.

There's actually a funny story I'd like to start with. It's becoming increasingly common to see hydrogen framed as a crucial molecule for the reduction of carbon emissions; some people are keen to exploit it under this framing. There are a lot of interests involved: to keep on drilling, build new infrastructure, and otherwise keep things 'business as usual'. But apparently, there are also some deposits of 'natural' hydrogen in certain parts of the planet, called 'white hydrogen', 'golden hydrogen', or geological hydrogen (which is perhaps a hint that this hydrogen belongs, first and foremost, to the planet).

SB

Where are these deposits? Are they underground or...?

SR

They are deep underground. The first one of these deposits was encountered in Mali in '95.[1] Yes, 1995, Mali. There is a whole myth about it. I'm not sure how real it is, or if it happened, but apparently people in Mali were looking for water underground, so they started drilling to make a very deep, huge hole. They didn't find water, or at the time, realise that anything else was there. Then, apparently, at some point, someone working there was inspecting this very deep hole, and decided there was nothing of interest. In disappointment or exhaustion, they took out a cigarette and lit it up. Then the whole...

SB

[gasps] Oh my God!

SR

Everything just caught fire. It wasn't a usual fire, because the flame of hydrogen is very light, almost invisible during the day – not red or blue. I'm not quite sure where the story turns into magical realism – because they say it's a first-hand account, but I'm like, 'hmmmm...' It's a huge hole filled with hydrogen, and someone accidentally lit it up with a cigarette. I'm not sure who lived to tell the story. But, apparently that's how they realised the presence of hydrogen, because of the fire. Then the exploitation began.

SB

What are the consequences for working in the field of chemistry, a field of research that is used by someone else to do something that you perhaps never imagined or didn't intend. How do we talk about that?

SR

Yes, that is rarely talked about. Some people might make these judgments of – 'Oh, hydrogen is not perfect... It might cause some things with' – I don't know – 'mining', or, 'You need to build these huge parks where you will split water into hydrogen and oxygen, which will take a lot of land, a lot of water'. 'It might have some negative consequences'... But they justify it and say 'overall it's worth it'. So questions like 'where does it all come from? Who is it for? Who decides that it's worth it?' Are answered by a few people, those who have and will benefit from it, because it's a top-down transition; something imposed on everyone.

SB

And it's also contributing to different ecocides, genocides, epistemicides. It's interesting when you're on the outside, this green energy thing, the public image of it is already made squeaky clean. 'Let the experts take care of it and let them handle it'. The general public might not have access to the language that can articulate it, through chemistry, through physics, through whatever. It's like how people just trust doctors, even though we should question them as well. What do you think hydrogen thinks about all of this? I know that's a very abstract question. Even water, H_2O, what do you think it thinks about all of this?

SR

I think for water, it might be violent. To produce this thing that *they* call 'green hydrogen' – that's, in principle, 'the cleanest hydrogen' – you use solar energy or wind energy to split the water molecule into hydrogen and oxygen. It requires energy to split them because they don't want to be separated, these hydrogen and oxygen atoms. So I think for water, this is a violent process. Like, 'Yo, why are you splitting me? I'm just chilling here'.

'Why do you take me and split me in this way?' Then hydrogen and oxygen become isolated. It's also violent because you use water to produce hydrogen in, as they say 'where the sun is shining', like Namibia, or Algeria, or Chile... Places that already struggle a lot with water scarcity. You produce it there to bring it here, to the 'Global North'. Even in the best possible case scenario, you need around nine kilos of water per kilo of hydrogen. That's in the best scenario, the case of green hydrogen, which already neglects a lot of ramifications of this production. You need lots of water. And they say that you can desalinate seawater, but then they often throw back the salt into the water.

SB

Then you make the current seawater even saltier than it should be.

SR

There's no way around it. There is going to be more water scarcity. For instance, Germany has these plans to bring water, in the form of hydrogen, from territories in Western Sahara, where the Sahrawi people are under occupation by Morocco. Germany is moving to recognise that territory as legitimate because they want their hydrogen. They call this 'hydrogen diplomacy' or something like that.

SB

Yes. It just never ends.

SR

You produce hydrogen *there*, using the water that was also from there. It's then brought here, to the Port of Rotterdam, for example, where it is allowed to react with oxygen from here, forming water *here*. You took water from there and you formed it again here. There is an effective water flux from one place to the other. It's like you are kidnapping water molecules.

SB

Oh my God. That's what I was thinking about. In a way, it's captured *through* the splitting. A capture that chemistry aids.

SR

In doing so, you might also affect atmospheric chemistry, because you are bringing all that water from all those places and you're releasing it here. That water also goes into the atmosphere. There is also a whole greenhouse thing going on. The other day they were showing that a kilo of hydrogen produced in the North Sea by windmills was like 13 Euros per kilo or something like that, and to produce it in the south of Spain and bring it all the way here was like 8 Euros. How is that possible? How does this make sense?

SB

How do you also quantify all of these things inside of the economic system of capitalism? Oh my God, all these molecules are capitalised. [laughs]

SR

Exactly.

SB

I never thought about it like that. When you really go into it, in terms of the makeup of water, which already is moving and constantly going from one place to the other, to do it this way, I just see a mechanism of violence.

SR

Yes. I think it can be seen a bit like you are introducing a new cycle of water, moved by economics and state power, and you are merchandising this new cycle. When I questioned some of the things at a port in the Netherlands, in the place where they handle and move all the hydrogen and hydrogen-based fuels and so on, they were annoyed. At some point, they were actually said , *'shh, shh, shh, shh'*.

SB

Oh, like silenced you?

SR

Yes. They told me, 'Shut up'. Then they also said, 'These are very important questions that are very crucial to have, but they are more suitable for the political arena'.

SB

This also allows us to think expansively about how people, I don't know, however many thousands of years ago, encountered hydrogen or any of the elements. Of course, there were other ways, maybe we don't know all of them, or maybe it's not important to know about all of them, but they have the possibility of expanding the Western chronology of science. We've previously spoken about all these scientific instruments named after all of these German men – I'm assuming most of them are men [chuckles]. Yet look at the Islamic Golden Age, and even in Mali, which you just brought up – it was a huge hub for science in the African continent.[2] People have been doing this for the longest time. For me, it's nice to also anchor this realisation, which I think in Euro-American contexts can become quite uncertain of itself because one is constantly inundated with this very particular ideology of the West – 'developed', 'access', 'resources', 'infrastructure'. It's like... hmm, no, people knew this 2,000 or 3,000 years ago. Thinking back to the explosive Mali incident you mentioned, they knew it was there because of an after-effect or a reaction to its presence, hindsight.

SR

Yes, you cannot see it but its presence changes the relationships around it, and you can read its effects on other bodies – and it can have a relationship to sound as well.

SB

Tell me about that.

SR

There is this tin can experiment, which is how I personally became really aware of hydrogen production for the first time. This was when I was about 15 years old. I was living in Cancun, in the hood with the kids, where kids do the things that kids do. [laughter]

The older kids were doing this activity, in which they would grab a plastic bottle – an empty one – and put the chopped pieces of a tin soda can inside, along with muriatic acid (which is basically an impure hydrochloric acid, or very diluted hydrochloric acid, that is used as a cleaning product in Mexico). Then they would close it, shake it, and then throw it onto the highway and at some point there is a big boom, because all of the hydrogen starts to form inside the bottle, produced by the reaction of the can and the muriatic acid, and there is no way for it to come out.

SB

The only escape is through the kinetic energy of sound?

SR

At some point, it shouts – you hear the gas leaving the system. So, in a way, one can sometimes only know gases are there through their absence.

SB

This is so fascinating to me. Also, when we were in the lab last week, you showed me a video about the camotero, the person on the street selling sweet potatoes in the metal cart, [whistling sound]. This is super, super interesting for me because I've been thinking about tools/instruments, not only scientific ones but also musical ones and the other correlations between science and sound, for example, sampling. During my research, I came across the Leiden Instrument Makers School; it's an entire institute dedicated to making scientific tools. I contacted them early in my research to find out more about hygrometers – an instrument used to measure the humidity, or amount of water vapour in the air.

SR

They make tools for people who need something specifically?

SB

They make and develop instruments and prototypes for scientific research, the medical industry, aviation, and space travel. I was thinking about how we become cognisant of humidity and water vapour, things that are often imperceptible to the eye. I found it fascinating because two hydrogens and one oxygen is water; it's literally everywhere.

What are the different ways of sensing that it's there? Is it through its relationship to other things, and those interactions with other things? These ways of knowing don't only come to be by using very specific high-tech scientific equipment from the Global North, but also from instances like this anecdote you shared from when you were a kid. What is the name of that sound bomb?

SR

I think people might call it a petardo.

SB

What does petardo mean?

SR

Petardo means an explosive. It's a very generic name, but I think it applies here.

SB

This is my point though, we have the language and the vocabulary to interact with chemistry on a day-to-day basis, these things don't only have to be encountered within labs. I just find all these techniques – or even when you show me all these experiments – start to remind me of how in school they break down or simplify certain experiments so we can understand the concept of what's going on.

Then, when you really think of it, it's like, 'Yes, we can also do this at home, or yes, we can use these tools elsewhere, or we can use other things to do the same thing da da da'.

SR

Yes, it's also a way of freeing these gases, these substances, from thinking that you need super sophisticated equipment. We are also sensing instruments, and part of the water cycle, but then it's funny to think that we are also – I imagine, or you imagine, like a cenote, or a river, or something like that. We are also evaporating. We ourselves.

SB

[Pause] And how would hydrogen feel, in all of this?

SR

I don't know. There's a bleak irony in the incompatibility of our economic cycles with our natural cycles, and how hydrogen is used as a resource. I imagine two things. If I would imagine hydrogen wants to exist, then on one side it's cool for hydrogen because they're like, 'you're making lots of me and I'm moving around, and I'm inhabiting new spaces. I used to not be here and now I'm powering cars or powering ships and I'm travelling through the ocean. I'm being produced in places where I was not produced in the past, although I'm also being consumed there'. If we're thinking about how hydrogen feels about its own 'artificial' production, then yes there will be a bit more hydrogen in the universe, although not drastically different to current levels, which is already very high as the most abundant element in the universe. So on the one hand, I think hydrogen might be happy, but on the other hand, it's also being exploited.

SB

Do you think it knows that it's being exploited? If we were to imagine that it has this awareness of, 'Yes, I'm everywhere. There's more of me'.

SR

Yes, because it's not free. Hydrogen is the tiniest molecule that exists. Being the tiniest molecule means it can easily escape from things. It's like if you have a fence; maybe a fence can stop a dog, but a cat can go through the fence. Hydrogen can escape from many materials. It wants to fly freely, but people will do their best to stop it and keep it locked through technology... Although some will manage to escape for sure.

SB

In the same way we can sense, thinking about hygrometers, for example, we are hygrometers as well. Our hair, our body.

SR

Or knees – I think some people's knees hurt when it gets too humid.

SB

Oh, yes.

SR

I've heard of people forecasting, 'Oh, it's going to rain'. [laughter]

SB

Oh my God. In relation to tools, and thinking about this 'hygrometer' that I'm [chuckles] proposing to make, spatially, as an exhibition. I've been struggling with questions like, 'Why make a hygrometer when you could buy one?' It's more about this process and thinking about other 'tools of knowing' that are far more interesting for me...

I should have gotten people who are annoying when it's humid and just put all of them in a room.

SR

> I have a friend who gets headaches with specific types of clouds related to certain pressures. It starts with a headache and, 'Oh there are going to be low clouds'.
>
> I think that's also one of the most common ways of relating and visualising gases, is through our senses, because of the fact that they push against you. They are constantly exerting a force. That can also make sense if you imagine what a gas is from a chemical perspective. For instance, we have water which is made up of gases...

SB

How did the two hydrogens meet the oxygen? Was it a dating app?

SR

> Yes, through a dating app. One couple looking for a third.

SB

Oh my God. [laughs]

SR

> First, what we'd have is pure hydrogen plus pure oxygen. Pure, that is, two oxygen atoms bonded together and two hydrogen atoms also bonded together. Then, when they meet and are allowed to share electrons and create new bonds with each other, this process relaxes them so they release some energy, and feel more chilled and stable as a water molecule than when they were separated and alone. An oxygen atom has about six electrons around it when it's alone.

SB

They're less stable when they're on their own?

SR

> Yes, let's put it like that. An oxygen atom has about six electrons around it when it's alone. Oxygen and most atoms – because of the magic rules of chemistry – really want to have eight electrons around them at all times.
>
> Hydrogen already has one, and it actually only wants two in total. So when it's around oxygen, it is happy to share its one electron, because the oxygen also shares one electron with hydrogen. Through this deal, they each share this extra electron, so hydrogen ends up

with the two electrons it wants. Sharing is caring. Once they are inside the molecule, they are not 'my' electrons anymore, they are 'our' electrons. So the hydrogen is satisfied. Its shell of electrons is fulfilled. And then oxygen also gets two more electrons, from the two hydrogens, so it has one, two, three, four, five, six, seven, eight. This one has eight and this one has two electrons. They are happy.

SB

Everyone's happy.

SR

They met probably in the very first, I don't know, thousands or millions of years of the universe, like before planets existed most likely. Especially because hydrogen formed so quickly apparently, I'd say. I was not there.

SB

Is it Big Bang related?

SR

Yes, it's Big Bang related. First, you just have small subatomic particles. I don't know, quarks, gluons, things like that. I don't really know about that. Then at some point, these quarks and gluons start to come together, and then they form protons. Then eventually, these protons meet electrons. When a proton meets an electron, that's it, because then they form hydrogen.

SB

The parents of hydrogen are protons and electrons?

SR

Yes! Hydrogen is 'very easy to make' because there is just a proton and an electron, and then you have hydrogen. Then two hydrogens come together and clash with a lot of strength, and when the two come together and clash, they form helium with two protons, and this releases a lot of energy in the process.

Then if two heliums come together and crash, then they would form beryllium, and there would be four protons and electrons around.

SB

Wait, they're all related? Maybe that's an oversimplification, but I didn't realise that some came from others. I didn't realise that these conversations were happening. I thought they were all independent.

SR

No, no, no, they are related, they also all have ancestors.

SB

This is wild; I had no idea, because I was speaking to a microbiologist, Professor Norbert [de Ruijter], and I was asking him about DNA and ancestry. It didn't cross my mind that I could apply the same questioning to this.

SR

Yes. Actually, hydrogen is an ancestor of oxygen. When you combine two helium, you get beryllium. It's four. If you combine two berylliums, then we have four, five, six, seven, eight.

Two, three, four, five, six, seven, eight. Then you have this thing going on, which has eight protons and around eight electrons. There are also some neutrons involved, but we will skip those. After its first, second, third, we have oxygen. It's like a fourth-generation, great-grandchild of hydrogen. Then they can combine to form water.

SB

Ohhh, this is so amazing. Hydrogen, you say, is the OG ancestor?

SR

Yes, hydrogen is the OG, the ancestor of all other elements. And this is happening inside the stars most of the time. These are very energetic things. Having two elements, two hydrogens, and forcing them to merge. For instance, these two protons are positive. They are positively charged. Have you tried to bring two magnets together?

SB

Yes. It's like **ehhhhhhh**.

SR

Exactly. You need somebody to say, 'No, no, now you kiss'.

SB

Then when they kiss, then it's next level.

SR

Then it's the next level. It releases lots of energy. There are lots of sparks going on. [laughter]

SB

Oxygen is the fourth generation from hydrogen – does that mean water is also a composite of this family tree?

SR

Yes, what would that be?

SB

At that stage, it's not linear anymore. It's something else.

SR

Maybe some form of quantum ancestrality?

SB

Wow. I am feeling so happy.

SR

You like this idea of the generations?

SB

I think it's just understanding that we're talking about something that you and I sitting here in the studio cannot see or smell, but that's with us.

SR

It's here, and also in all of our bodies. It has been forming for so long now. It connects us to, I don't know...

SB

Even the dinosaurs, everybody.

[1] This encounter took place in Bourakébougou, Mali. Some sources mention that this occurred in 1987, not 1995. Hand, Eric.'Hidden Hydrogen'. *Science* 379, no. 6633 (17 February 2023): 630–36. https://doi.org/10.1126/science.adh1477.

[2] Timbuktu – from the 11th century and during Mali Empire, which reigned between the 13th to 17th centuries, founded by Soundiata Keita and subsequently notably led by Mansa Musa, and later the Songhai Empire – was a wealthy city and intellectual site for the production of knowledges in – but not limited to – science, mathematics, medicine, and astrology. A significant amount of this knowledge was recorded in the distinguished Timbuktu manuscripts. Farouk-Alli, Aslam. 'Timbuktu's Scientific Manuscript Heritage: The Re-Opening of an Ancient Vista?' Journal for the Study of Religion 22, no. 1 (2009): 43–61. http://www.jstor.org/stable/24764276.

Dating App

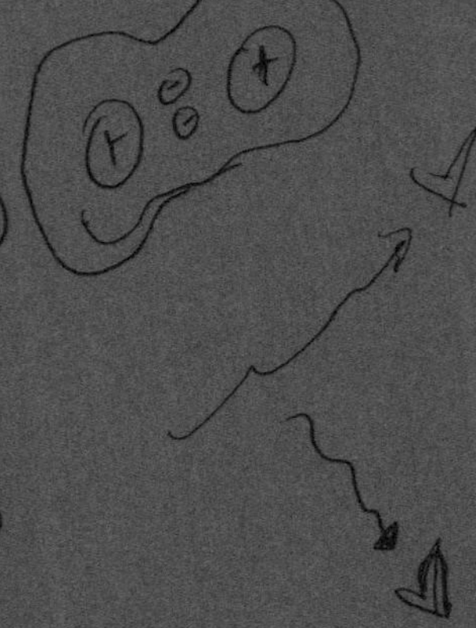

$$2H_2(g) + O_2(g) \rightleftharpoons 2H_2O(g)$$

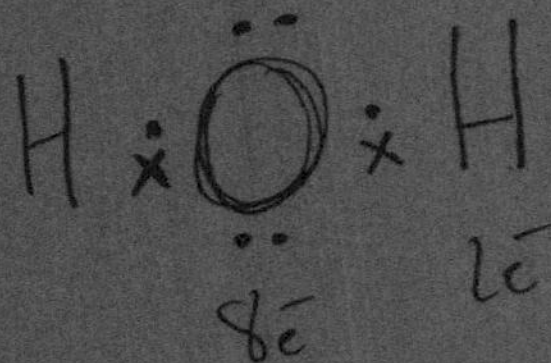

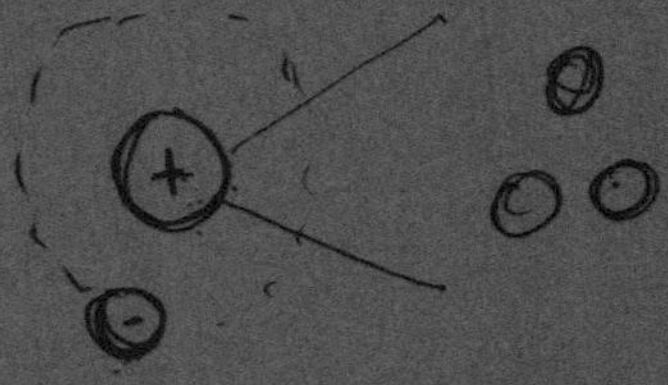

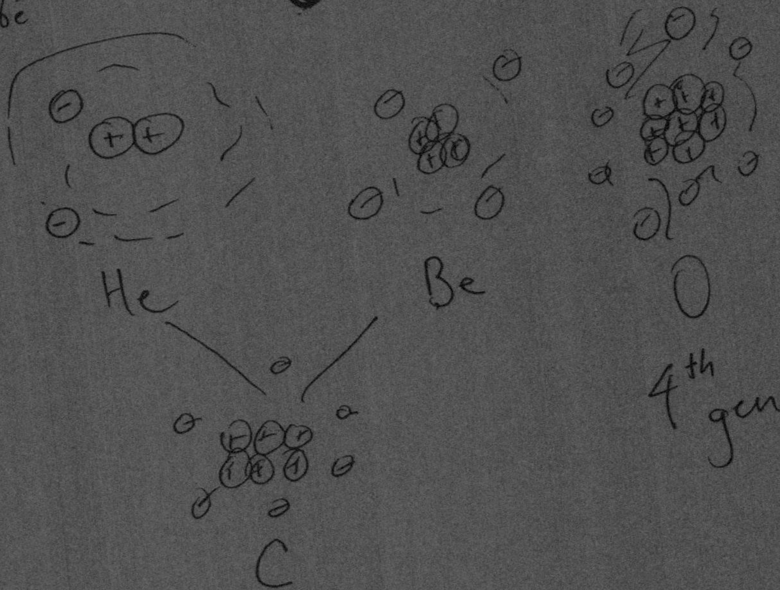

4th generation

ausencia

$$NaHCO_3 + HCl \longrightarrow NaCl_{(aq)} + H_2O_{(l)} + CO_2(g)$$

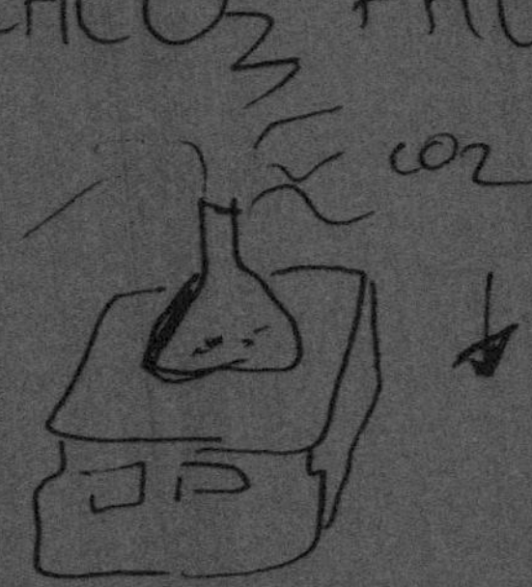

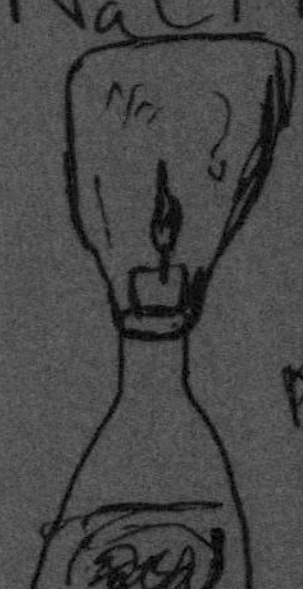

→ types of Bakng soda + vinagre

$PV = nRT$

Pressure, Volume, number of moles, temperature

H_2 ideal gas

$n = 1$

$T = 300°C$

$P = 5 atm$

$V = ?$

$$V = \frac{nRT}{P} = \frac{(1)(8.314\ J/K\,mol)(573K)}{(5atm)}$$

$V = 22.4L$

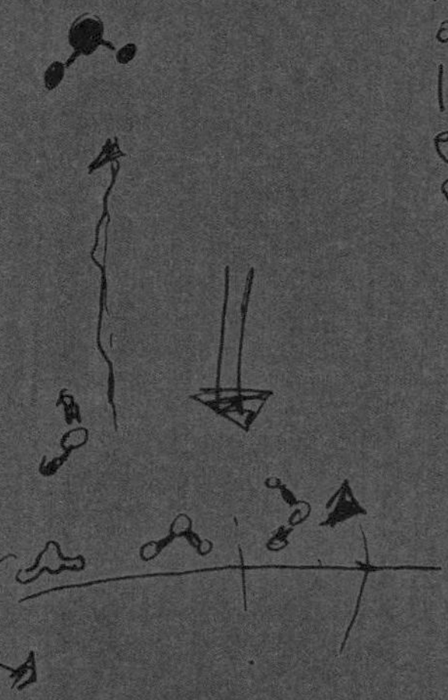

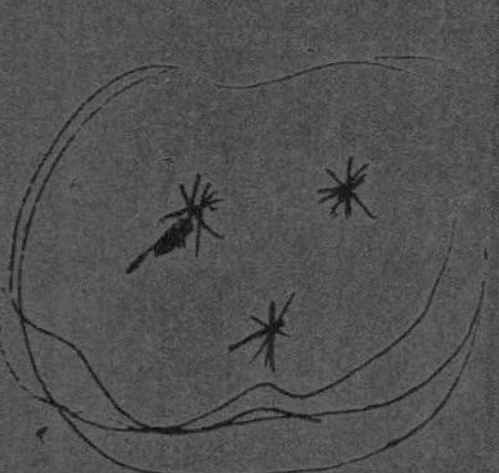

AgI

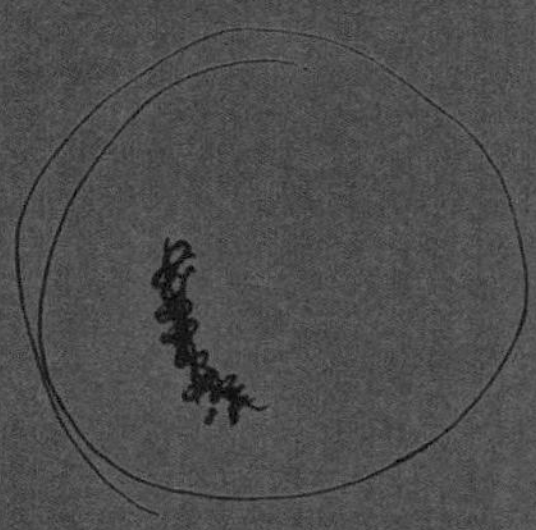

nucleation point

PLACES OF INTEREST ALONG THE TSWAING CRATER TRAIL

The listed numbers below refer to the numbers on the concrete plinths along the trail

1 To the right (east) is an open space where the old cattle pens (kraal) of the former Zoutpan research farm used to be

2 Remains of a trench that carried the main pipeline between the crater and the soda and salt reduction works (site 19) through which saline liquid flowed that was pumped from the crater

3 Foundations of the residence built in the 1940s for the Mine Manager of SA Alkali Ltd, the company that mined soda and salt at Tswaing between 1912 and 1956

4 Crater viewpoint with a morula tree Due to changes in the slope angles of the crater rim and in the soil types and nutrients, broadleaved woodland trees cover the upper slopes and thorny trees cover lower slopes of the inner crater rim

5. Crater rim cutting, named after W Mauss who designed the reduction works It carried the pipeline that pumped back waste liquid, remaining after the extraction of soda and salt, back into the Crater Lake

6 Crater viewpoint with foundations of another building

7 One of the concrete survey beacons erected in 1953 to demarcate the mining area

(No number) Granite plaque commemorating Dr Eugene Shoemaker, an American geologist who pioneered the study of meteorites and their impact. This viewpoint is named after him

8 The Tswaing Crater is a bowl-shaped geological feature, caused by the impact of a 50m chondrite (stony meteorite) 220 000 years ago which exploded and vaporized on impact. The crater can host four simultaneous football matches and half a million spectators!

9. At Shoemaker Viewpoint you are 60m higher than the surrounding landscape and 100m above the crater floor The distance to the opposite crater rim is 1.13km You are standing on top of large granite boulders that were ejected by the force of the meteorite impact. Please beware of the steep drop

10 These granite boulders show how weathering (breaking up into small fragments) by lichens takes place Lichens are minute organisms, consisting of algae and fungi living together

11. Stone tools and weapons, dating back to the Middle Stone Age, have been found here, showing that as long as 150 000 to 30 000 years ago people came to Tswaing to hunt, gather edible plants and collect salt.

12 Segment of dyke consisting of igneous (volcanic) intrusive rock known as lamprophyre This rock was present before the impact

13. Research boreholes, made in 1972 by Pratley Company (pressure tap to collect water for medicinal purposes), 1988-1989 (hidden) and 2001-2002. The 1988-89 and recent boreholes explored the sedimentary deposits below the present crater floor

14 The Crater Lake water originates from surface springs, underground water and rainwater. Because the lake is rich in dissolved carbonates and chloride salts, predominantly of sodium (originating from the soils and groundwater), it was mined. The sulphurous smell emanates form bacteria in the lake.

15. Close to the road, made for ox wagons in the 19th century, is a place where Sotho- and Tswana- speaking communities produced salt by filtering, boiling and evaporating the lake water during AD 1200-1830 They left behind many fragments of clay pots that disintegrated during this process Please do not remove these potsherds

16. Remains of central pumping station from where the saline liquid, collected through many boreholes (visible above the lake surface) was pumped over the crater rim to the reduction works

17 Section of crater rim showing granite that was folded, displaced and overturned as a result of the impact.

18 Whitewash, used in an unsuccessful attempt to change the colour of salt, briefly produced in the 1960s, from brown to white.

19. Ruins of the reduction works where the saline liquid from the crater was transformed into soda ash and salt between 1922 and 1956. Beware of snakes and hidden underground reservoirs!

20. These ponds, part of the reduction works used to store and warm up the ice-cold saline liquid, left over from the soda production process, before salt was extracted from it.

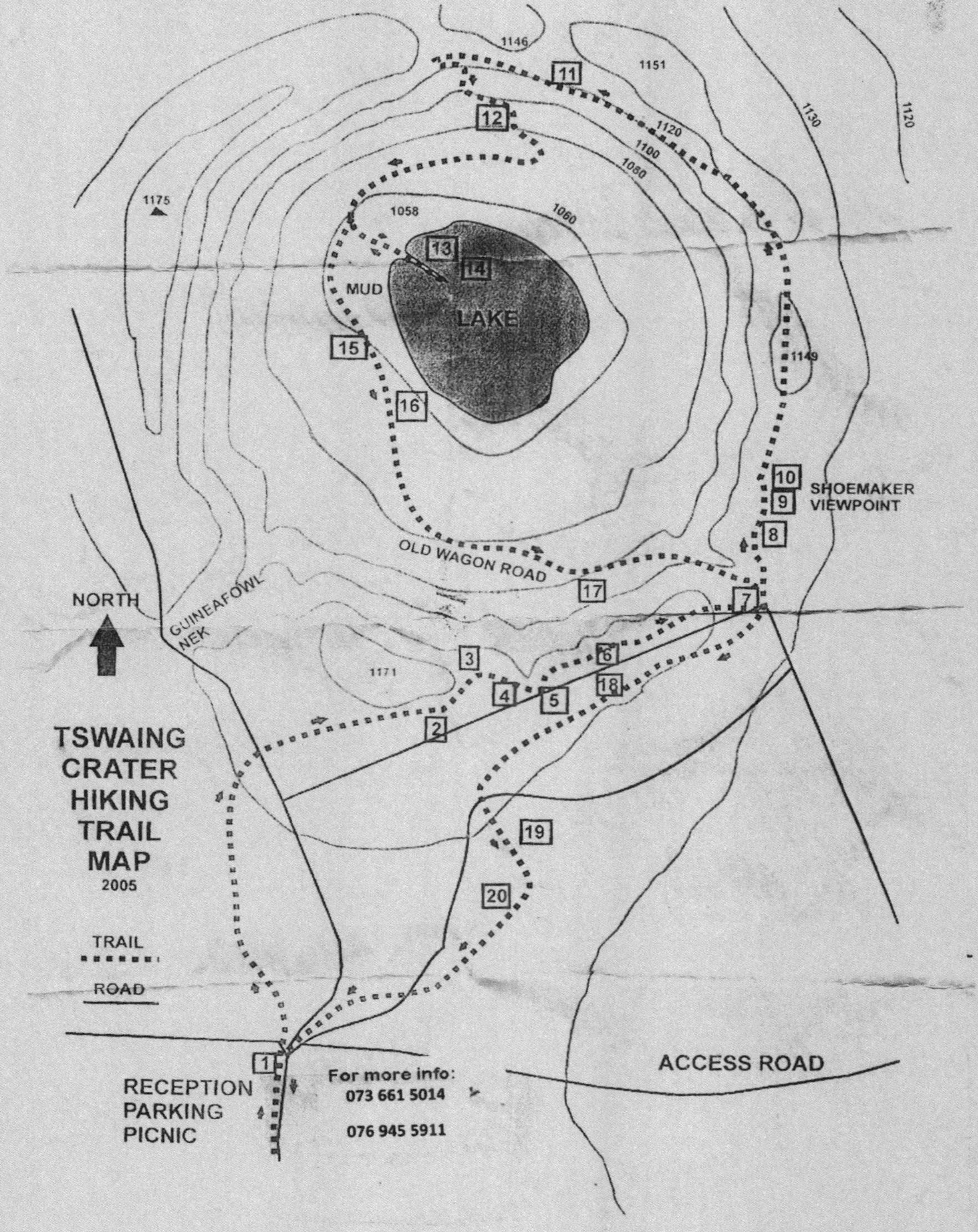
TSWAING CRATER HIKING TRAIL MAP
2005
TRAIL
ROAD
NORTH
LAKE
MUD
OLD WAGON ROAD
GUINEAFOWL NEK
SHOEMAKER VIEWPOINT
ACCESS ROAD
RECEPTION
PARKING
PICNIC
For more info:
073 661 5014
076 945 5911
1146
1151
1120
1130
1120
1100
1080
1060
1058
1175
1149
1171
1
2
3
4
5
6
7
8
9
10
11
12
13
14
15
16
17
18
19
20

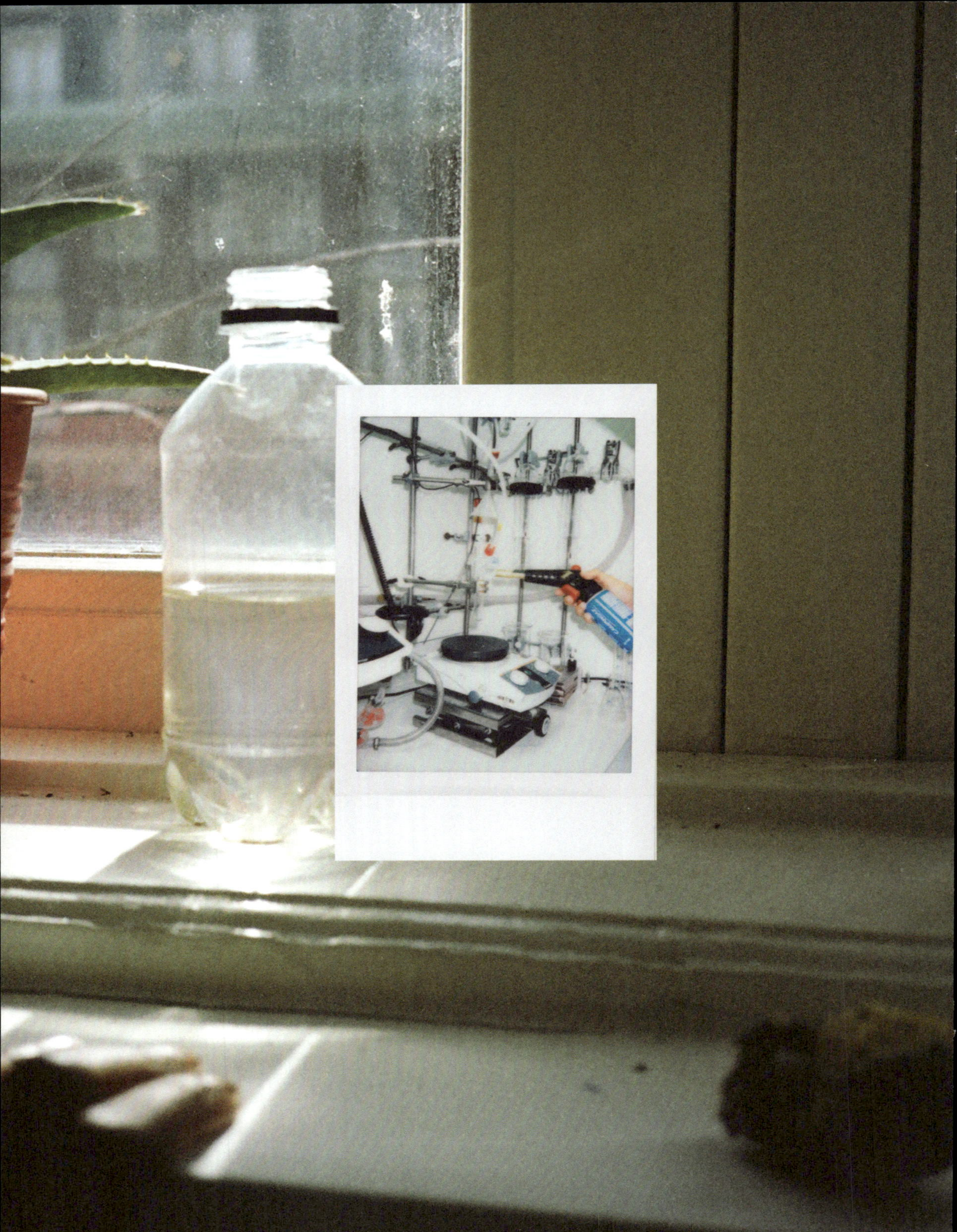

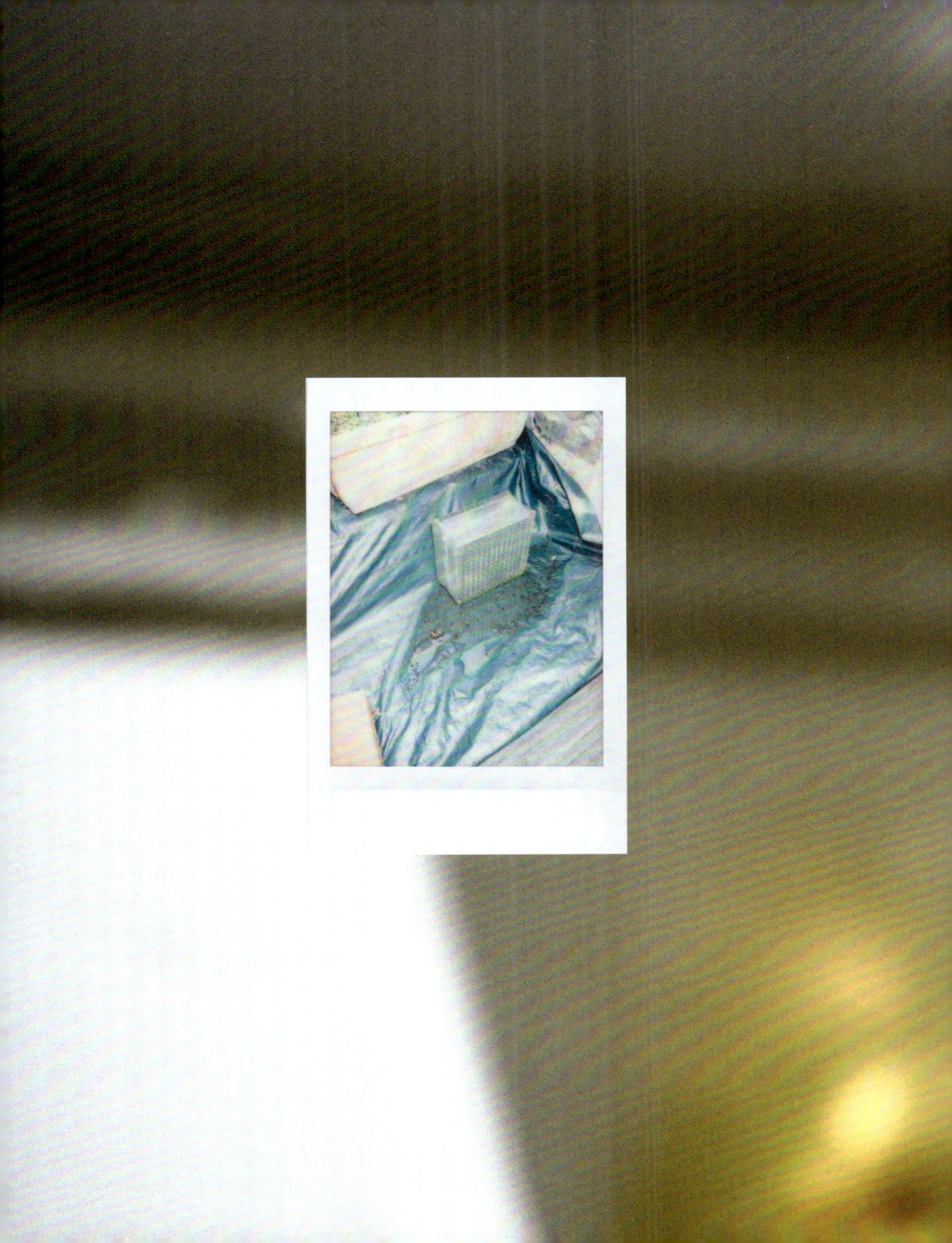

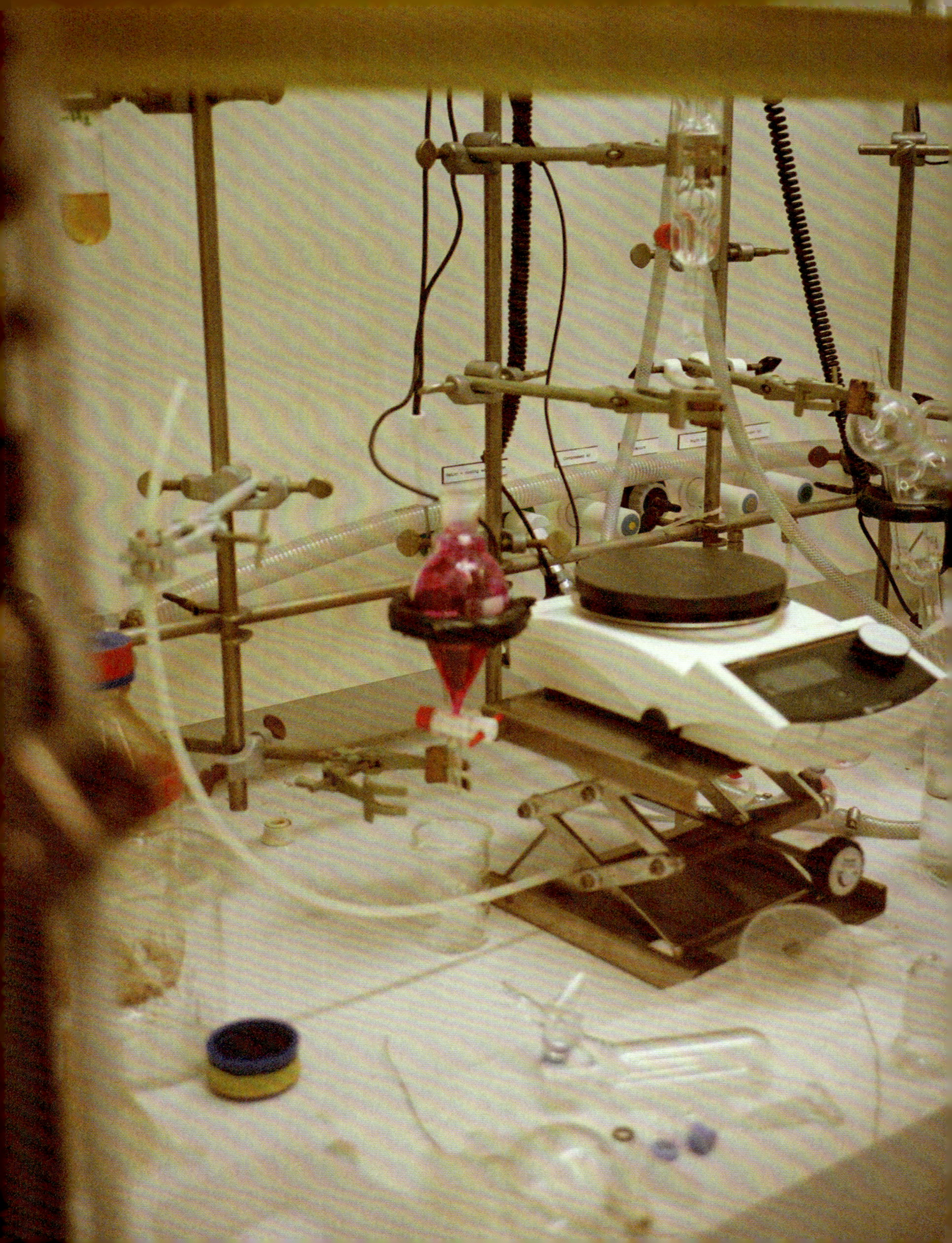

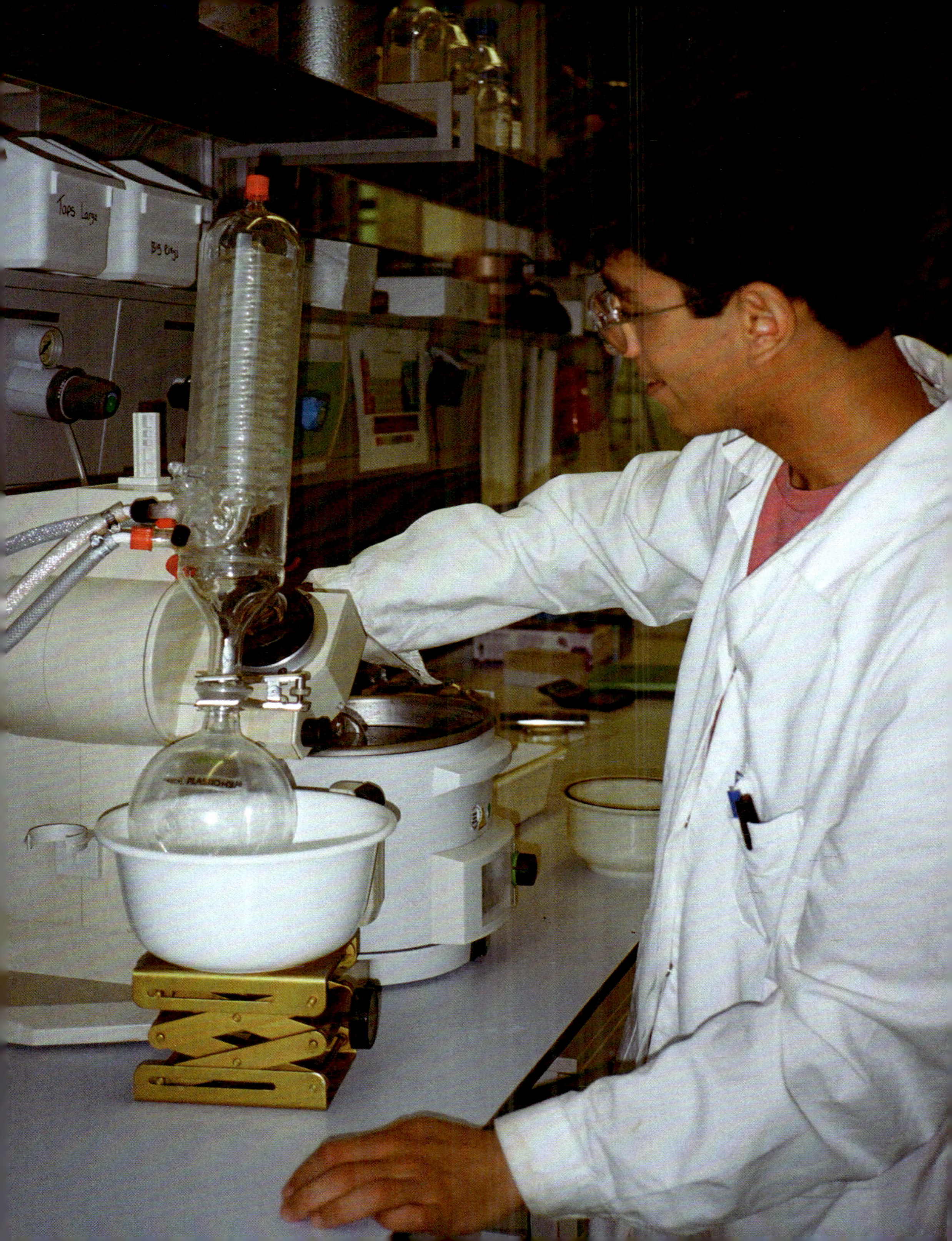

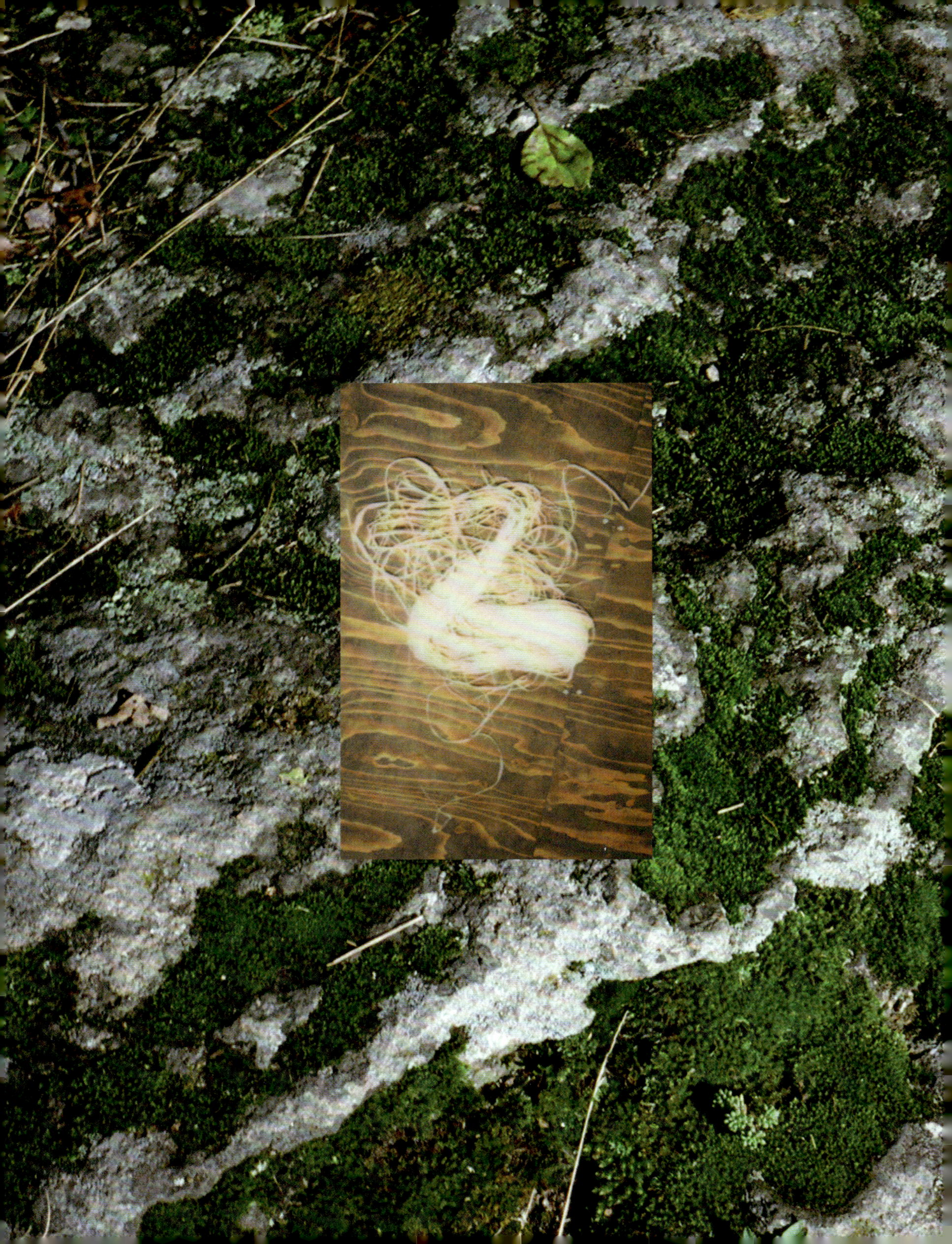

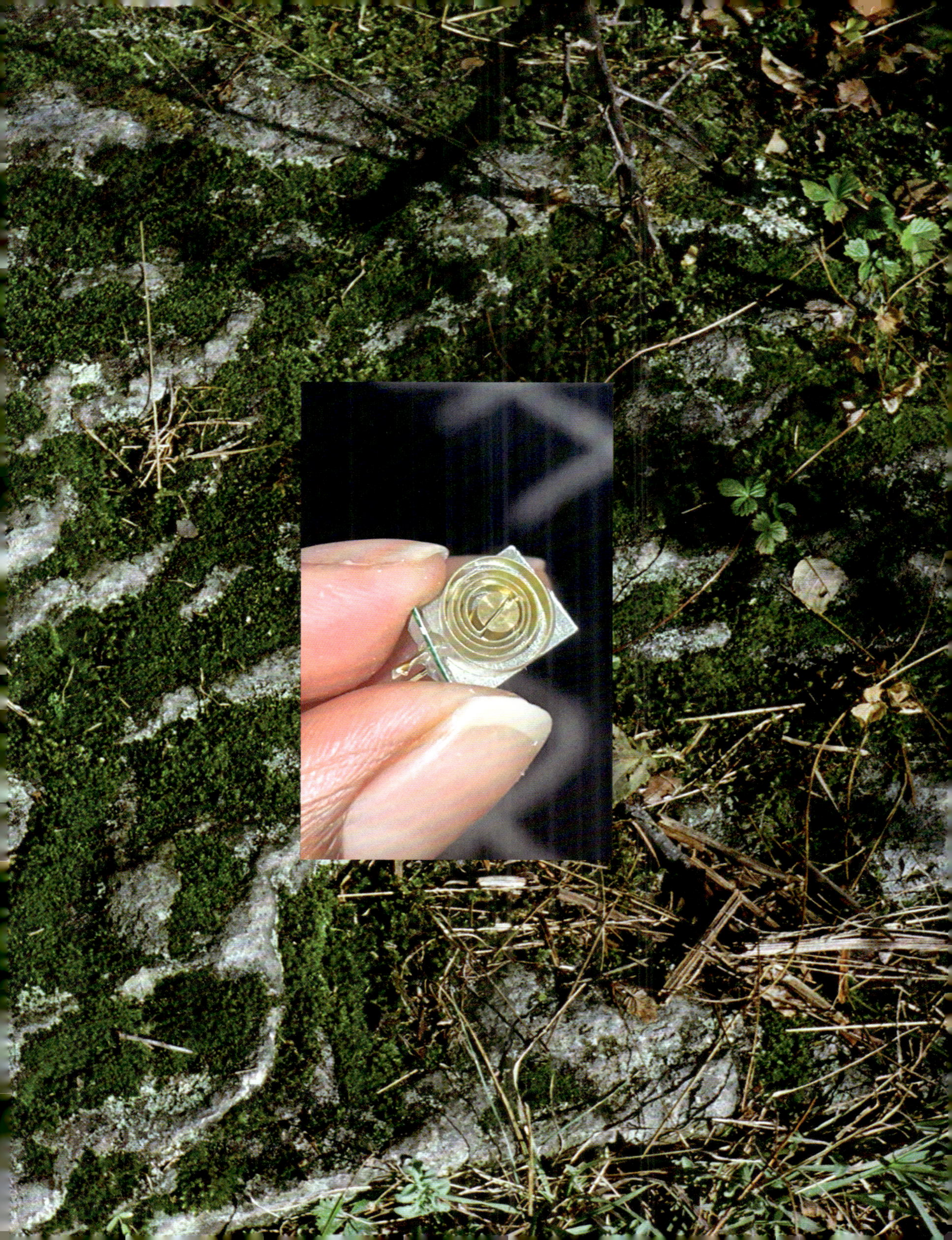

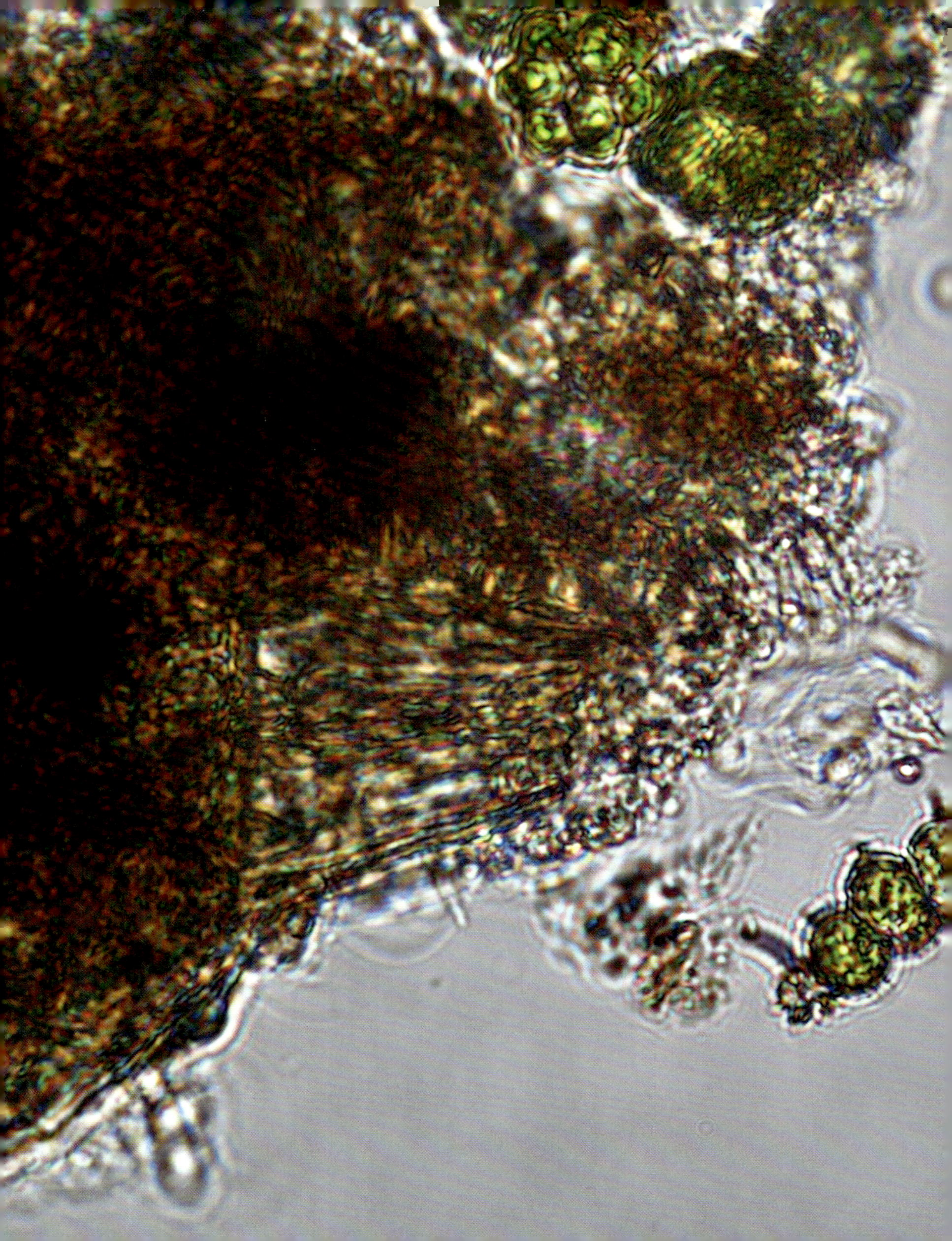

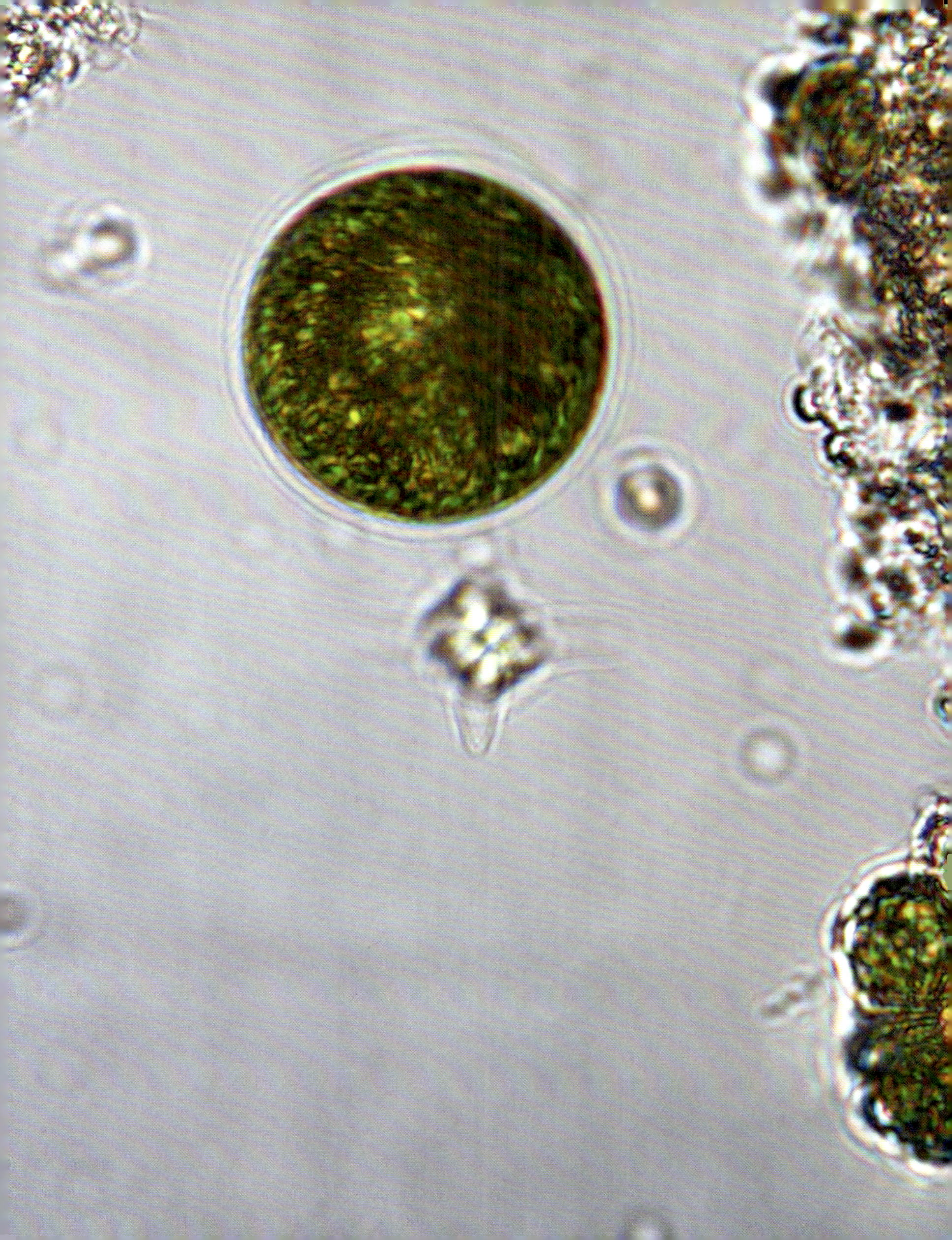

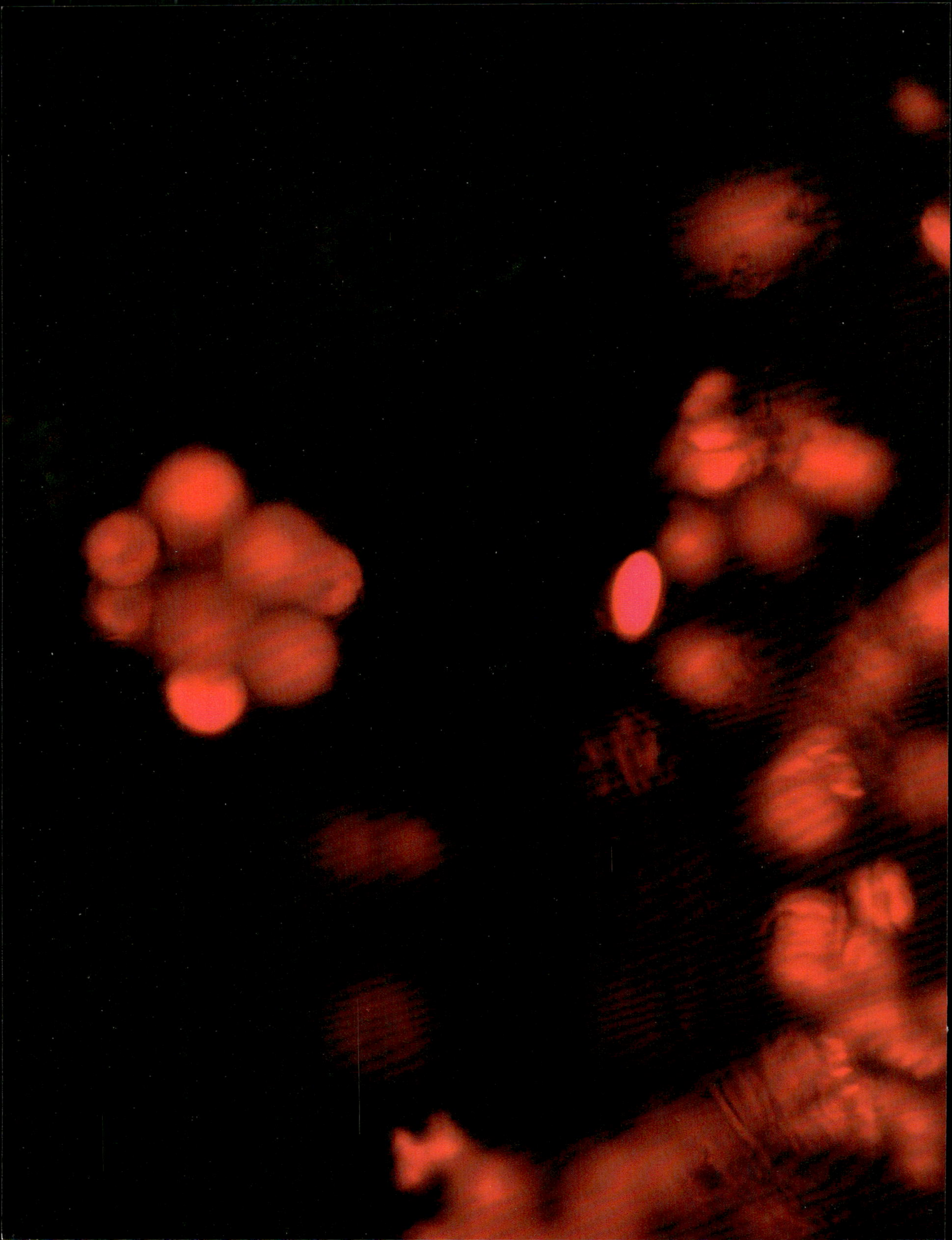

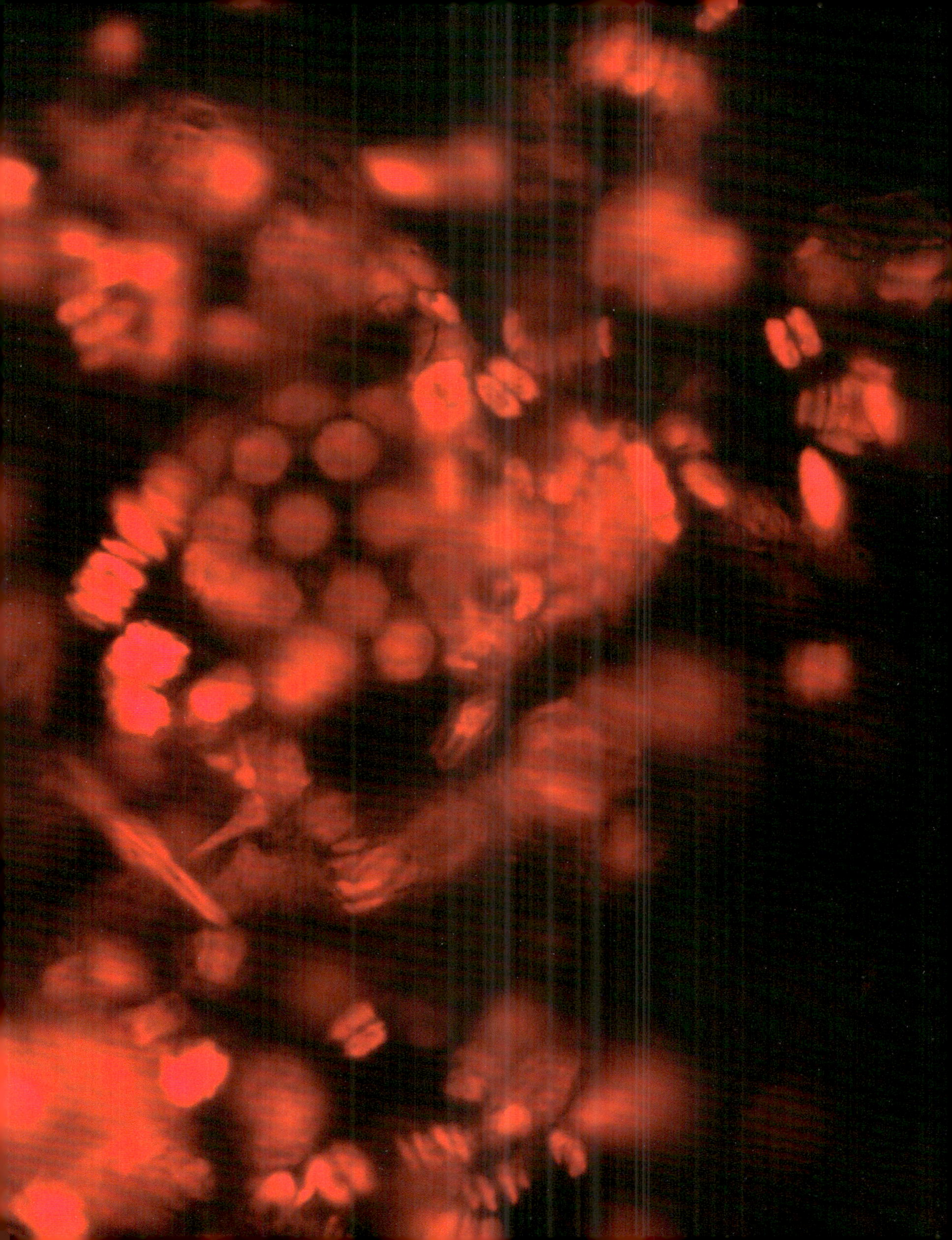

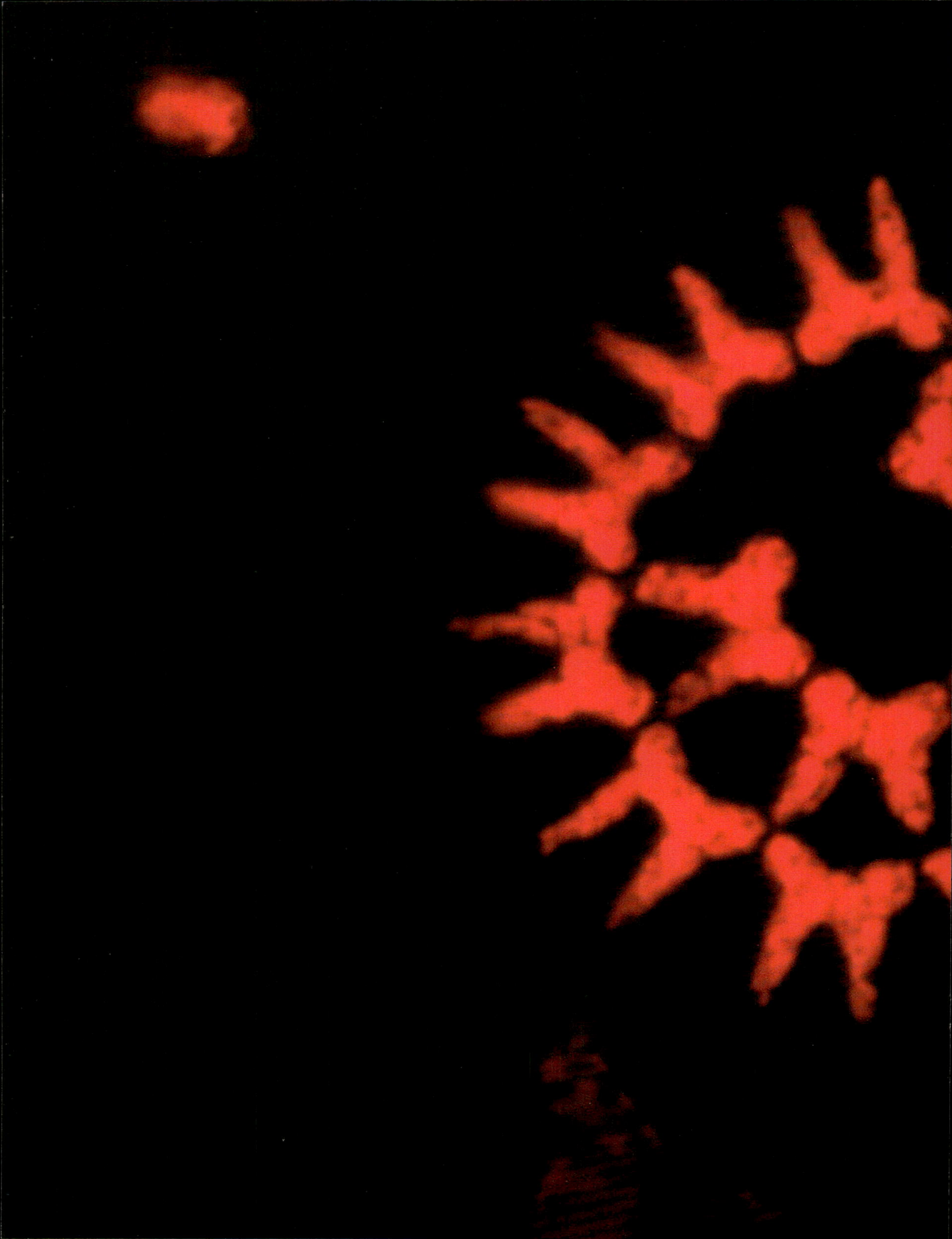

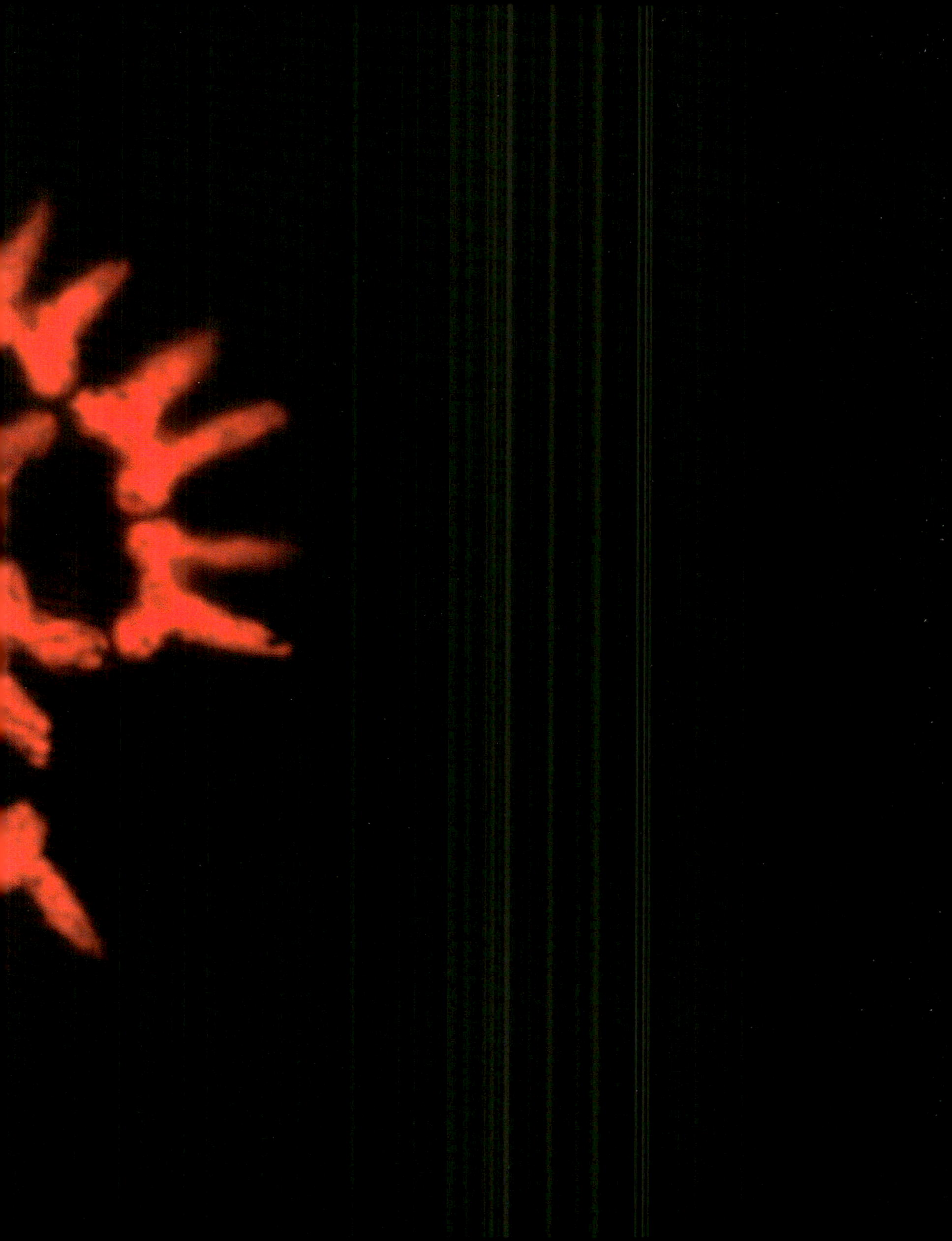

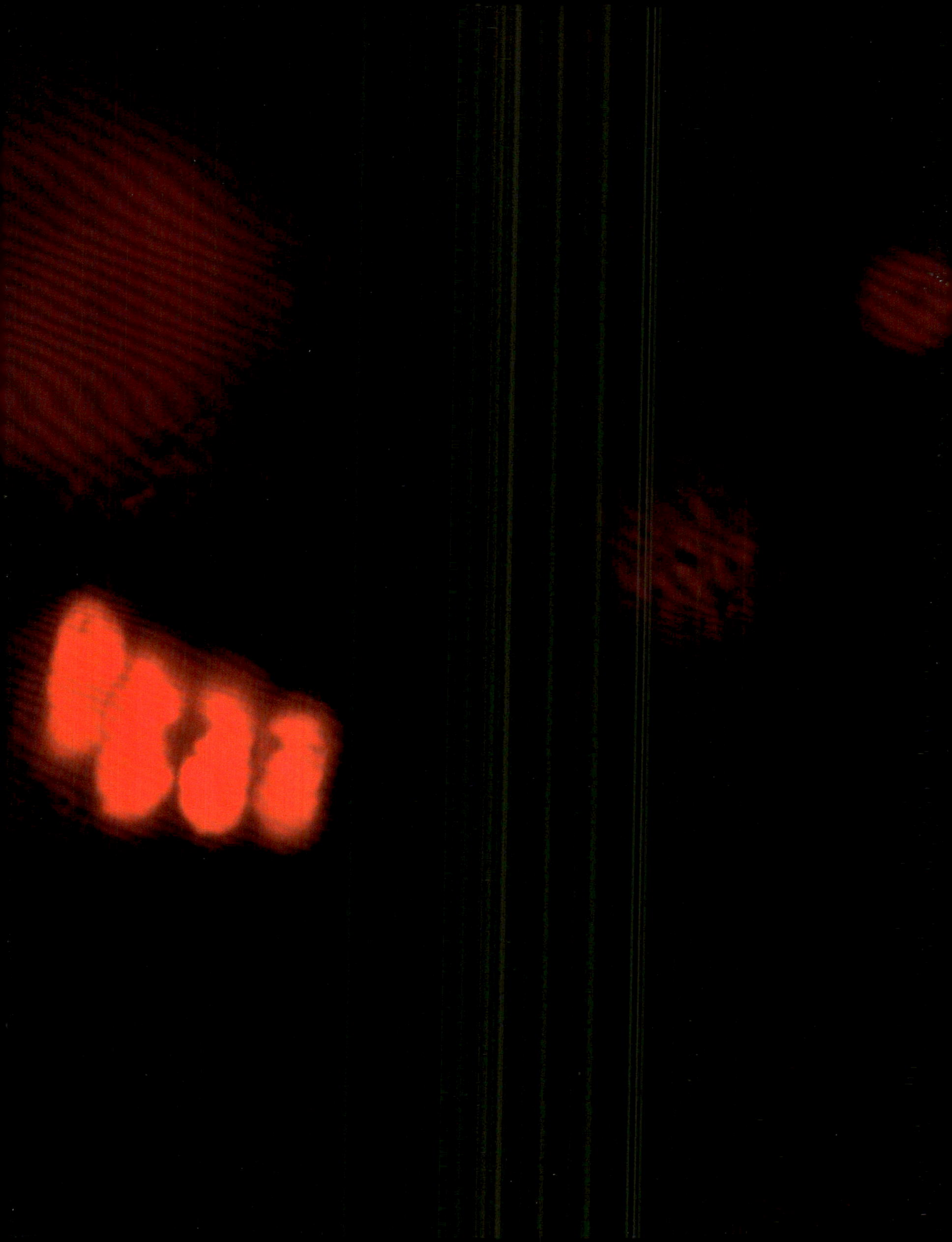

Simnikiwe Buhlungu & George Mahashe

Simnikiwe → George; George → Simnikiwe

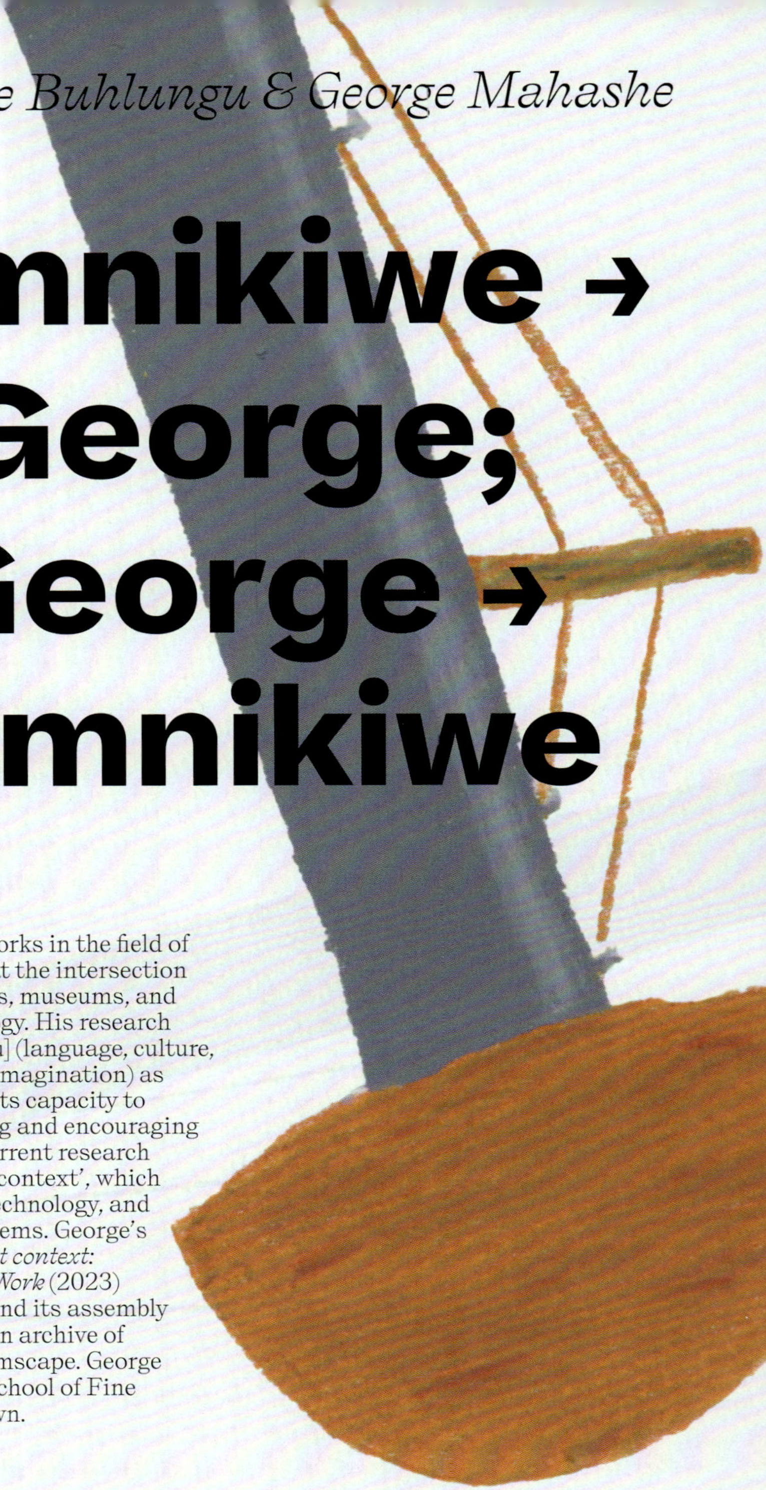

Tebogo George Mahashe works in the field of photography, particularly at the intersection of artistic practice, archives, museums, and the afterlives of anthropology. His research takes khelovedu [khelobedu] (language, culture, practices, philosophy, and imagination) as a central idea, drawing on its capacity to complicate ways of knowing and encouraging trans-disciplinarity. His current research project includes '—defunct context', which engages the nexus of art, technology, and indigenous knowledge systems. George's recent publication *—defunct context: Ambivalence to Important Work* (2023) explores the artist's book and its assembly as a process of inscribing an archive of practice as a physical dreamscape. George is based at the Michaelis School of Fine Art, University of Cape Town.

BERENSTRAAT 20—1
1016 GH
AMSTERDAM
16TH OCTOBER 2023

Dearest George

I write to you, on the verge of an afternoon nap I'm trying to fight off, to insert you into one of my conundrums.

Hehe. It's not bad at all!

In fact, this letter is an open attempt to think alongside you, should the proposal be remotely interesting.

I need to build a hygrometer.

I do not know how.

A few weeks ago, I sent a WeTransfer link to you, which contained a rather extensive PDF of Helaine Sellin's "Encyclopaedia of the History of Science, Technology and Medicine in Non-Western Cultures – Second Edition (2006)". As an echo of your work with the camera obscura, – defunct context and your methodologies of [de]constructing various apparti within the more socio-scientific-astrono-geometric-mathematic realm. I really appreciate the curiosity you have of this world and the delicate yet thoughtful and critical manner through which you mull over this vocabulary – but take it elsewheeeeeere!

Anywho, in this PDF, Sellin describes a hygrometer – a mechanism/device – which measures the amount/presence of humidity of air and other gaseous friends. If you Google 'hygrometer', the internet will usually prioritise 'sources' that claim that some swiss dude 'invented' the world's 'first' hygrometer. The words I have placed in inverted commas are keywords that particular historical writings are just utter hogwash.

Ok, so I thought to check again as this chronology of the Swiss dude's hygrometer iteration from the 1780s was far too unconvincing and made it seem like humans have been doing absolutely nothing by way of being curious of humidity prior to the 18th century.

Streeeeeeeeeeeeeeeetching the timeline a bit further back, it turns out more dudes [who] were experimenting with hygrometers before the 1780s (albeit; not really "elsewhere"); in the 15th century (Leonardo da Vinci); the 17th century (Francesco Folli) and in the 1750s (Johann Heinrich Lambert), then we end up in the 1780s with the Swiss dude I mentioned earlier (Horace Bénédict de Saussure).

'Inventors'.

What is interesting about Sellin's PDF is that it articulates that an early usage/iteration of the hygrometer was developed not by an individual per se, but a context. In writing, at least. So, it is said that in the → [in China!] western Han dynasty* (circa 206 B.C. – 9 A.D.), folks made hygrometers using a "lump of earth and a bar of charcoal (or a feather) → [Sellin 2006:1664] [on a staff.] When the humidity would rise the coal/feather would absorb the moisture and drop a little. Like some kind of scale the dry weight vs. humid weight of the charcoal would be measured, with the difference being the quantifiable 'amount' of humidity.

I'm going to be boring and quote the rest of the description of the hygrometer as I have struggled to find a visual representation of it.*also not sure here, other sources state it was the → [in China!] Shang dynasty (circa 1600 B.C. – 1045 B.C.). I don't know. The inconsistencies are worrisome for me...

So, Sellin says:

> By hanging a lump of earth and a bar of charcoal (or a feather) on the two ends of a staff separately and fixing a lifting string on the middle point, making the staff horizontal in the dry air, a humidometer was made. When the air became humid, the end which had the charcoal fell down.

That's the most vivid description I have encountered. My suspicion, driven by speculation and very desperate curiosity, is that maybe it was something like this?:

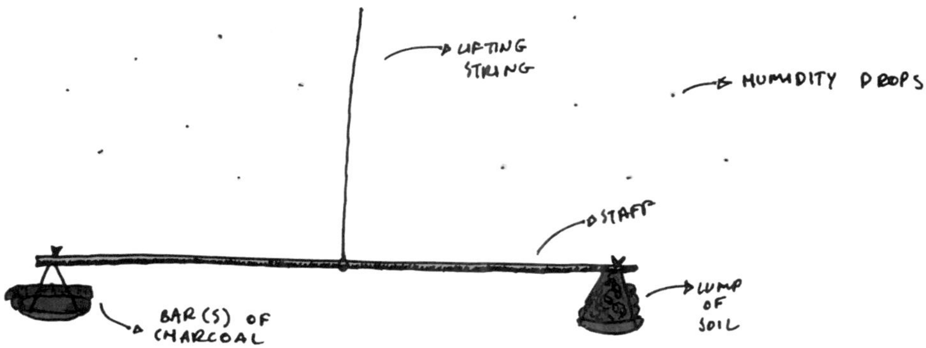

It definitely looks like a scale. But I'm wondering how to balance the coal and soil, and what material would the staff be made out of? I do not understand how the feather would work; wouldn't it be offset by the weight of the soil in any case? Maybe this speculation is too much like a scale. Also, wouldn't the hygrometer just keep spinning 360 degrees? What mechanism keeps it still for a credible reading? It also doesn't specify what kind of soil is apt. Loam? Clay? Sand? Silt?

The power of the coal does make sense to me [though]. Growing up, we always had a lump of coal in the back of the freezer.

Upon asking my mother, 'Mama, why is there coal in the fridge?', I recall her telling me that it is because the coal would absorb the smell of frozen goods (looking at the chickens and beefs, especially!). So I don't doubt the porousity of coal. Apparently my grandmother does it, too.

Now, going back to this letter as a proposal, I wanted to ask you what you think Sellin's description of this ancient hygrometer could've looked like/visually existed? And beyond that, how else do you think we can imagine (with an intentional invitation of the speculative within 'science') an apparatus to measure the presence of humidity?

- [short break to eat a snack. The snack is a banana] -

I need to build this hygrometer as I am working on a project with a puddle. The project is in London at the Chisenhale Gallery, and the puddle is...somewhere in Johannesburg. I want to invite the puddle – visa free travels, all expenses paid – to the exhibition space of Chisenhale Gallery. There are many loose conceptual threads, I'm still working on it. Anyways, since the puddle is likely to leave on its own terms shortly after arriving (by way of the water cycle), I'm reaching this moment is not about the spectacle of a sentient body from the global south temporarily inhabiting a space in the west (I mean, who needs *another* one of those?!), but allowing the puddle to live on its own terms, which is likely to include eschewing capture. So then, I was thinking about the messenger (maybe even "one who gossips") who remains behind to share what happened and who was there. Like a griot.

*I should WhatsApp them to double check.

But specifically a griot who remained "on site" as the source of info for passersby.

I'm not sure if a puddle[s] is enough water/liquid to offset a hygrometer, but...Ja I'm also interested in apparati that shows us phenomena we can't see. Like some of the equipment in a chemistry lab, when one is working with gases, specifically. How to know they are present if we cannot see/smell/taste etc. them? Then we're left with apparati whose sole purpose is to ‘tell’. Apparati we trust. Apparati we are already surrounded by, that we have beeeeeeeeeen using. And untangle things; how to make do with the threads? Which might have a lot say on their own.

So. Ja. What do you think/ what can it look like to measure humidity? How do we know something – that we cannot ‘see’ – was [t]here?

I’ll leave this letter/proposal here.

I look forward – with the utmost excitement – to your reply.

Otherwise? I hope you are well and that this finds you somewhere between your vertical travels from Cape Town, through the equator, to Bern.

Please send my regards to Kabelo and Nani!

Take care!

Hugs,

SIMNIKIWE

x x

Simnikiwe Buhlungu:

Hiiiiii! Aside from Kalk Bay, what are some good fish restaurant recommendations? Xx
13:12

George Mahashe:

Hey, crazy day. The only one is lucky fish which is really a kfc. Have not eaten fish out in Cape Town.
23:16

Re: proposal. The first thought is a song that i know of but do not know the words to. A story of some women that call forth a puddle when they sing when drunk. Women taken as slaves but in reality are the punishment for colonial arrogance. Instrument-device-technology-wise I think of telluride interference meter. A vacuum with a light film that spins based on the moisture in the air. But I think the fridge device is the one. Excited to think with you.
23:21

Got a book for you
23:21

Love the format of the letter
23:22

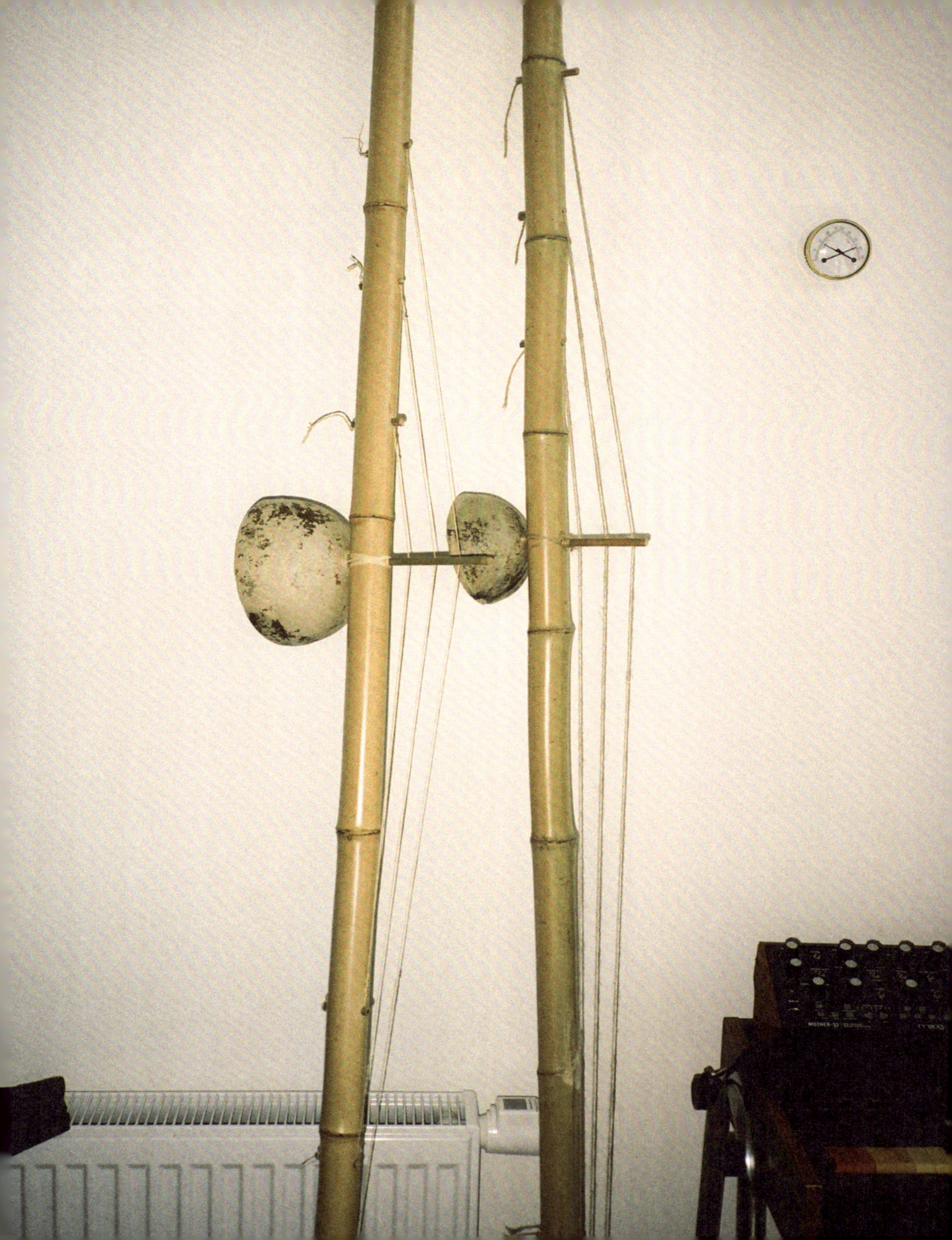
MOTHER-32
moog

Khwezi Gule

Izigemegeme ZamaGwibgwib

UKhwezi Gule is an arts administrator based in Johannesburg, South Africa. The drawings presented in this publication are a reflection of his attempts to escape the drudgery of bureaucracy, as in the movie Brazil (1985). UKhwezi has worked in various curatorial contexts, leading many people to think of him as a curator. He has contributed texts to anthologies, catalogues, and mainstream media publications. His favourite form of written text however, is the handwritten letters he sends to friends and other special people. These missives allow him to wrestle with ideas in an authentic way. UKhwezi is currently pursuing an MA in Curatorial Studies at the University of Witwatersrand. UKhwezi's pronoun is "u-".

IZIGEMEGEMES ZAMAGWIBGWIB

... the adventures of amaGwibgwib

GLOSSARY:

* umkhathi - space
* inqwelo-mkhathi - spaceship
* ixhaphozi - a puddle
* abavakashi - visitors
* ukudlala - to play
* amafu - clouds

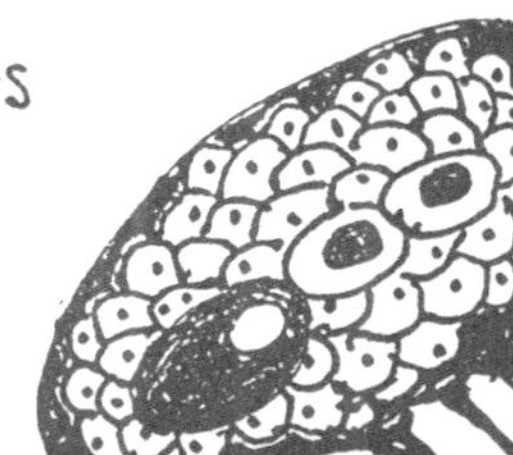

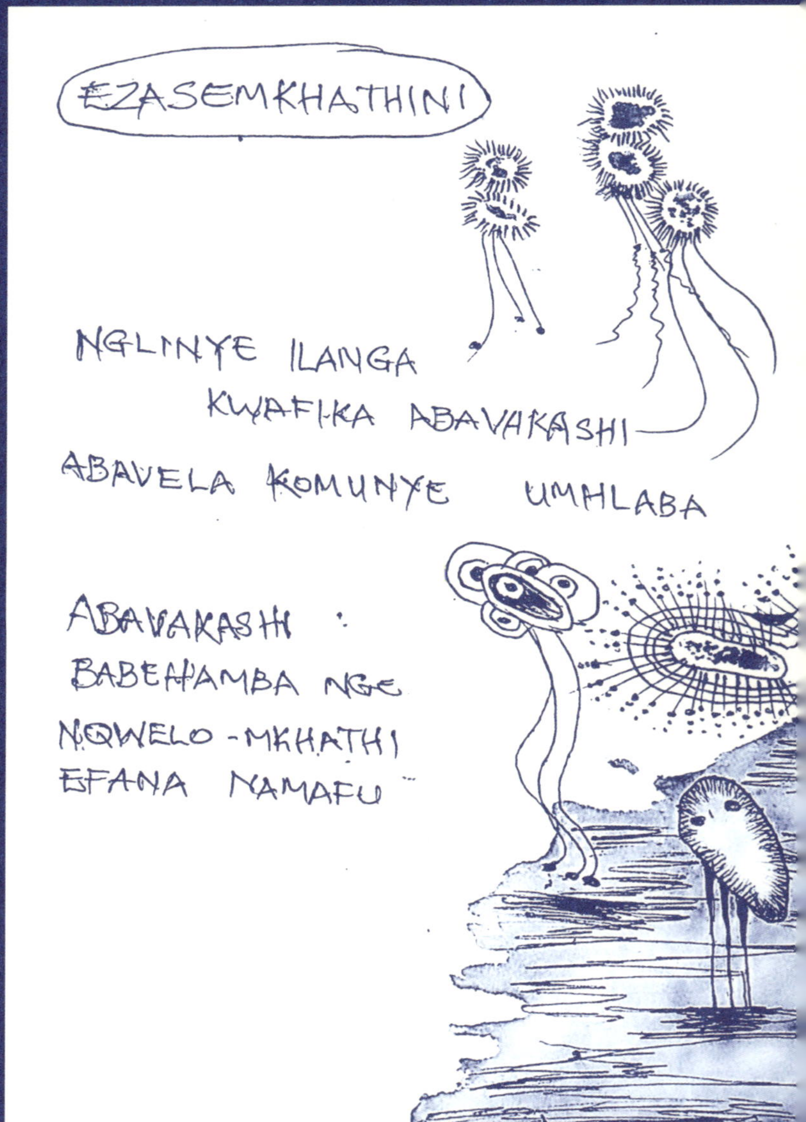
EZASEMKHATHINI
NGLINYE ILANGA
KWAFIKA ABAVAKASHI
ABAVELA KOMUNYE UMHLABA
ABAVAKASHI :
BABEHAMBA NGE
NQWELO-MKHATHI
EFANA NAMAFU

ABAVAKASHI
BASE
MKHATHINI

BABEBIZWA
NGAMA
GWIBIGWIBI

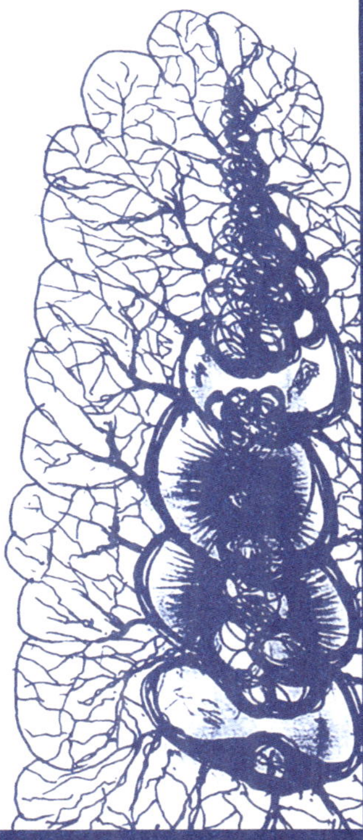

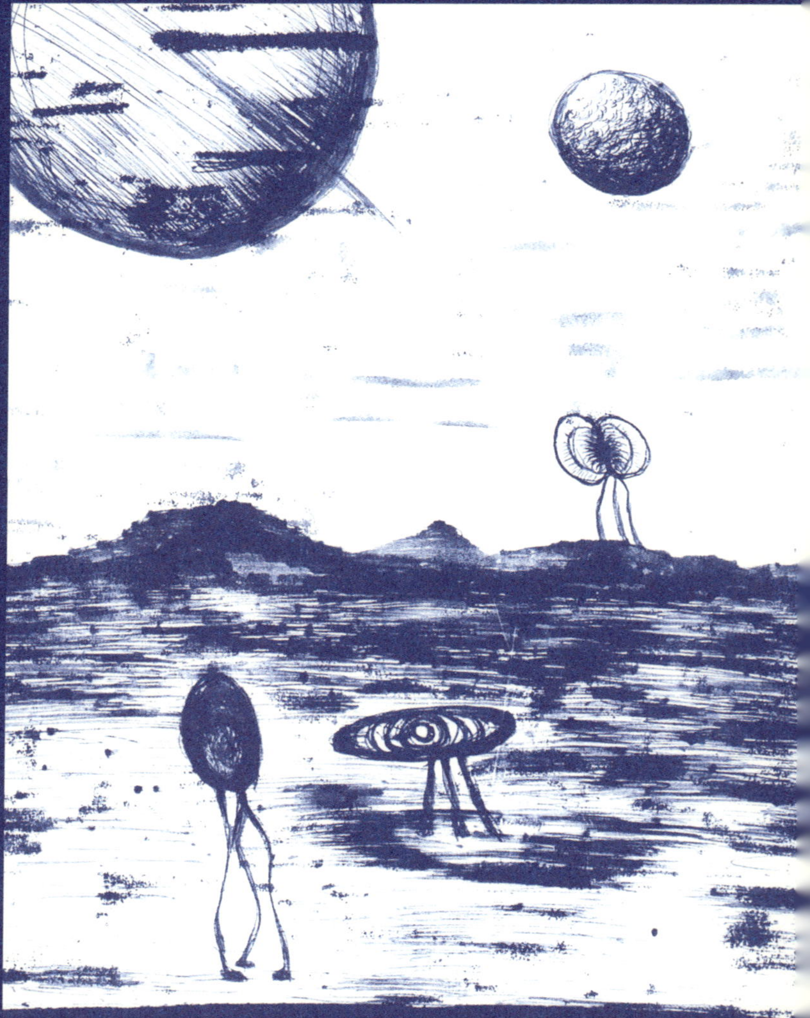

UMHLABA WAMAGWIBGWIB
WAWUNAMAXHAPHOZI AMANINGI

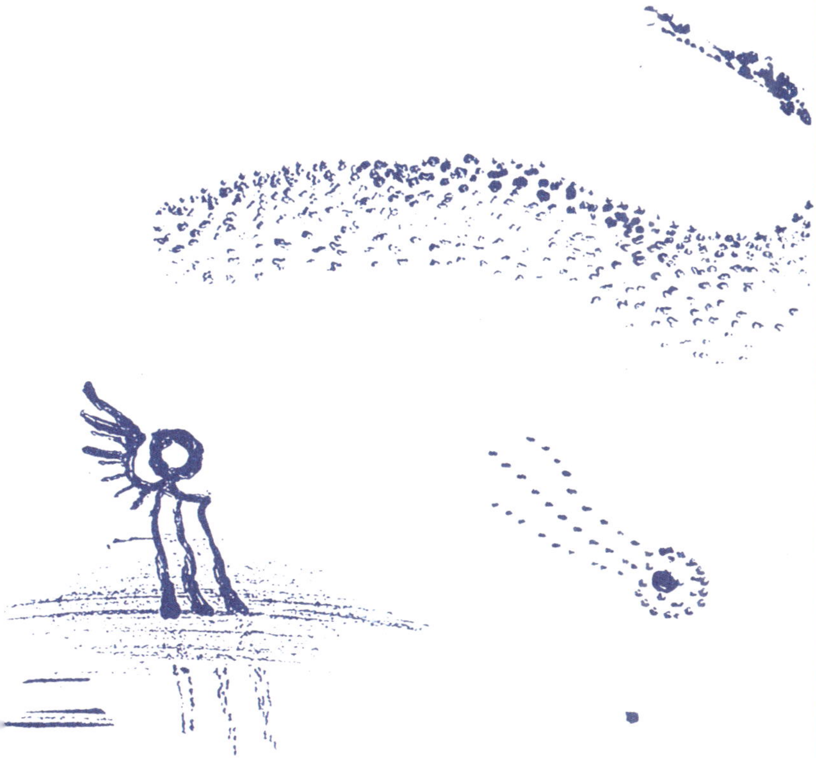

AMAGWIBGWIB AYEDLALA

KUMAXHAPHOZI

ASEMKHATHINI ...

The puddle is a fugitive!!!!

The hygrometer isn't merely a passive sensing apparatus; it — again through humidity — can call and subsequently anticipate responses.

Regarding the samples and their genealogy, I have been thinking of clan names and kinship and how humidity could also be a messenger (in its ubiquitous but inconspicuous state).

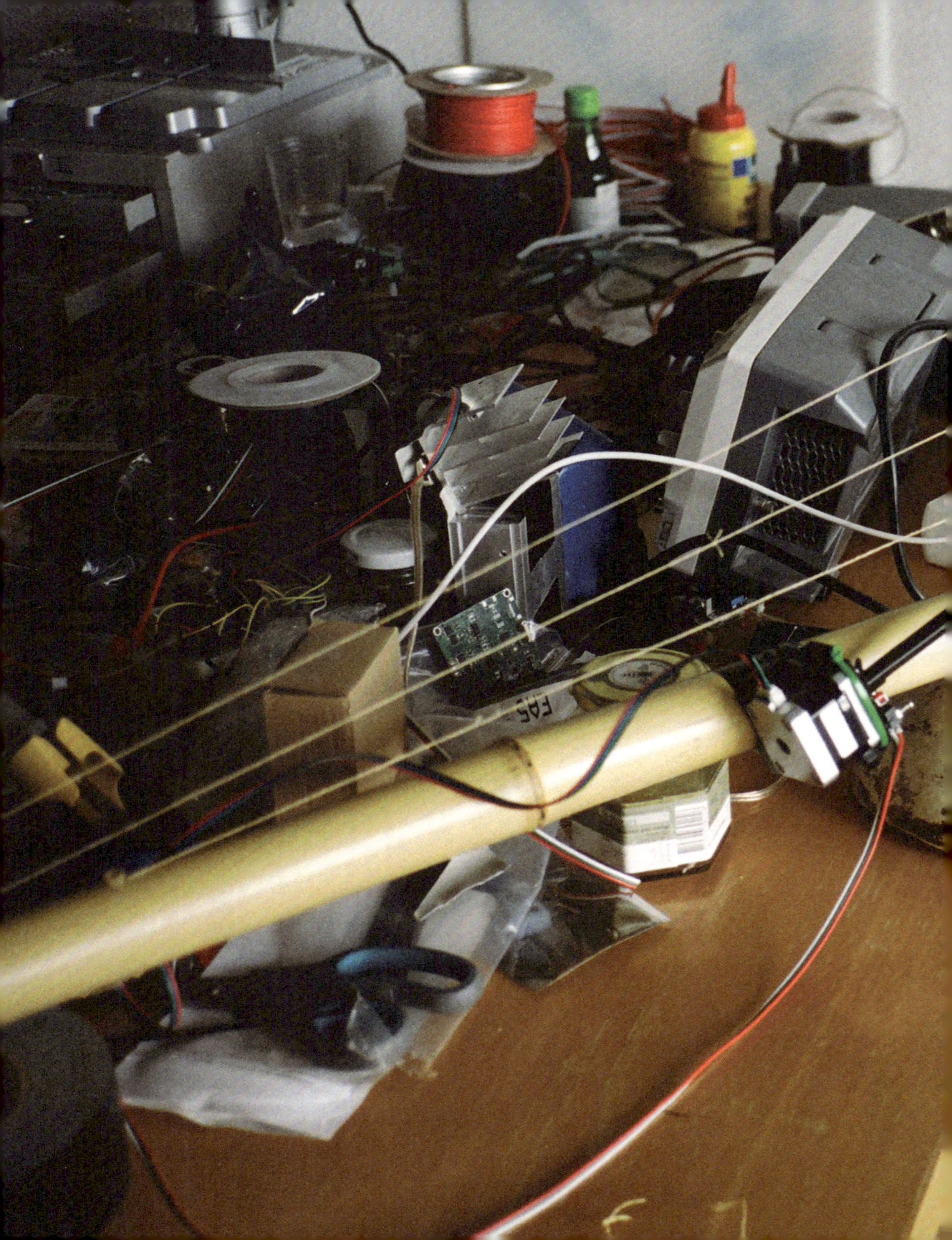

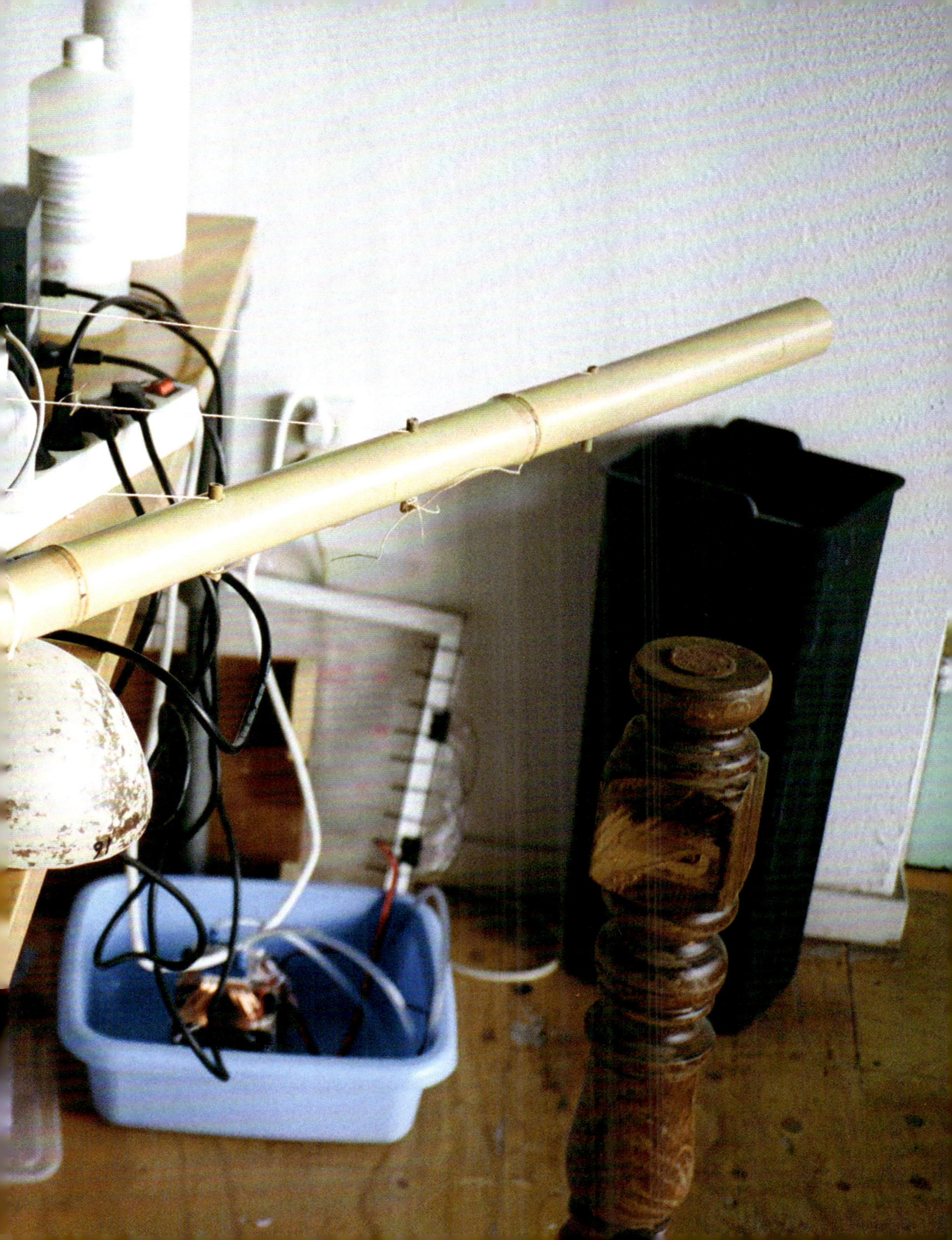

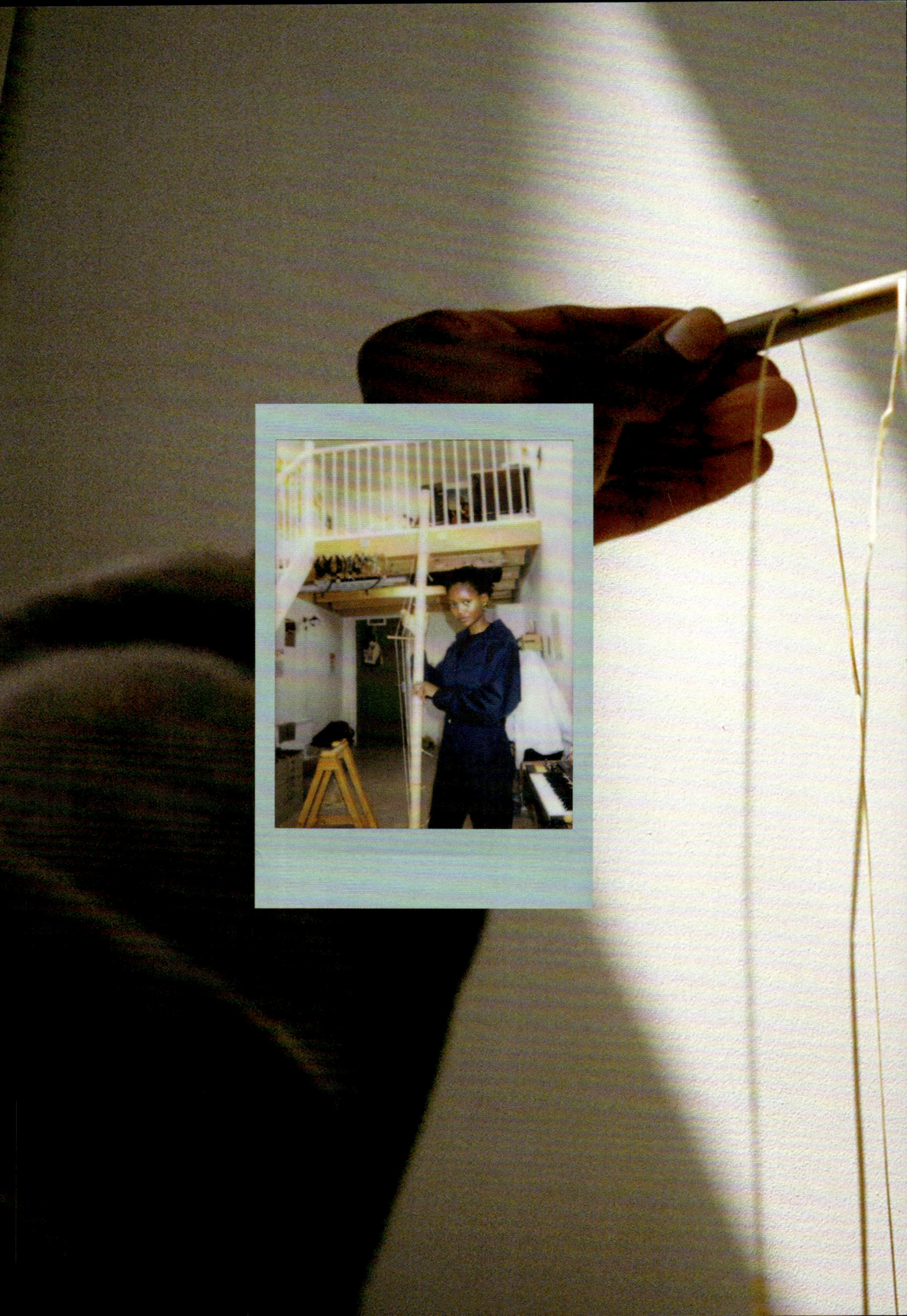

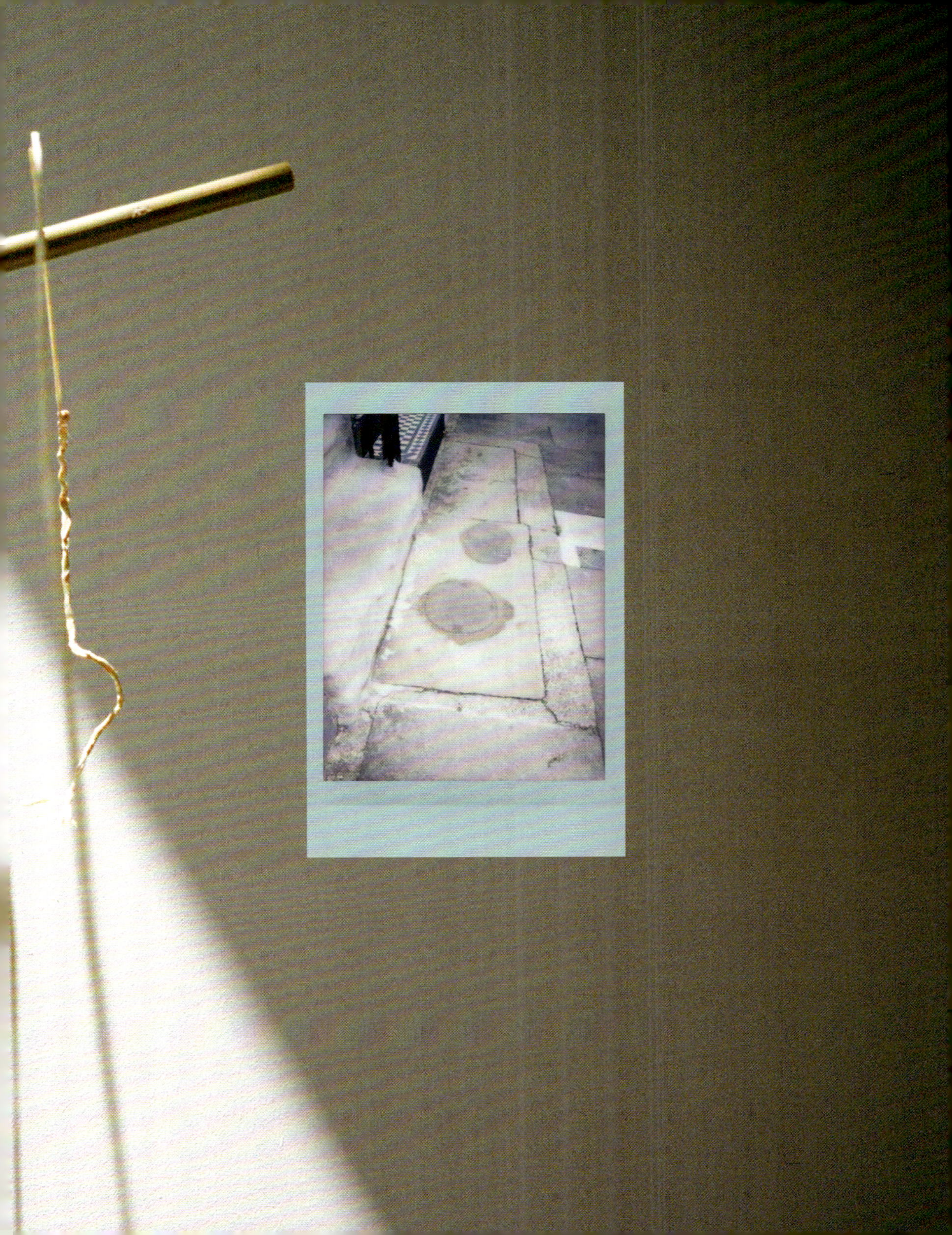

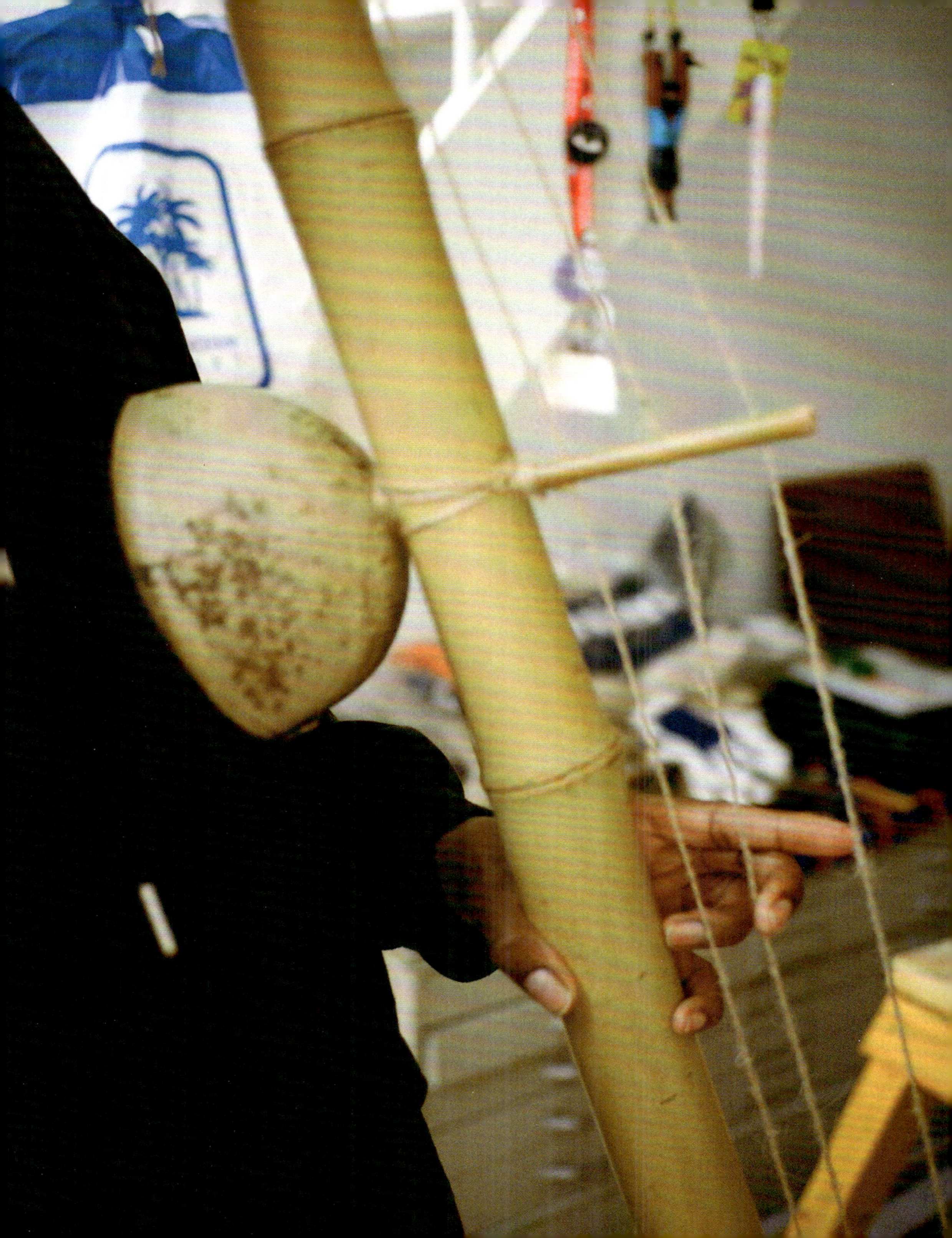

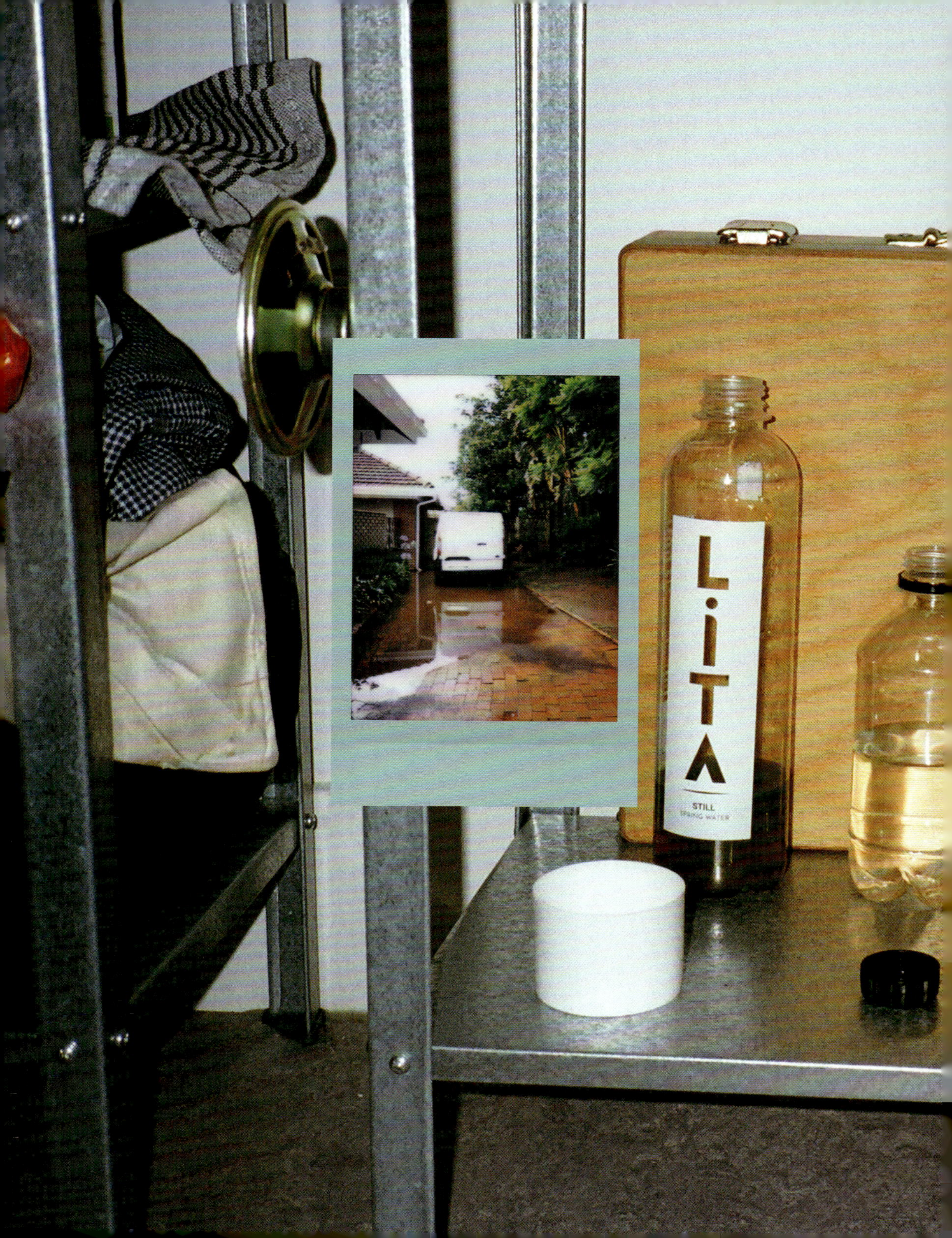
LiTA
STILL
SPRING WATER

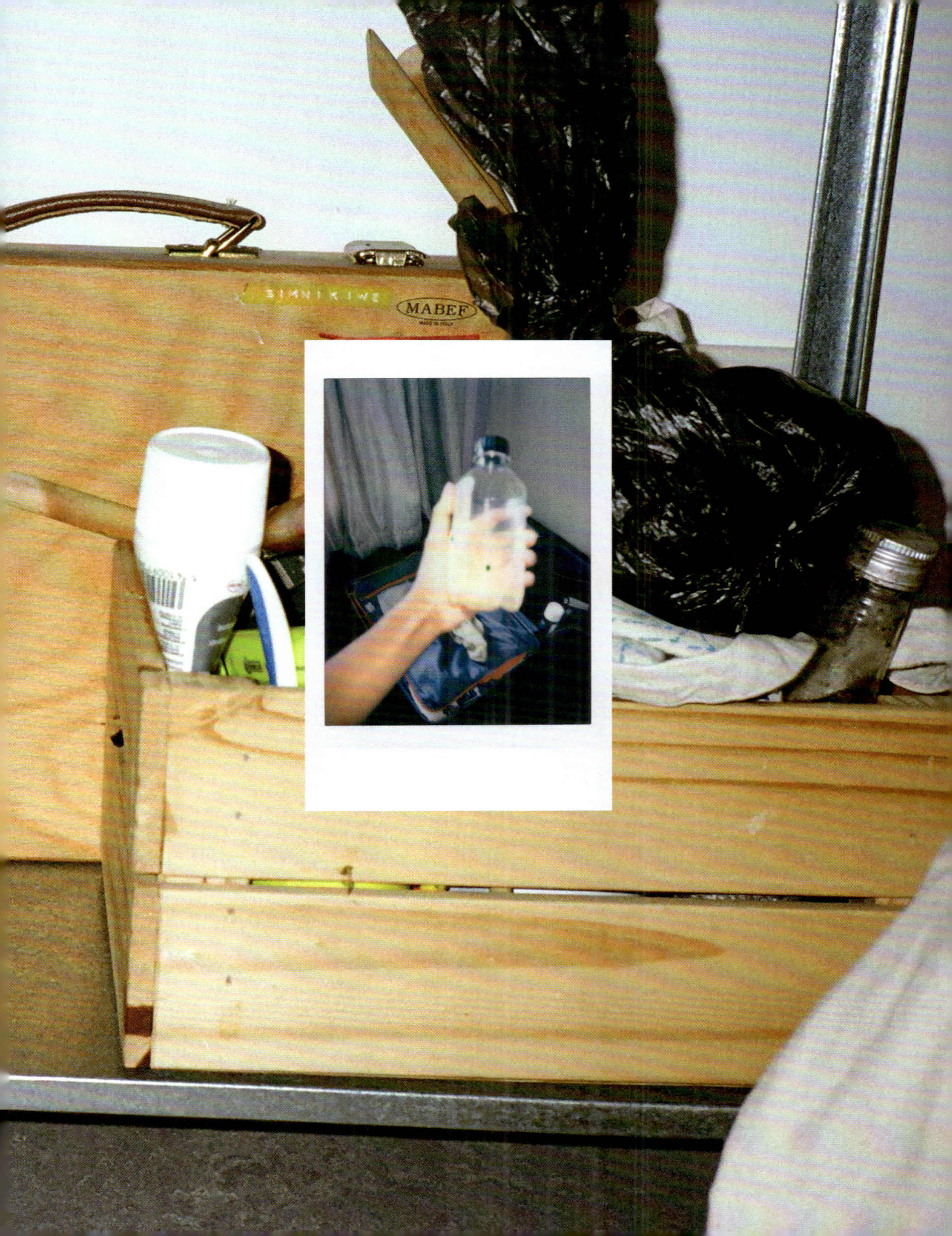
SIMNIKIWE
MABEF

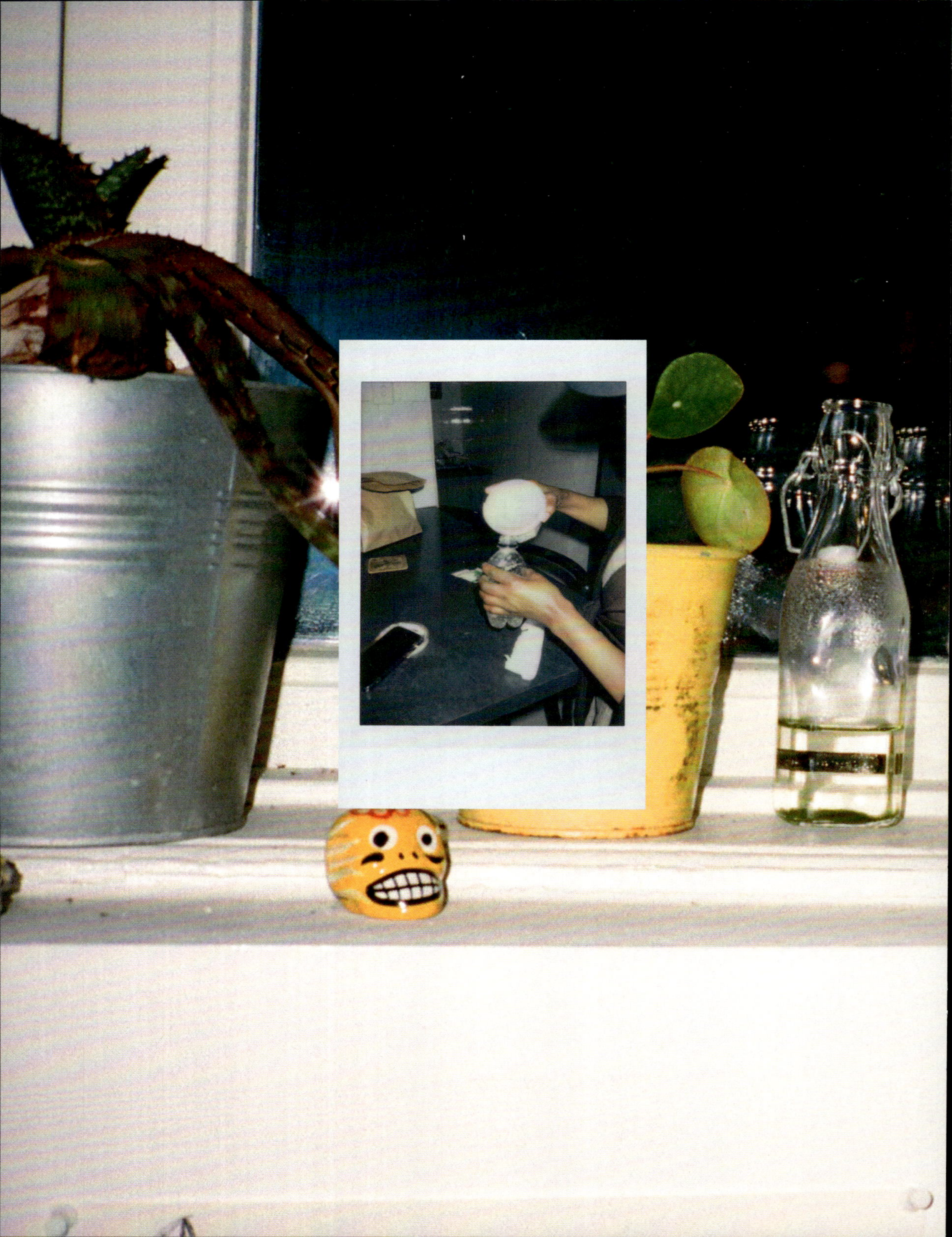

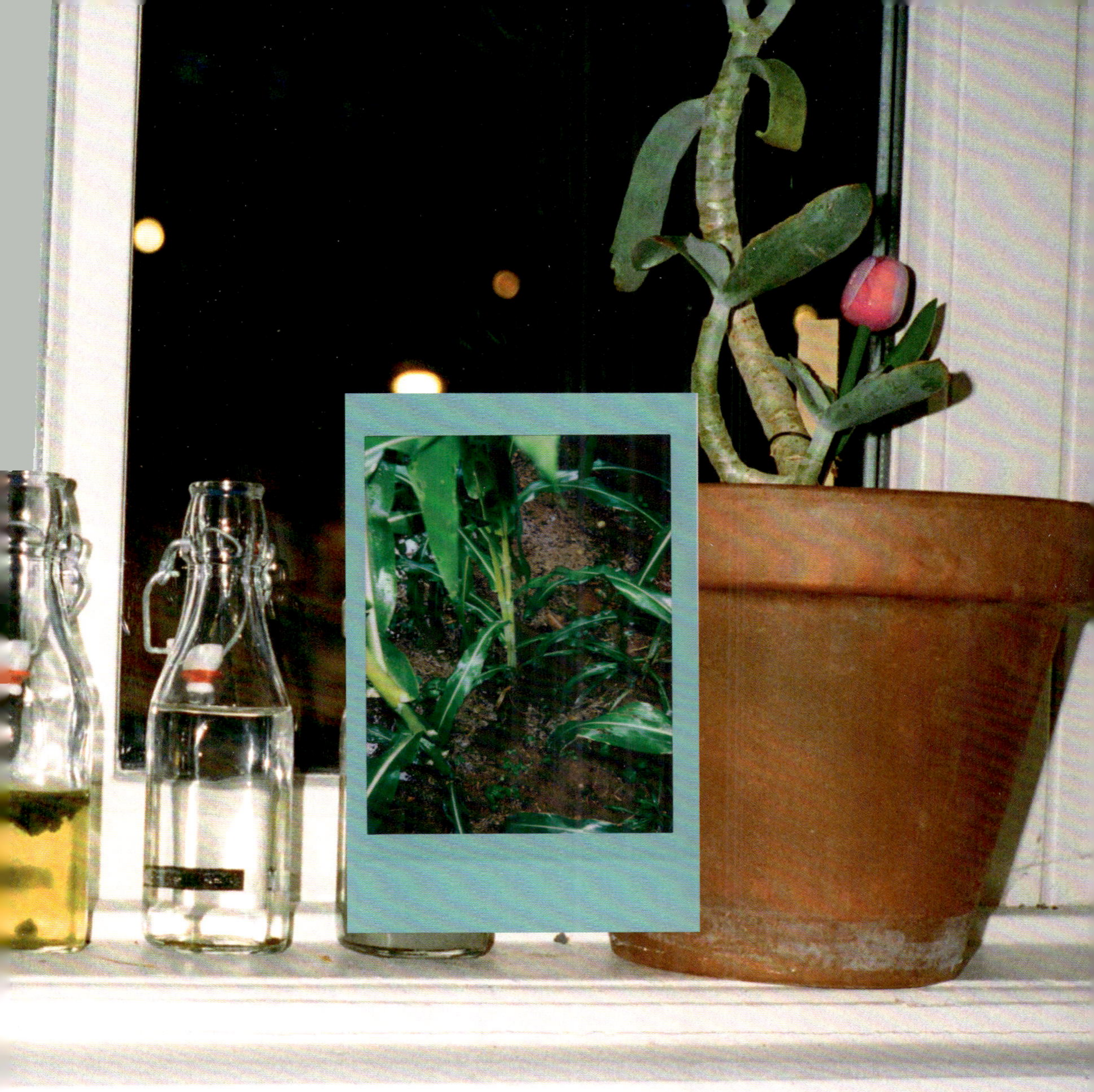

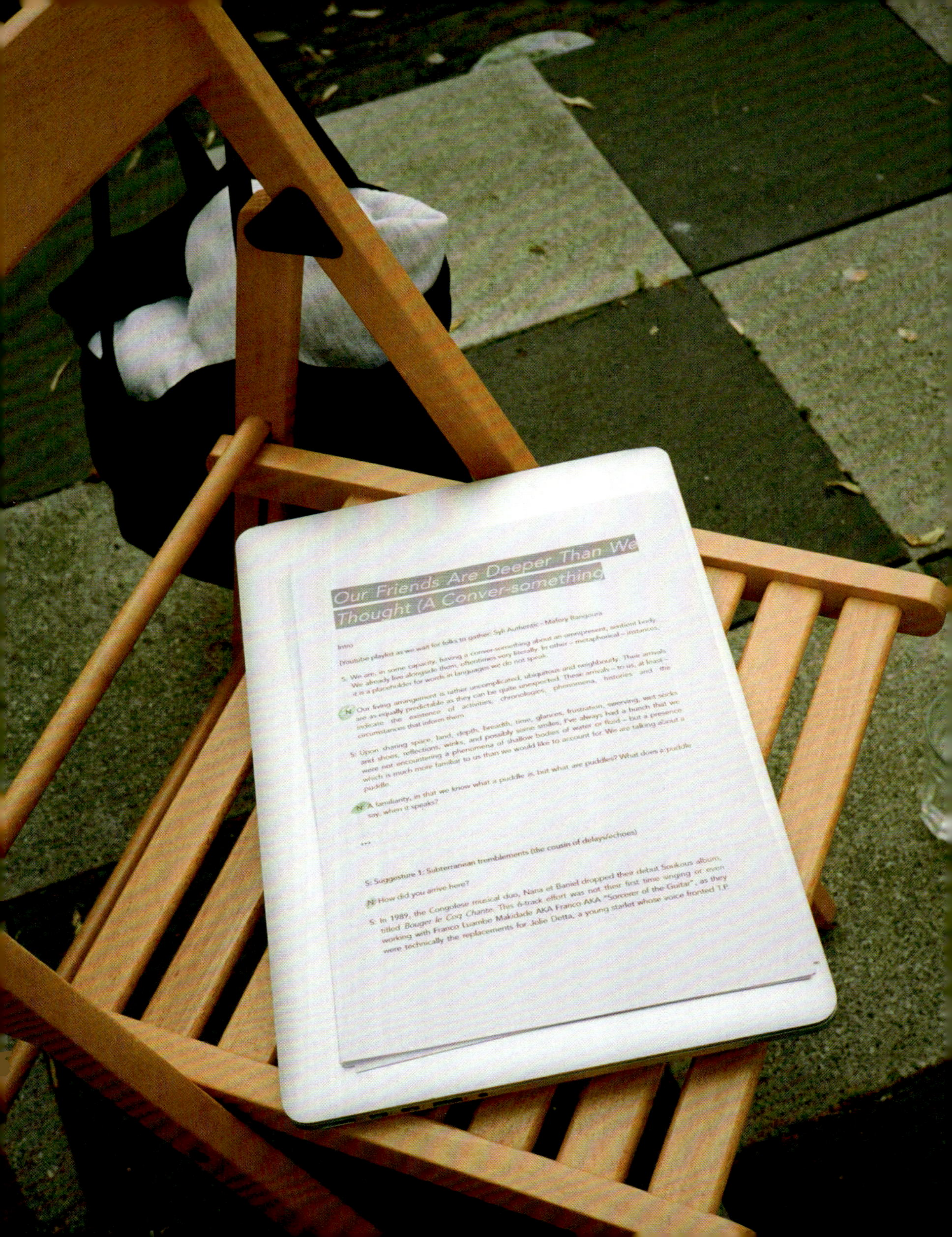
Our Friends Are Deeper Than We Thought (A Conver-something
Intro
[Youtube playlist as we wait for folks to gather: Syli Authentic - Mafory Bangoura
S: We are, in some capacity, having a conver-something about an omnipresent, sentient body. We already live alongside them, oftentimes very literally. In other – metaphorical – instances, it is a placeholder for words in languages we do not speak.
N: Our living arrangement is rather uncomplicated, ubiquitous and neighbourly. Their arrivals are as equally predictable as they can be quite unexpected. These arrivals – to us, at least – indicate the existence of activities, chronologies, phenomena, histories and the circumstances that inform them.
S: Upon sharing space, land, depth, breadth, time, glances, frustration, swerving, wet socks and shoes, reflections, winks, and possibly some smiles, I've always had a hunch that we were not encountering a phenomena of shallow bodies of water or fluid – but a presence which is much more familiar to us than we would like to account for. We are talking about a puddle.
N: A familiarity, in that we know what a puddle is, but what are puddles? What does a puddle say, when it speaks?
***
S: Suggesture 1: Subterranean tremblements (the cousin of delays/echoes)
N: How did you arrive here?
S: In 1989, the Congolese musical duo, Nana et Baniel dropped their debut Soukous album, titled Bouger le Coq Chante. This 6-track effort was not their first time singing or even working with Franco Luambo Makiadi AKA Franco AKA "Sorcerer of the Guitar", as they were technically the replacements for Jolie Detta, a young starlet whose voice fronted T.P.

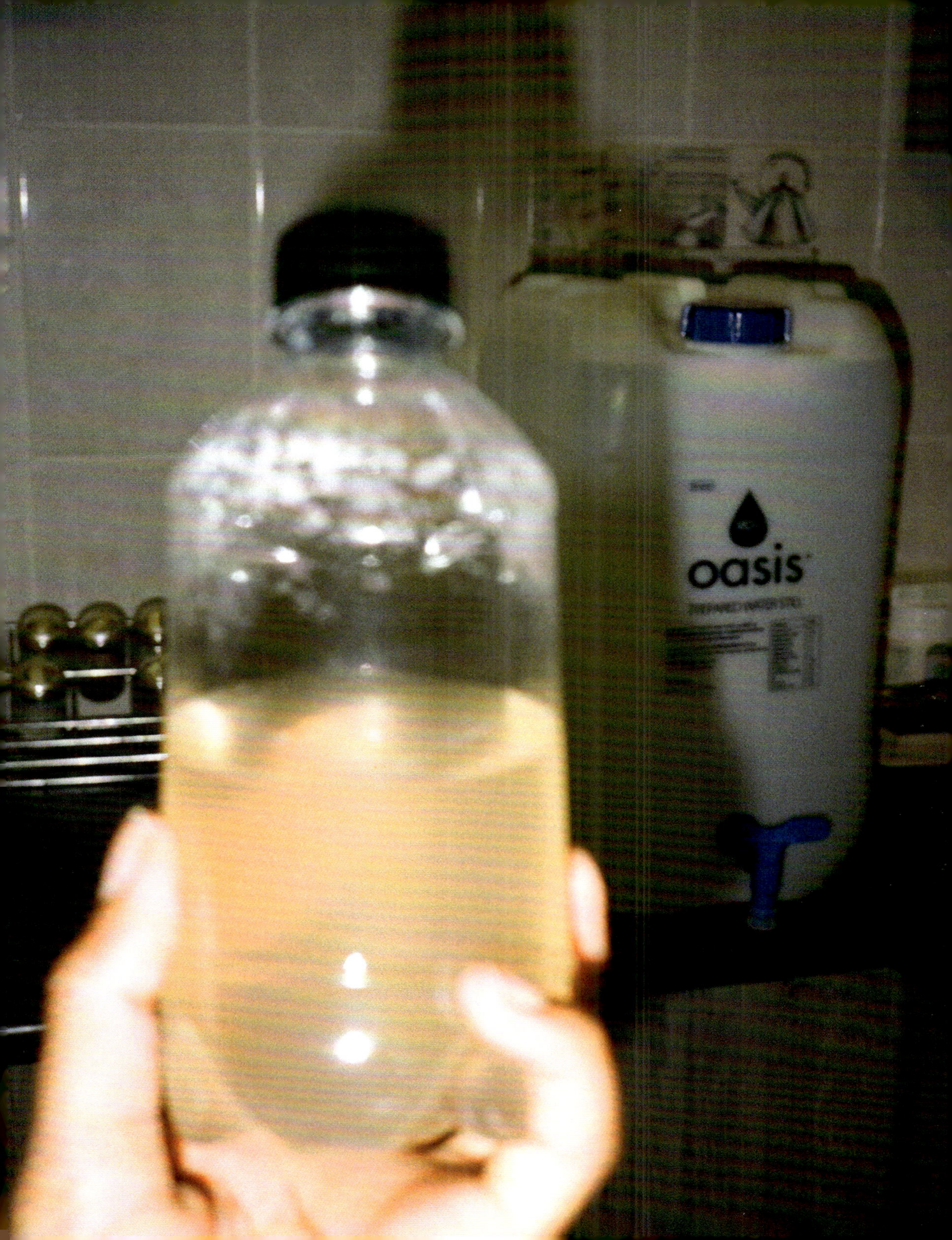
oasis

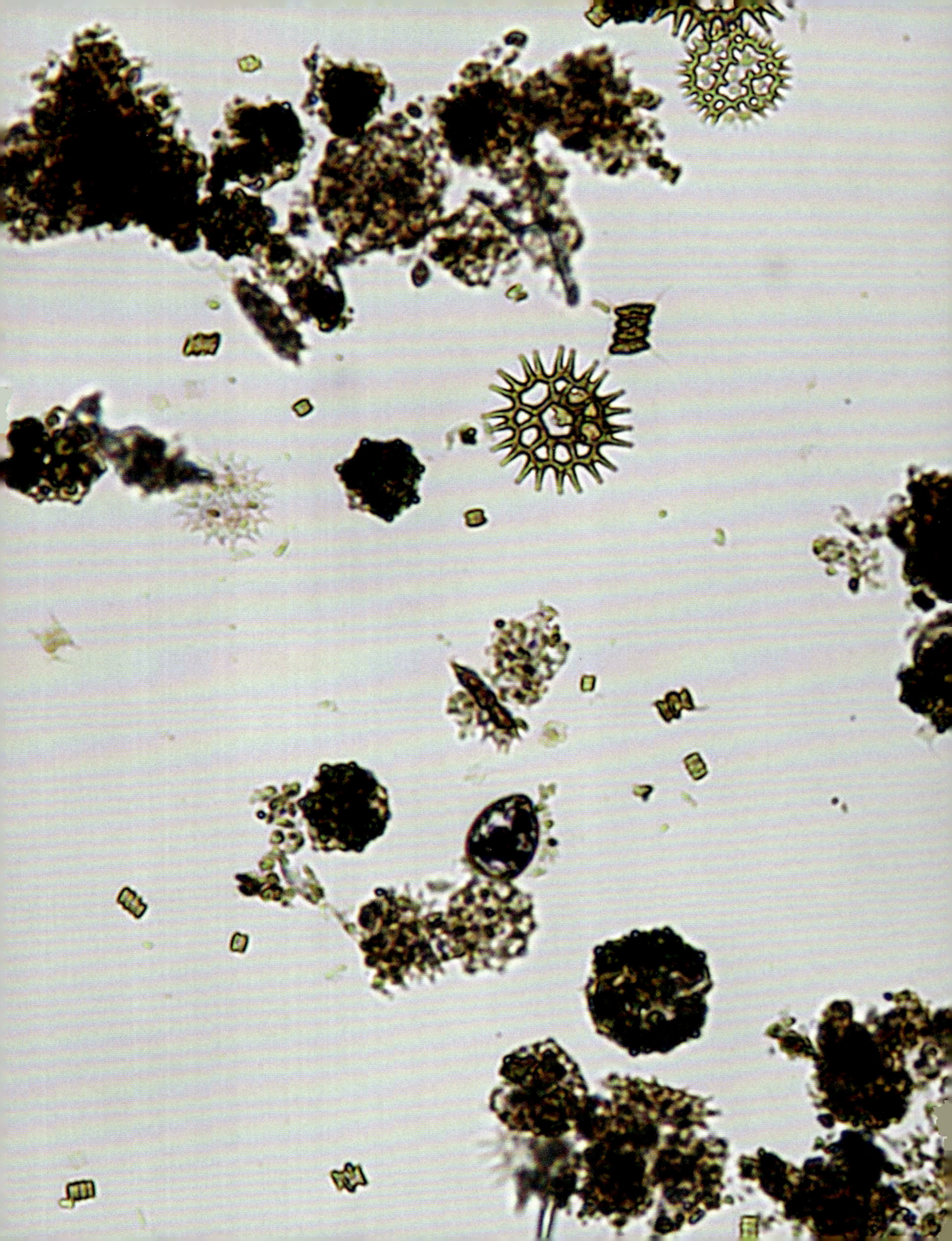

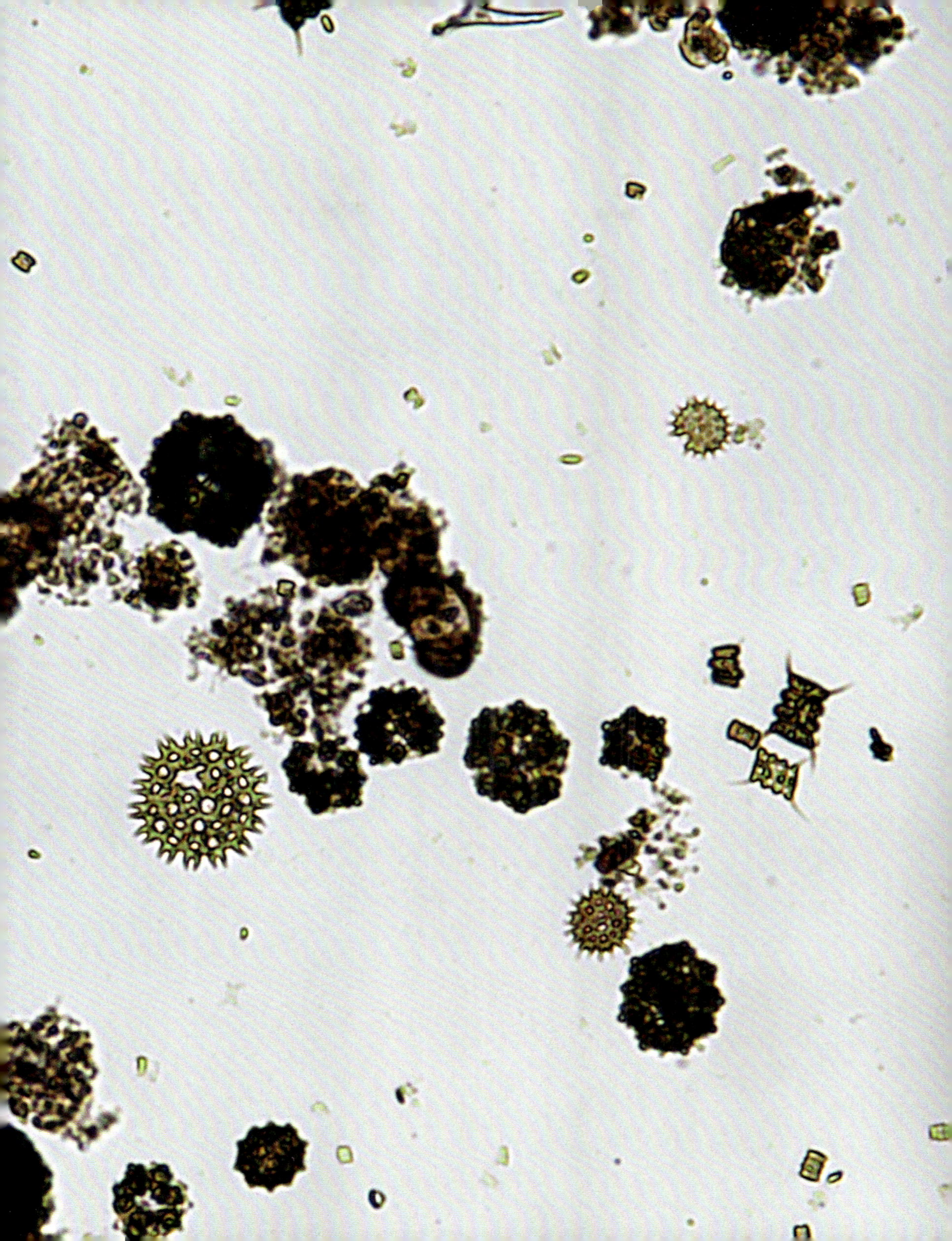

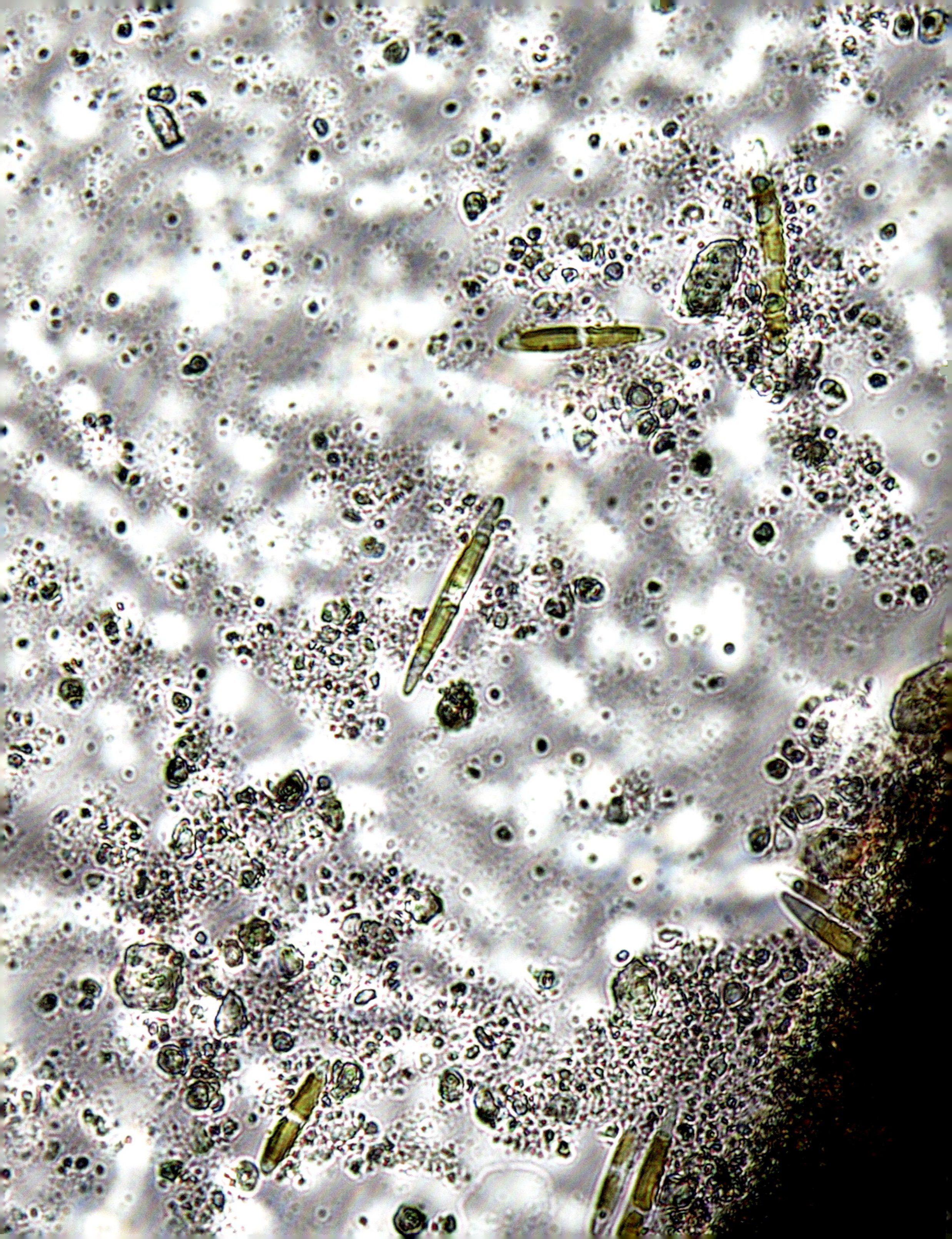

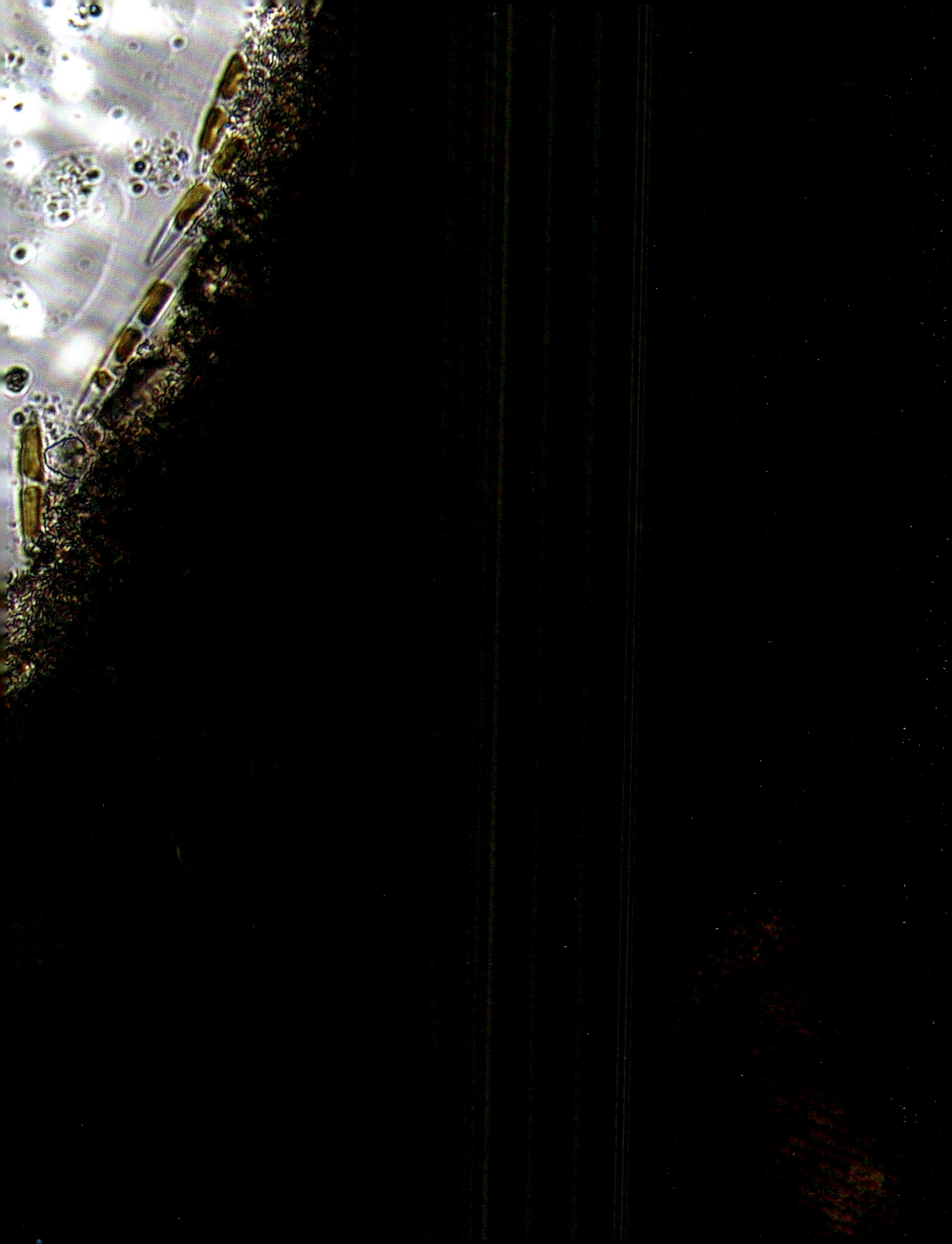

Taylor Le Melle

The Thief, Navigating the Small Francophone Inside

Taylor Le Melle works as a curator (of sorts); and certainly as a writer of ante-modern and anti-modern criticism; off-kilter catalogue essays; and artistic subgenres of fiction. Taylor is also founding co-director of the London-based workers cooperative not/nowhere, which is concerned with building just infrastructures for artistic practice through the circulation and distribution of 8mm and 16mm moving image formats. Recent presentations of their work have been held at Rijksakademie van Beeldende Kunsten, Amsterdam (2024); Sandberg Instituut, Amsterdam (2022); Amant Foundation, Brooklyn (2021; Felix Gaudlitz, Vienna (2020); Wysing Arts Centre, Cambridge (2019). Recent writing has been featured in *Anthea Hamilton: Mash Up*, Triangle Books (2023); *Otobong Nkanga: Unearthed*, Kunsthaus Bregenz (2022); *Renee Green: Inevitable Distances*, Hatje Cantz (2022); *DNA6: Carrier Bag Fiction*, Spector Books (2021).

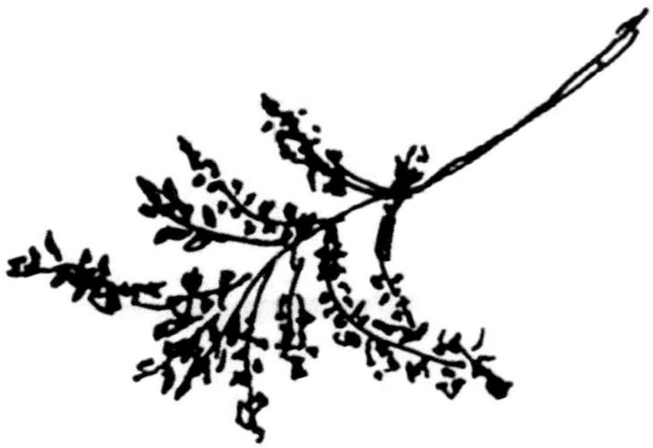

These poems and drawings speak to foraging, landscapes, the imperfections of translation, and practices of observation.

Can you provide some alternate translations for the first poem I asked you about?:

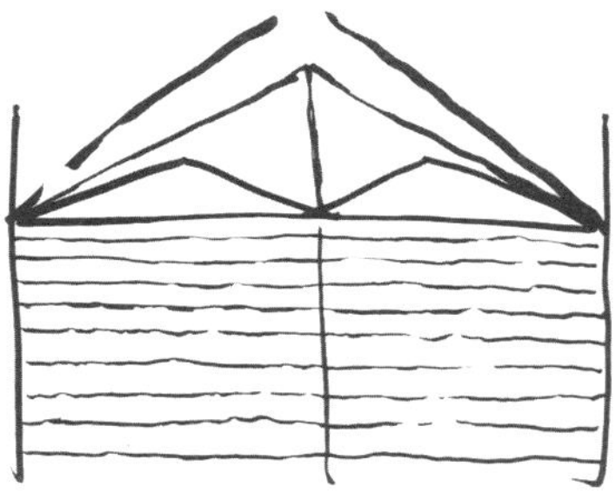

des piqûres de jaune
fleur de colza
officiellement interdites
limites, mais en regardant de loin–
identifiant les moments
où je peux me retenir
pour ouvrir
la peur de
mes propres
impulsions dictatoriales

Les épines se dressent vers
les ouvertures émotionnelles, hachant
leur fleur

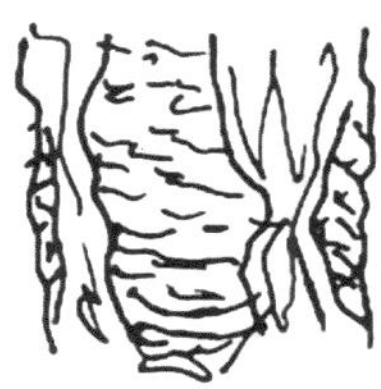

des pointes de jaune
fleur de colza
officiellement interdites
limites, mais en regardant discrètement –
identifiant les moments
où je peux me retenir
pour ouvrir
la peur de
mes propres
impulsions dictatoriales

Les épines se dressent vers
les ouvertures émotionnelles, coupant
leur fleur

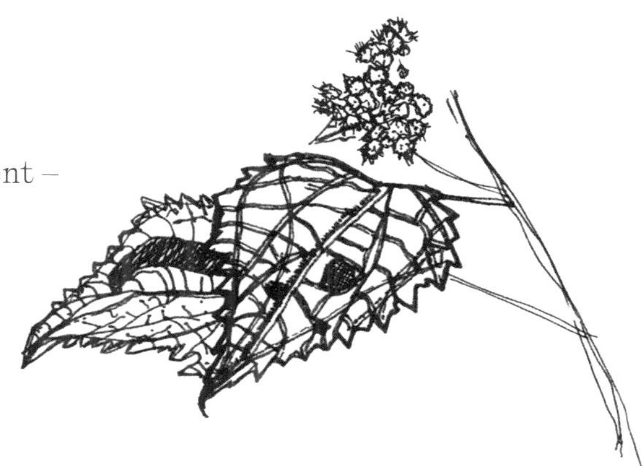

With a consideration
of 18th-century
French style?:

des piqûres de jaune
fleur de colza
officiellement interdites
limites, mais en regardant de loin–
identifiant les moments
où je peux me retenir
pour ouvrir
la peur de
mes propres
impulsions dictatoriales

Les épines se dressent vers
les ouvertures émotionnelles, hachant
leur fleur

des pointes de jaune
fleur de colza
officiellement interdites
limites, mais en regardant discrètement–
identifiant les moments
où je peux me retenir
pour ouvrir
la peur de
mes propres
impulsions dictatoriales

Les épines se dressent vers
les ouvertures émotionnelles, coupant
leur fleur

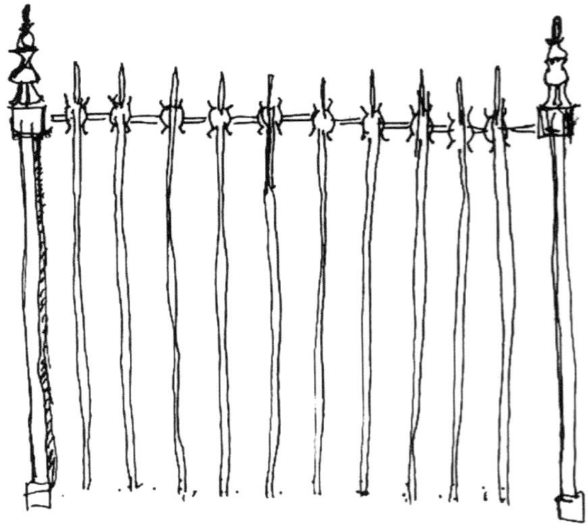

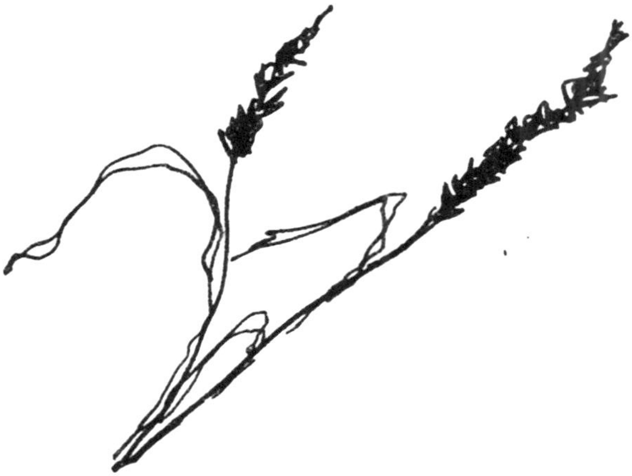

As an 18th century
French Botanist?:

des éclats de jaune
fleur de colza
officiellement interdite
des limites, mais en observant discrètement–
mais en regardant de loin–
identifiant les moments
où je peux me retenir
pour explorer
la crainte de
mes propres
impulsions autoritaires

Les épines se dressent vers
les ouvertures émotionnelles, coupant
leur fleur

The Brother Moves On

Descents and Descendants

The Brother Moves On (TBMO) is a South African performance art ensemble based in Johannesburg, South Africa. The group was founded between the years 2008 and 2010 by broad-based artist Nkululeko Mthembu and his brother Siyabonga Mthembu. Beginning as a loose art collective including graphic and performance artists, TBMO is most widely recognised as a band fronted by Siyabonga Mthembu as lead vocalist, Zelizwe Mthembu on lead guitar, Ayanda Zalekile on bass and Simphiwe Tshabalala on drums. This core group is regularly joined by a shifting cohort of collaborators and members from various disciplines.

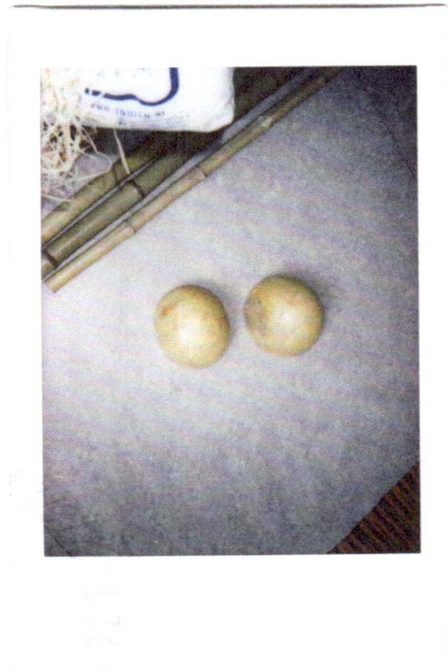

The following text is excerpted from a WhatsApp call between Zelizwe Mthembu – lead guitarist of the renowned performance art ensemble, The Brother Moves On (TBMO) – and Simnikiwe Buhlungu on the 24 July 2024 at 13:06 (SAST).

This text explores the narrative anchor of the song 'Puleng', the introductory track with an extended [instrumental] version on TBMO's album, *$/he Who Feeds You...Owns You* (2022). Birthed long before the album, 'Puleng', its descents, and descendants, become departure points to explore the interweaving aspects of orature, notation, uncle-ing, niece-ing, recollections, and chordal accumulations.

Ke mang eo?

(on songwriting)

In the process of writing 'Puleng', I initially wrote a melody for a saxophone. It was the first time I ever wrote a melody intended for an instrument I don't play.

It's the combination of chords I learned in my first few weeks of learning how to play guitar. I put them all in a song because my cousin – Nkululeko Mthembu, who actually started The Brother Moves On – used to love hearing them. I remember when I first played with a drummer and a bassist, they were at my house and we were in the backyard, and then a storm descended amidst us playing the composition.

So, we called it 'Puleng', but not because of a girl's name but rather because of *being* in the rain. Ka Sesotho, 'Ey! Ke tsamaya ka gare a pula.' Wang'thola? Because I'm umZulu. I don't know if I named it correctly, but then it took a life of its own. That's when the character that Siyabonga [Mthembu] plays at the beginning of the song comes alive. He embodies the character of a child just before we go on our trip as The Brother Moves On, asking for us to return home with a red balloon. In the intro of our album, we play those chords again to evoke the feeling of a storm's beginning.

The song has also changed throughout time, and there are parts that have come and gone, in reflection of significant moments in my life. For it to be the way it is now, I rewrote it again to celebrate the birth of my niece. The feeling I had the day when we wrote the song of being in the rain resurfaced when she was born in similar weather conditions.

My sister's friend texted me and my other sister, saying, 'Look, I got something to tell you'. She bought a burner phone with the intention to secretly text us. She said, 'Your sister's going to give birth at the hospital in Hillbrow'. I literally had band practice that day, and then that message came through and hit me. I looked at it again. After band practice, I walked towards Hillbrow, and it started raining.

The writing process has taken years. Everybody we've ever played with basically has a hand in that song. At the beginning, we used to play with this guy called Legae Blaky Hukxz. Then Gugu Ra Ntsu, and myself. Later, Mthunzi [Mvubu] would play the melody on guitar because we didn't have a horn; we were a 'rock band!' We also didn't have a sax at the time, but in my heart of hearts, I knew that someday a sax would have to sing this melody.

It wasn't even the first time we made this kind of instrumental substitution; at times we would play with our previous guitarist, as well as Ayanda [Zalekile], myself, Siya, and Simphiwe [Tshabalala]. We also had Raytheon [Moorvan]. Basically, the current horn melody is now filling the space Raytheon left behind. There are similar lines and melodies evoked by guitar parts that he left.

It used to be really pretty. It didn't work out the first time we recorded it, so we saved it for this album. The beauty of it, actually, is also how many people perfected it over time. The individual stories that people have in relation to the song affects what it means for themselves. To people listening to the song, it's never actually the state of being in rain, but it's always Puleng, the person. Some people are like, 'Eish, I used to love this girl called Puleng'. Others are like, 'Puleng broke my heart!' or, 'I know this place called Puleng'.

I let it flow because you cannot force meaning upon people. Especially when your song is instrumental. I do, however, notice that people are connecting it to rain. People are starting to understand because I have more opportunities to explain it to people and tell my story behind it, while also interacting with the stories that people have created for themselves in relation to it. That's been the most beautiful thing, to actually see it grow from where it was to where it is now. It's quite amazing; and while it's on our latest album, I also consider it to be our first song.

The weird thing is Siya asked me *way* later, 'What do we call the song?' I reminded him about our niece being born and that's how the child character who says, 'UMalume uyahamba!' comes about (who he plays in the beginning). That child is a living memory of that idea.

When my niece was born and I arrived at the hospital, I named her Puleng after the song.

(Ref)rains

(on call and response)

My Sesotho is really, really not that great but I think that's the language the lyrics would resonate with and come from. That's the language I would look towards in order to find what I'm saying. I don't think it would be a song with many verses. I don't hear that. I hear the instruments existing within large space in the expression of meaning; I do hear... so it would follow the melody, like:

Puleng ngoana ke
Puleng ngoana ke
Ke go ratile

This would come about whenever we were far away from home, in places where it's not easy to drive down the road and see a mountain or a big tree. You know how nice it is here in South Africa, sometimes we forget how much the scenery keeps us happy, you know? You'd be stuck in another world like Paris, for instance, where it's not as green. When we become homesick, that melody would always come up. We started singing that melody. It wasn't really part of the song until we started singing it because we missed home on tour. That's another thing that 'Puleng' does for us whenever we're far from each other. Whenever we feel like we haven't been chilling together, the first song we'll start with on stage is 'Puleng'. It's sort of like a prayer for when we want to come closer to each other and to home. It does that. It gives us that connection.

We start with it because it reminds us, 'okay, we don't do this just for us'. We do it for home, and home is important. That's why we do it.

Modjadji

(do you think about her?)

I think about her a lot.

I believe I'm a rainmaker. To be honest with you, ngoba izithakazelo zasekhaya zithi, 'Mnisi wemvula ilanga libalele'. Recalling this ritual – that I used to perform *through* music – was a way I could actually make it rain.

That's how Modjadji connected to me most because I wondered, 'could I not be related to her somehow, because of izithakazelo zami?' It turns out that I'm related to a guy, uJama kaNdaba, uNdaba kaMnisi, so that's where that comes from and all the way down to uMthembu.

I used to hear a lot about rain magic, and people like Modjadji were superheroes to me. That sounds like Storm from the X-Men when I think about it!!

I love the prospect and the idea of a Queen who rules over men, marries women, and can control the sky. I love the idea that I could have been related to her. There are times when I would close my eyes and literally pray and humbly ask for rain while the song is playing, and it would rain. I try really hard to not let that get to my head. I've definitely seen it happen. Rain is miraculous!

I believe anybody can do anything they put their minds to, especially with music. The crazy thing is that all those chords and the way it sounds now stayed the same in terms of music theory, but those chords all came the first day someone said, 'Come here, I'm teaching you how to play guitar'.

She ['Puleng'] won't leave us alone. She has us held together. That song means so much to me. The most painful thing about it is hearing The Brother Moves On play it without me. There was once a tour the guys went on to Paris and I watched it online.

Yoh, it was so painful.

Kempton Park

(this one, not that one)

It's funny because we also come from a place that is known for having special puddles; Kempton Park has these water pans. They don't even have names. There are so many all over the place. Our area is known for having the most in the world.

They're protected areas. Apparently, there are certain wind formations that are particularly hectic, and its energy will concentrate like a mini-tornado and dig a little hole in the ground. Then when it rains over time, those water pans collect water and then give rise to life.

Erosion is what shapes our mountains, our valleys, our hills. It's what shapes us. Like, what happens to your skin when you take a bath: it loosens and you get rid of the dead skin, and that's how your growth also happens.

Water has a really important part in my existence especially in relation to music. In the intro of our album, we are trying to evoke the feeling of a storm that's coming. It's the intro of 'Puleng' that we made into a separate track. There's another song by Sello Galane, which is interesting, called 'Pula'. (If you know it, if you miss home, you should bump that right now!) It'll touch you. It's also where I gained awareness of the rhythm that 'Puleng' has.

Sello Galane, he's Molobedu. He's a traditional healer and also a doctor. When he plays his percussion, it's like a seance into space. That's literally what he does. He doesn't just perform, he's a conduit.

He says, 'Puuuuuuuuuuuuuuuuuula!' It's a really, really beautiful song

Circle of fifths

(amanz' azobuya)

In my geography class – because my teacher was very, very kind to me – as long as I finished all of my work, I was allowed to play guitar in class. The water cycle starts from water, then it evaporates and eventually forms clouds. Then the clouds get heavy, then rain falls. I learned that in geography and biology. I was in school when I came into contact with the water cycle and found it special; the miracle of that process! The simplicity of what keeps us all alive is gorgeous. It's mind-blowing. The cycle of life, it's even amazing to consider how that all is related to reincarnation. Music, by the way, also works in a circle of fifths.

There's a way in which you can write songs. To put it simply, we have 12 notes. What's happening with these 12 notes is that they're just increasing in pitch. They're getting higher or they're getting deeper. The circle of fifths is a way you can create music by choosing your flow. We have

do, re, mi, fa, so, la, ti, do.

If you start from do, to get to the next fifth would be so. If a song goes

do, so,

that's a recognisable pattern that comes up in music writing: the circle of fifths. There's that important cycle I see in music and all of this. I don't write or read music in the same way that everyone else does. I know my music theory, but I don't read music. I don't know if I could create a document that someone else can read; I play by ear and then pretend to read it. It works!

When we started recording, it was not necessary to write music on paper to register it. That's what made me a bit lazy, but it happened. I write music this way and I think it's my blessing. I am actually getting somebody to write the guitar parts that I play in The Brother Moves On, because if somebody wants to learn how to play it, I should put that up online, you know?

Especially because music, from an African perspective, has always been called to preserve our history, our traditions, and our beliefs. That's how we share it with the coming generations – through song and poetry and storytelling. It always has that function. I think it's quite important for me to also start visualising how 'Puleng' looks on paper – even as something painted.

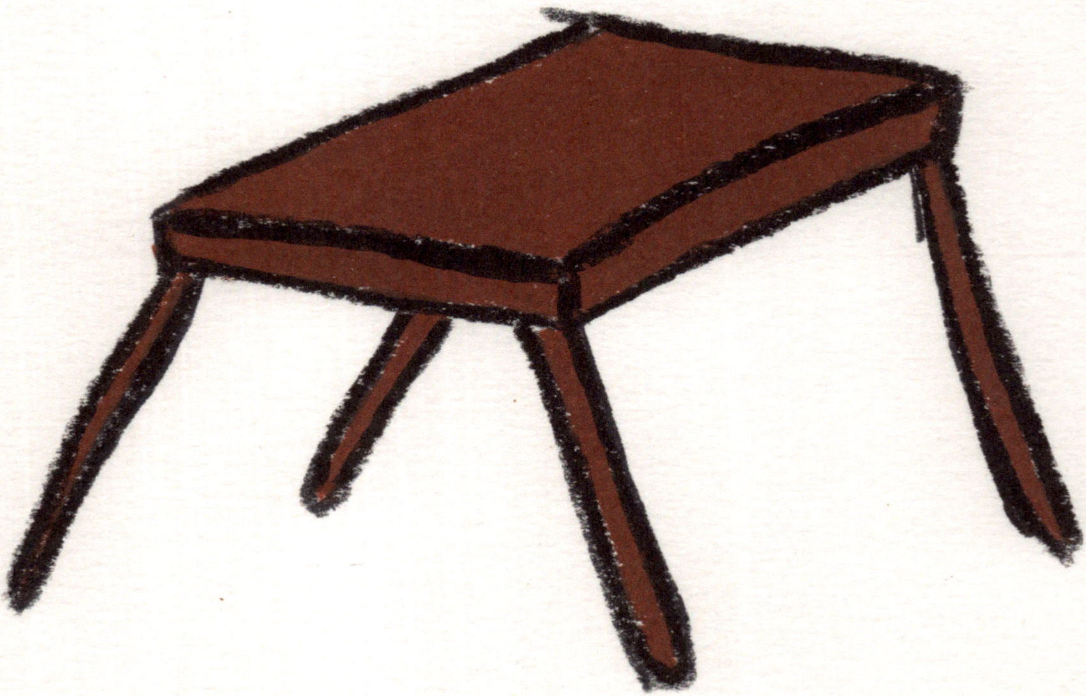

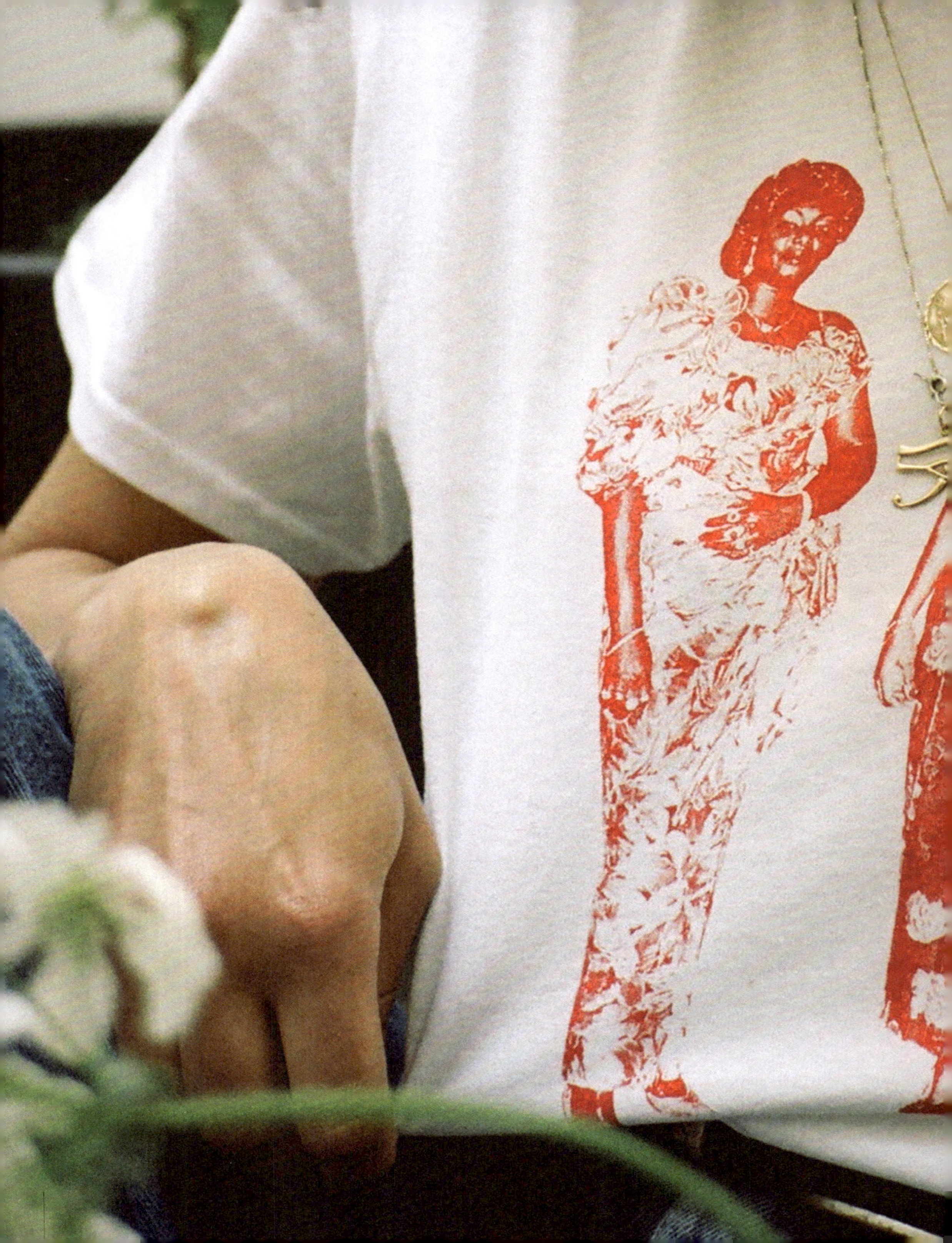

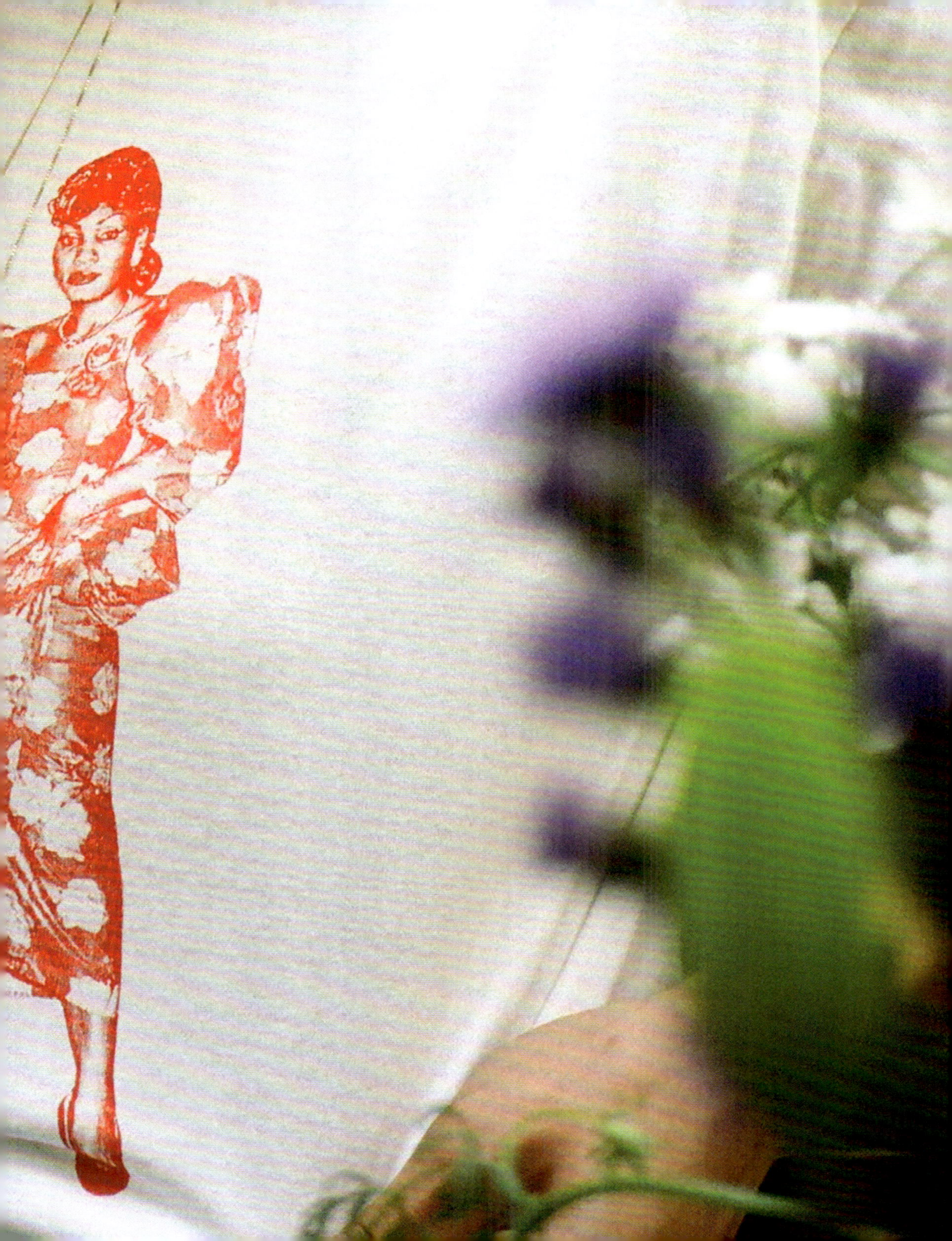

Simnikiwe Buhlungu

Simnikiwe Buhlungu is an artist from Johannesburg, South Africa and is currently based in Amsterdam, the Netherlands.

Interested in knowledge production[s] – how it is produced, by whom and how it is disseminated – Buhlungu locates socio-historical and everyday phenomena by navigating these questions and their inexhaustible potential answers through research based methodologies. By doing this, she maps points of cognisance which situate various layers of awareness as reverberated ecologies.

Simnikiwe attended the Rijksakademie van Beeldende Kunsten in Amsterdam (2020–2022); notable exhibitions include *A Lasting Truth Is Change*, Van Abbemuseum, Eindhoven; *The Milk of Dreams*, The 59th Venice Biennale, Venice; **dissonated underings [hic!], after-happenings and khuayarings (sithi "ahhhh!")*, Kunsthalle Bern, Bern (all 2022). Her work has been collected by The Stedelijk Museum, Amsterdam, and KADIST, Paris.

Lately, she has been listening to djelis, thinking about geologic burps and attempting to distribute publications via Simunye Resource Works (a publishing house that is forever yet-to-exist).

Tremblement de Terre [1234567]

[1] Side A; Track 3.

The dusty fingers and lack of Dettol wet wipes was worth it. Place du Jeu de Balle, situated in the Marolles district of Brussels, would be one of many inconspicuous invitations into the subterranean. Possibly the sole purchase of the day – which was unusual considering how frequently I visited this flea market back in 2018 – was a cassette tape. The cover featured two women, finely adorned in matching-but-opposite floral dresses, permed afros, bright makeup indicative of the late 1980s/early 1990s, and pointed high heels. The photo is underexposed but that is none of my business.

Their second album as a duo, titled *Bouger le Coq Chante*, is affectionately dedicated to Franco [Luambo Makiadi] with whom they worked alongside in TPOK Jazz, a Congolese rumba ensemble which Franco founded in 1956.

Nana Akumu Bolenge and Baniel Mbambo – known by their musical duo name, Nana et Baniel – harmonise abreast the singing guitar solo. Listening through the tape hiss, I suspect that they must be singing in Lingala (?) and I am struggling to access a trace of the lyrics in the liner notes or online (Discogs wasn't so helpful). I'm not sure if there is some French in this particular song, aside from this alliterative title. But, pulling from my high school-level French, I know that it means 'earthquake'. I surmise that they must be singing about a heartbreak. Or an argument with an unfaithful partner(s)? Rumours? Seismology?

About halfway through the song, it switches to its 'second movement'.

Is it possible they're singing about the 1966 Toro earthquake?

[2] There was a modest congregation dressed in white, tranquil from afar, praying at the foot of the Tswaing Crater. While walking on the hiking trail, I noticed the surface of an Ntsu snuff lid buried in the ground. Later, one of the security guards of the crater – whose name I cannot recall – pulled up on a quad bike for a routine safety check.

Skkkkkkkrvrvrvr!

[3] Land reclamation ≂ water displacement?
∴ Land reclamation ≂ making puddles of land in water?
* What is being reclaimed? Because it insinuates it was lost, when perhaps it was already at home, submerged?

[4] A lot of the discourse on puddles fails to go beyond the obvious; they are water, they are wet, they tell us it has rained, children like to jump in them despite the common sense that one should avoid stepping in them because...why get your shoes and socks wet?

And, further! 'Is it a pond?', 'Or a lake?', 'Is it a puddle?', 'Ah, are you sure?', 'No it's too big to be a puddle', 'It's too deep to be a pond', 'it's too small to be a lake'. This is tautological. These markers of size, depth, and time are relative, inconsistent, not epistemologically universal, and distract us from a fundamental philosophical line of questioning, which is, 'Where have you been? What did you see? Where are you going?'

Maybe puddles are on the run; in fugitivity. Maybe they're young adults moving out of home for the first time. Maybe they don't like living in cities and are relocating to the countryside for some quiet; or they're nosey and curious about us; or they're taking a break from being responsible for sustaining life. Maybe they took a left instead of a right. Perhaps they cannot stay long because their schedules are increasingly fully booked because of climate change. Maybe they are witnesses to something that 'never happened'; something traumatic? exciting? and urgently need to tell someone. Perhaps they cannot stay long because it is more fun in the clouds and they prefer to be a little closer to the sun than down here, with us.

Still, this tautology is revealing. A word which I landed on, ngesiXhosa, in my quest for expanding the 'definition' of 'puddle' beyond its noun-centric existence was 'amanz'amileyo'.

It literally means 'water that is still', yet poetically resounds as 'water that is waiting'.

[5] Umchamo *(noun)*.

Sometimes evidence just smells bad.

It wasn't his mother's, as I had confusingly kept thinking, but Mam' Martha Maduma's shebeen that the South African author, Bloke Modisane, pointed out to in the early pages of his 1963 memoir, *Blame Me On History*, published by Thames and Hudson.

Cue the arrival of an ungovernable, clandestine pooling. An offensive olfactory presence.

Modisane writes how, upon approaching Mam' Martha Maduma's shebeen, he spotted a puddle of urine.

Stench aside, he wrote that this sighting was – to him – a reminder of the forced removals of Sophiatown's 60,000 residents on 5 February 1955, following the passing of the apartheid regime's segregationist Native Resettlement Act (1954), in which Black South Africans were displaced to make way for white residential and business settlements. Less than three decades prior, the Liquor Act was passed on 28 January 1928. In a sequence of many laws, the Act prohibited Black South Africans from brewing and selling their own alcohol. In resistance to this and as a crucial part of a need to live, sustain life and community, have a site of gathering, a place for good times, a space to listen, to learn and foster intellectual and cultural production, people – especially Black women – continued to brew and sell alcohol regardless.

The ungovernable, clandestine pooling was not only a drunk person's piss, but was both a witness and evidence to this spatial resistance in a time of destruction, displacement, and land theft.

[6] Giambastiani, B.M.S., Antonellini, M., Nespoli, M. et al. 'Mud flow dynamics at gas seeps - Nirano Salse, Italy -'. *Environ Earth Sci* 81, no. 480 (2022). https://doi.org/10.1007/s12665-022-10615-2.

Covered in dry grey mud – along my thighs, behind the knees, and just below the buttocks of my denim trousers – I imagined that people who saw me in public assumed I was working in construction or, at the very least, was in the midst of attempting to fix something. However, the reality was that I had been tripping and falling into a slurry of cold mud, whose perpetual supply was burped up from below the surface of the ground, every few minutes, from puddles and 'volcanoes'.

Salse di Nirano Regional Nature Reserve was established in 1982. Located in the Municipality of Fiorano Modenese, Modena, in Italy, the reserve currently protects one of the most fascinating ongoing phenomena concerning mud, clay, and the underground.

From afar, they look like grey mountains; from above, like the breasts of the ground. Depending on the time of year and whether it has rained weeks before, you can hear bubbling in different tones and cadency. Some sound like babies burped after meal time, and others, like 'bloop!' Some are one metre high volcanic cones; others are flat, quiet puddles, and some have miraculous clay that surround their mouths. Some are closed; others are newly emerging. When it's dry, the surface is cracked and ashy, and looks like it needs some Vaseline.

The mud is composed of high salt content, water, some petroleum, hydrocarbons, and methane which occasionally accompanies it as it projects upwards. Beneath all of these layers is a bed of organic matter.

Which is to say, that these subterranean movements are vestigial resurrections of those who were here before us (i.e. Agongointo-Zoungoudo). A roll call of what is here now (from macroscopic organisms of botany to microscopic organisms of microbiology), and an indication of happenings that are yet to come (the entropic nature of mud that swallows borders). 'Grounding' is but a sliver of all the activities that cycle, circle, churn, migrate, hide, build, bury, store, and archive from below.

All the while, emerging from/through this depth, Salse's collective burps murmur, '...you have no idea what's going on down here'.

[7] Someone(s) made a mobile app, Operation Vala Zonke, where you can report sightings of potholes on roads in South Africa. Each filed report is directed to the South African National Roads Agency Limited (SANRAL) (a state owned enterprise), in the Department of Transport. These reports indicate there are potholes that need filling and roads that need maintenance and repair, as if the nationwide decay of governance and infrastructure wasn't apparent enough. Launched in 2020, Operation Vala Zonke has garnered 111,850 downloads and 75,650 potholes have been reported, as of writing.

Someone(s) made an app where you can snitch on potholes rather than the state.

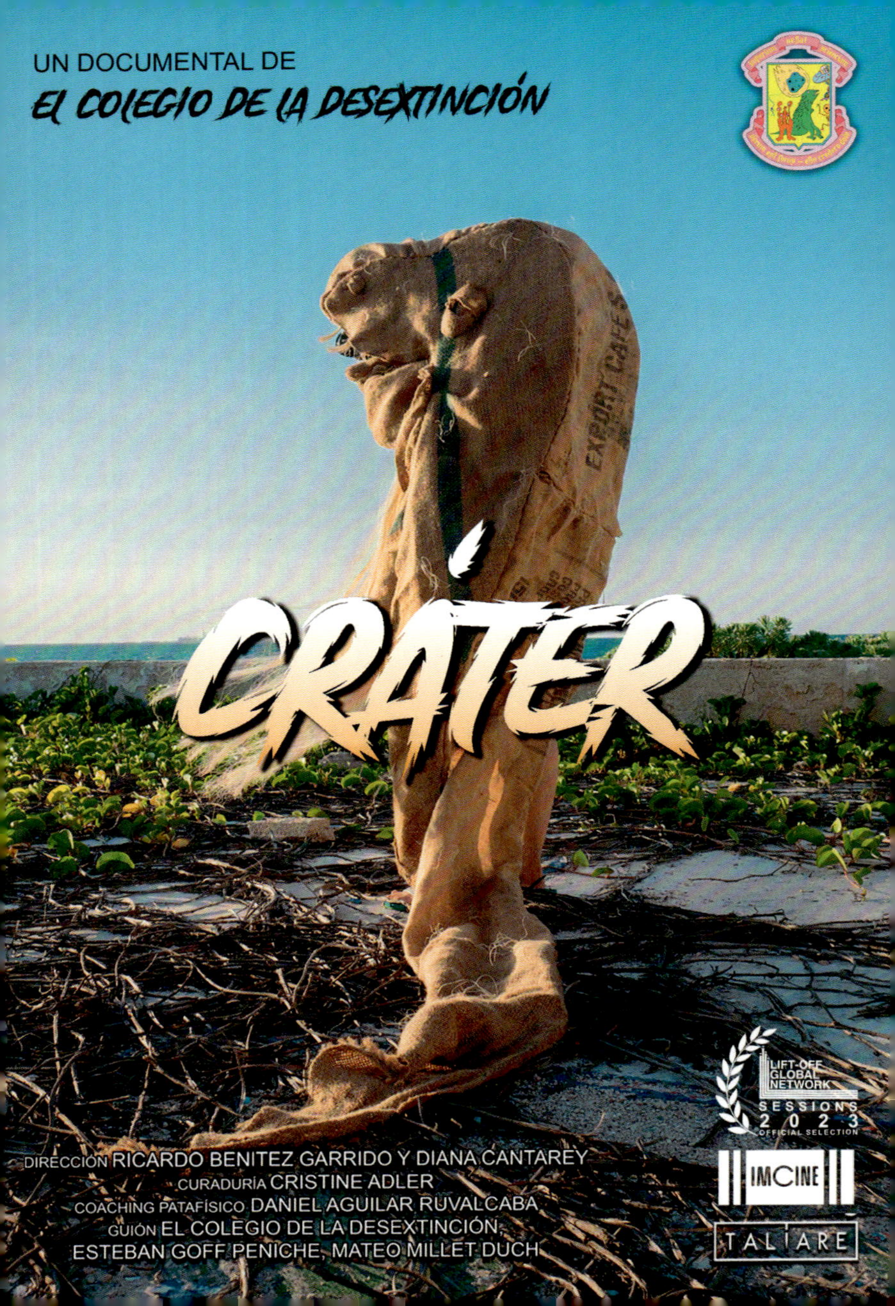

UN DOCUMENTAL DE
EL COLEGIO DE LA DESEXTINCIÓN
CRÁTER
DIRECCIÓN RICARDO BENITEZ GARRIDO Y DIANA CANTAREY
CURADURÍA CRISTINE ADLER
COACHING PATAFÍSICO DANIEL AGUILAR RUVALCABA
GUIÓN EL COLEGIO DE LA DESEXTINCIÓN,
ESTEBAN GOFF PENICHE, MATEO MILLET DUCH
LIFT-OFF GLOBAL NETWORK
SESSIONS 2023
OFFICIAL SELECTION
IMCINE

El Colegio de la Desextinción

El Colegio de la Desextinción is a slow production house that investigates processes of disappearance of species, practices, and objects. It was formed during the filming of the documentary feature film *Cráter*, supported by the Mexican Film Institute for scriptwriting (2019) and project development (2020), and released in 2022. Their research on coloniality and extinction led them to carry out an artistic residency at Taliare in Mérida, Yucatán (2020), as well as the curatorship of the Tres Pesos Triennial (2020, 2023).

www.youtube.com/watch?v=arUI-ayjWiA&ab_channel=ElColegiodelaDesextinci

Image credits

Page 2
Simnikiwe Buhlungu, research image, 2024. Produced by Chisenhale Gallery, London, and commissioned by Chisenhale Gallery and Kunstinstituut Melly, Rotterdam. Courtesy of the artist.

Page 5–17
Simnikiwe Buhlungu, research images, 2024. Produced by Chisenhale Gallery, London, and commissioned by Chisenhale Gallery and Kunstinstituut Melly, Rotterdam. Courtesy of the artist.

Page 24–29
Simnikiwe Buhlungu, research images, 2024. Produced by Chisenhale Gallery, London, and commissioned by Chisenhale Gallery and Kunstinstituut Melly, Rotterdam. Courtesy of the artist.

Page 44–61
Simnikiwe Buhlungu, research images, 2024. Produced by Chisenhale Gallery, London, and commissioned by Chisenhale Gallery and Kunstinstituut Melly, Rotterdam. Courtesy of the artist.

Page 46–47
Professor Norbert de Ruijter, *Diatoms with olive green chloroplasts slide over a granular surface of debris*, 2024. Courtesy of Professor Norbert de Ruijter. All figures display micrometre sized single celled organisms of water samples of different origins.

Page 50–51
Professor Norbert de Ruijter, *Flagellated green algae (left) and threadlike colonies of cyanobacteria (right)*, 2024. Courtesy of Professor Norbert de Ruijter. All figures display micrometre sized single celled organisms of water samples of different origins.

Page 62–63
Simnikiwe Buhlungu, production image, 2024. Produced by Chisenhale Gallery, London, and commissioned by Chisenhale Gallery and Kunstinstituut Melly, Rotterdam. Courtesy of the artist.

Page 68–75
Simnikiwe Buhlungu, *Nomvula Diphororo Crèche log*, 2024. Produced by Chisenhale Gallery, London, and commissioned by Chisenhale Gallery and Kunstinstituut Melly, Rotterdam. Courtesy of the artist.

Page 76–77
Simnikiwe Buhlungu, research image, 2024. Produced by Chisenhale Gallery, London, and commissioned by Chisenhale Gallery and Kunstinstituut Melly, Rotterdam. Courtesy of the artist.

Page 78–85
Simnikiwe Buhlungu, *Nomvula Diphororo Crèche log*, 2024. Produced by Chisenhale Gallery, London, and commissioned by Chisenhale Gallery and Kunstinstituut Melly, Rotterdam. Courtesy of the artist.

Page 92–95
Simnikiwe Buhlungu, research images, 2024. Produced by Chisenhale Gallery, London, and commissioned by Chisenhale Gallery and Kunstinstituut Melly, Rotterdam. Courtesy of the artist.

Page 108–109
Saïd Rosales, *Sketch from conversation on hydrogen*, 2024. Courtesy of Saïd Rosales.

Page 110–111
Tswaing Crater Hiking Map, n.d. Courtesy of Tswaing Meteorite Crater, Ditsong Museums of South Africa.

Page 112–117
Simnikiwe Buhlungu, research images, 2024. Produced by Chisenhale Gallery, London, and commissioned by Chisenhale Gallery and Kunstinstituut Melly, Rotterdam. Courtesy of the artist.

Page 118–119
Professor Norbert de Ruijter, *Bright field image of single celled green algae (size: 1 to 5 micrometre)*, 2024. Courtesy of Professor Norbert de Ruijter. All figures display micrometre sized single celled organisms of water samples of different origins.

Page 120–121
Professor Norbert de Ruijter, *Fluorescent image showing chlorophyl autofluorescence in single celled green algae*, 2024. Courtesy of Professor Norbert de Ruijter. All figures display micrometre sized single celled organisms of water samples of different origins.

Page 122–123
Professor Norbert de Ruijter, *Fluorescent image of colony of green single celled algae (Pediastrum sp)*, 2024. Courtesy of Professor Norbert de Ruijter. All figures display micrometre sized single celled organisms of water samples of different origins.

Page 124–125
Professor Norbert de Ruijter, *Fluorescent image of colony of green single celled algae (Coelastrum sp)*, 2024. Courtesy of Professor Norbert de Ruijter. All figures display micrometre sized single celled organisms of water samples of different origins.

Page 126–127
Professor Norbert de Ruijter, *Fluorescent image of colony of green single celled algae (Scenedesmus sp)*, 2024. Courtesy of Professor Norbert de Ruijter. All figures display micrometre sized single celled organisms of water samples of different origins.

Page 135
Simnikiwe Buhlungu, production image, 2024. Produced by Chisenhale Gallery, London, and commissioned by Chisenhale Gallery and Kunstinstituut Melly, Rotterdam. Courtesy of the artist.

Page 142–143
Simnikiwe Buhlungu, research images, 2024. Produced by Chisenhale Gallery, London, and commissioned by Chisenhale Gallery and Kunstinstituut Melly, Rotterdam. Courtesy of the artist.

Page 144–147, 149
Simnikiwe Buhlungu, production images, 2024. Produced by Chisenhale Gallery, London, and commissioned by Chisenhale Gallery and Kunstinstituut Melly, Rotterdam. Courtesy of the artist.

Page 148, 150–153
Simnikiwe Buhlungu, research images, 2024. Produced by Chisenhale Gallery, London, and commissioned by Chisenhale Gallery and Kunstinstituut Melly, Rotterdam. Courtesy of the artist.

Page 154
Simnikiwe Buhlungu, *Our Friends Are Deeper Than We Thought (A Conver-something)*, 2023. Ellen de Bruijne Projects, Amsterdam. Courtesy of the artist.

Page 155
Simnikiwe Buhlungu, research image, 2024. Produced by Chisenhale Gallery, London, and commissioned by Chisenhale Gallery and Kunstinstituut Melly, Rotterdam. Courtesy of the artist.

Page 156–157
Professor Norbert de Ruijter, *Bright field microscope overview shows a variety of green algae*, 2024. Courtesy of Professor Norbert de Ruijter. All figures display micrometre sized single celled organisms of water samples of different origins.

Page 158–159
Professor Norbert de Ruijter, *Diatoms with olive green chloroplasts slide over a granular surface of debris*, 2024. Courtesy of Professor Norbert de Ruijter. All figures display micrometre sized single celled organisms of water samples of different origins.

Page 165
Simnikiwe Buhlungu, production image, 2024. Produced by Chisenhale Gallery, London, and commissioned by Chisenhale Gallery and Kunstinstituut Melly, Rotterdam. Courtesy of the artist.

Page 174–175
Simnikiwe Buhlungu, research image, 2024. Produced by Chisenhale Gallery, London, and commissioned by Chisenhale Gallery and Kunstinstituut Melly, Rotterdam. Courtesy of the artist.

Page 176–177
Simnikiwe Buhlungu, *Our Friends Are Deeper Than We Thought (A Conver-something) with Negiste Yesside Johnson*, 2023. Ellen de Bruijne Projects, Amsterdam. Courtesy of the artist.

Page 197
Simnikiwe Buhlungu, research image, 2024. Produced by Chisenhale Gallery, London, and commissioned by Chisenhale Gallery and Kunstinstituut Melly, Rotterdam. Courtesy of the artist.

Page 200
Professor Norbert de Ruijter, *Green algae attached to soil particles in water sample*, 2024. Courtesy of Professor Norbert de Ruijter. All figures display micrometre sized single celled organisms of water samples of different origins.

Artist acknowledgments

Leonardo Ciarleglio
My mother, Nokusa Buhlungu
My father, Sakhela Buhlungu
Tswaing Crater (to the security guard whose name I cannot recall and the secretary who was sleeping upon arrival)
Salse di Nirano (Chiara Campion and Astrid Degli Esposti)
Ellen de Bruijne Projects
Negiste Yesside Johnson (for the cover-something and tender listening)
Nana et Baniel
Umbona Wasekhaya
Kunstinstituut Melly and their team
Chisenhale Gallery and their team
Wageningen University & Research (WLMC)
Imperial College London Microbiology department (Tom P. Smith and Dr. Thomas Bell)
Amy Jones
Olivia Aherne
Rachel Be-Yun Wang
Niels de Bakker
Nomvula Diphororo Crèche (and to Chad Cordiero for caretaking duties)
Rijksakademie van Beeldende Kunsten
Key Color Foto Lab, Amsterdam

To all the lakes, ponds, reservoirs, brine pools, tears, drops of honey, reservoirs, dams, seas, and oceans.

My friends and family, whose support (calls, texts, check-ins) has been a lifeline in the challenges that presented themselves and creative breakthroughs I eventually met.

To each and every one of the contributors of this publication, whose rich voices have made puddles – all that we know of them and all that we don't – much deeper than we thought.

Chisenhale Gallery

Board of Trustees

Staff

Caoimhe Rogan, Development Coordinator
Adam Shield, Technician
Josie Spalla, Digital and Communications Manager
Nkara Stephenson, Events Assistant
Rachel Be-Yun Wang, Asymmetry Curatorial Research Fellow
Zoé Whitley, Director
Daniel Wilkinson, Technician
Lucy Woodhouse, Head Technician

Kunstinstituut Melly

Supervisory board

Fariba Derakhshani
Timme Geerlof
Yolande Zola Zoli van der Heide
Annet Lekkerkerker (chair 2019 – 2024)
Annuska Pronkhorst
Yin Yin Wong

Staff

Emilia Aivazian, Education & Mediation Manager
Rachel Carey, Financial Controller
Laura van den Enden, Hospitality Coordinator
Luke Fentross, Marketing & Communications Coordinator
Rosa de Graaf, Curator of Exhibitions & Art Commissions
Jessy Koeiman, Coordinator Collective Learning
marjolijn kok, Archivist & Data Organizer
Angélique Kool, Executive Assistant & HR Coordinator
line kramer, Lead Preparator & IT Supervisor
Jeroen Lavèn, Community Relations & Operations Manager
Shana Lewis, Program Assistant
Alexis Medina Trejo, Program Assistant
Simon Mensger, Financial Assistant
Gabi Ngcobo, Director
Sarah van Overeem-van der Tholen, Director Development
Wendy van Slagmaat-Bos, Program Coordinator
Erik Visser, Bookshop Assistant
Vivian Ziherl, Research & Programs Manager

Art Mediators

Ezgi Aktuğ, Nurdan Arioz, Lotte van Dooremalen, Folke Janssen, Berdan Kaplan, Maria Mombers, Sabrina Schoop, Floor Snels, Kirti Soekaloe, Nabil Tkhidousset, Ilidia Medina, Emmelie Mijs, Bram Verhoef, Gino van Weenen, Roos Wijma, Jo Willoughby, and Femke van Zanten

Hospitality Team

Bergur Anderson, Silvia Arenas, Nathan Bastien, Rabin Huissen, Franklin Lopes, Elvis de Launay, Eun Lee, Shearey Pinas, Yusser Salih, Britte Tegelaar, Ioana Tomici, Gino van Weenen, Karin Westendorp, and Jo Willoughby

Installation Crew

Bergur Anderson, Ties Ten Bosch, Jonathan Breejen, Carlo van Driel, Folke Janssen, Johannes Langkamp, Judy van Luyck, Hilde Onis, Sandro Setola, Luuk Smits, Hans Tutert-Smits, and Liza Wolters

Exhibition credits

hygrosummons (iter.01) is produced by Chisenhale Gallery, London and commissioned by Chisenhale Gallery and Kunstinstituut Melly, Rotterdam.

Lead Supporters: Mondriaan Fund and the Embassy of the Kingdom of the Netherlands.

Headline Supporters: Marcus and Alexa Waley-Cohen and The African Arts Trust.

With additional support from the Chisenhale Gallery Commissions Fund.

Chisenhale Gallery's Schools' Programme 2024 is made possible through the generosity of Goodman Gallery and Freelands Foundation.

The 2023–24 Asymmetry Curatorial Research Fellow is hosted by Chisenhale Gallery.

Kunstinstituut Melly is supported by the city of Rotterdam and the Ministry of Education, Culture, and Science in the Netherlands. Simnikiwe Buhlungu's experiment forms part of the *Call and Response* exhibition program supported by Ammodo.

Supported using public funding by ARTS COUNCIL ENGLAND

mondriaan fund

Kingdom of the Netherlands

The African Arts Trust

Gemeente Rotterdam

AMMODO

Ministerie van Onderwijs, Cultuur en Wetenschap

besides Puleng; dontsa-ring and roving preoccupations was published on the occasion of the exhibition *hygrosummons (iter.01)* by Simnikiwe Buhlungu at Chisenhale Gallery, London (6 September – 3 November 2024) and Kunstinstituut Melly, Rotterdam (May – October 2025)

Series Editor
Zoé Whitley

Editors
Olivia Aherne
Simnikiwe Buhlungu
Amy Jones

Managing Editor
Anita Dawood

Publishing Editor
Micola Clara Brambilla

Assistant Editor
Rachel Be-Yun Wang

Proofreader
Wendy van Slagmaat-Bos

Design
Rose Nordin

Contributions
Alunamda Buhlungu
Simnikiwe Buhlungu
El Colegio Desextinctión
Khwezi Gule
Taylor Le Melle
George Mahashe
Gabi Ngcobo
Saïd Rosales
Norbert C.A. de Ruijter
The Brother Moves On
Zoé Whitley
Riet Wijnen

First edition 2024

Co-published by
Chisenhale Gallery, London, Kunstinstituut Melly, Rotterdam, and Mousse Publishing, Milan.

64 Chisenhale Rd, London E3 5QZ England
chisenhale.org.uk

Witte de Withstraat 50, 3012 BR Rotterdam, the Netherlands
kunstinstituutmelly.nl

With the generous support of:
Mondriaan Fund, Mercedes Vilardell, Frank Bowling and Rachel Scott

Distributed by
Mousse Publishing
Contrappunto s.r.l.
via Pier Candido
Decembrio 28
20137, Milan–Italy

Available through
Mousse Publishing,
Milan
moussemagazine.it

Printed by
Pureprint, London
ISBN 9788867496617
£23 GBP / €27 EUR /
$29 USD

A catalogue record for this book is available from The British Library.

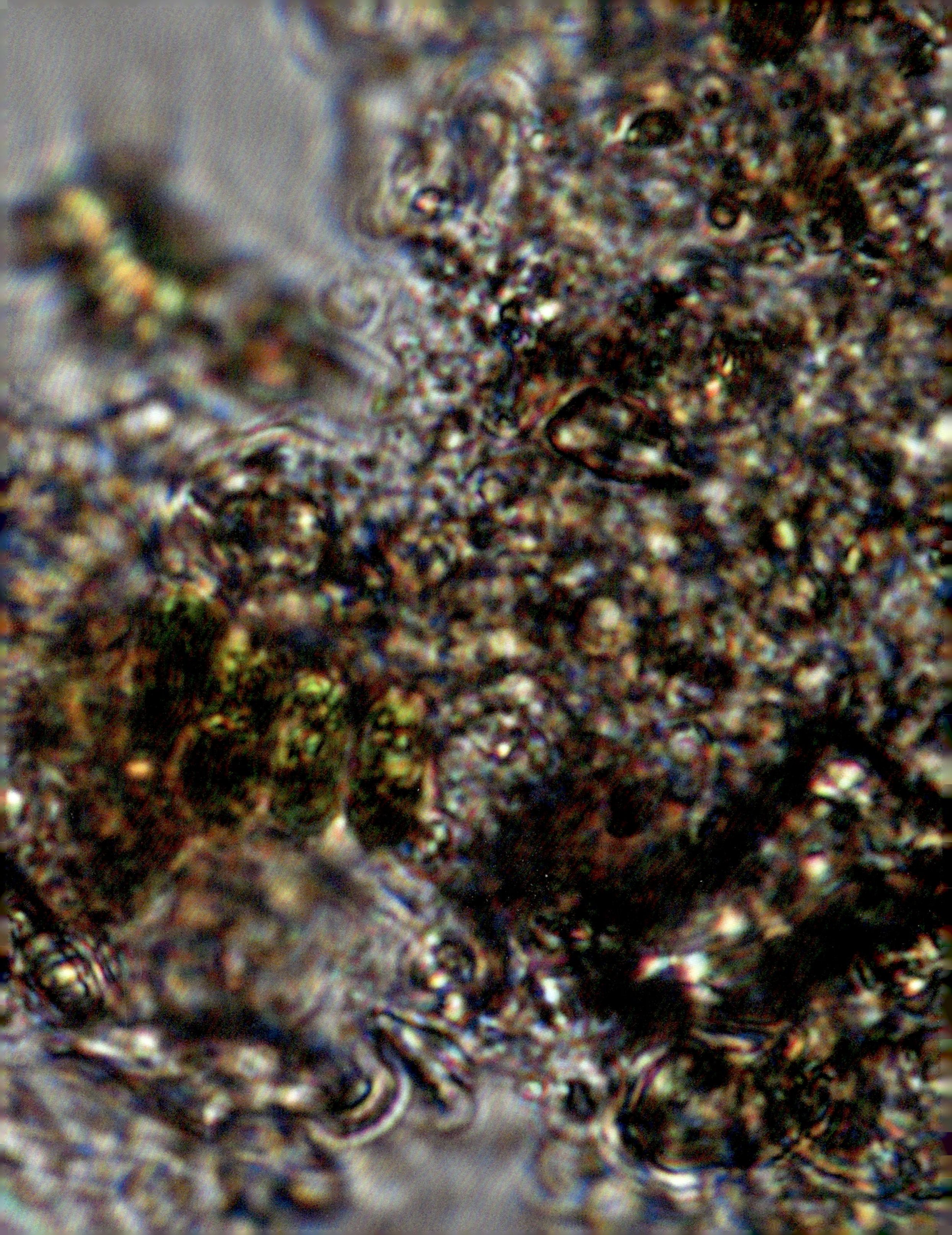